WHERE ARE ALL THE LIBRARIANS OF COLOR? THE EXPERIENCES OF PEOPLE OF COLOR IN ACADEMIA

WHERE ARE ALL THE LIBRARIANS OF COLOR? THE EXPERIENCES OF PEOPLE OF COLOR IN ACADEMIA

Coedited by
Rebecca Hankins, CA, MLS and
Miguel Juárez, MLS, MA

LIBRARY JUICE PRESS
SACRAMENTO, CA

Copyright respective authors, 2015

Published in 2015 by Library Juice Press

Library Juice Press
PO Box 188784
Sacramento, CA 95822

http://libraryjuicepress.com/

This book is printed on acid-free, sustainably-sourced paper.

Library of Congress Cataloging-in-Publication Data

Where are all the librarians of color? : the experiences of people of color in
academia / coedited by Rebecca Hankins, CA, MLS; Miguel Juarez, MLS, MA.
     pages cm.
   Includes bibliographical references and index.
   ISBN 9781936117833 (pbk.)
   1. Minority librarians--United States. 2. Academic librarians--United States.
3. Minorities in higher education--United States. 4. Diversity in the workplace-
-United States. I. Hankins, Rebecca, editor. II. Juarez, Miguel, 1958- editor.
   Z682.4.M56 W48 2015
   027.7092--dc23
                          2015032617

Contents

PREFACE

Loriene Roy, Ph.D.

Librarians are concerned with reflecting diversity in their professional education and their workplaces—from library collections to services and outreach—and in the make-up of library staff. Highly visible efforts, such as the Spectrum Initiative Scholarships, were established to increase enrollment of students from underrepresented groups in master's programs accredited by the American Library Association (ALA) or in school library certification programs accredited by NCATE, the National Council for Accreditation of Teacher Education (now part of the Council for the Accreditation of Educator Preparation [CAEP]). Yet although librarians acknowledge a strong belief that library staff should reflect the diverse communities that they serve, the demographics of library employees remain relatively stable. The average library worker today is still a white woman in her mid-fifties. Much work therefore remains to be accomplished in achieving the goal of diversity. There is no single route to changing the characteristics of the workforce, and even scholarship support only produces results over much time. Meanwhile, the few current librarians of color are in need of support and attention.

Despite overt attention to diversity in the recruitment of prospective librarians into graduate programs, little attention is given to the experiences of librarians of color as they transition from student to information professional, particularly after they enter the workplace.

As a librarian of color and current faculty member of color helping graduate students prepare for their careers in information studies, I know how intimidating the process of seeking, accepting, and stepping into employment can be. A library and information science student may eventually find herself/himself hired as the sole person of color in a work environment that, while potentially satisfying, does not reflect her/his own culture—much less that of the communities of color in the prospective patron audience. In my case, the isolation is magnified: Indigenous librarians are even more marginalized because reporting and writing on diversity issues less frequently discusses librarians who are American Indian, Alaska Native, First Nation, or affiliated with another indigenous community than it does Black, Latino/a or Spanish Speaking, or Asian librarians.

Mentorships are often offered as the best answer for facilitating a smooth adjustment into the workplace and for further advancement within the field. Mentoring may be integrated not only directly into accomplishing day-to-day work activities, but also into pursuing continuing education and advancement. Formal mentoring takes many faces and is often an initiative hosted by a professional organization. Informal mentoring can be the process of a professional librarian choosing a likely mentee for long-term contact, or it may be a brief contact between employees, with the senior employee providing advice or assistance whenever possible or needed. Thus, a librarian of color may find one more layer of isolation if he or she is not aware of or is not included in either formal or informal mentoring. Professional organizations— especially the ethnic library organizations affiliated with ALA—can serve as advocates for their members, largely through enlisting them into conducting work for the organization, although not all potential beneficiaries will be able to take advantage of these opportunities. Such involvement is voluntary and both membership and association work are usually dependent upon the individual paying personal dues and creating a plan of involvement—from attending meetings and conferences to serving on committees and/or election to various offices.

Once hired, the new work environment might be particularly foreign and challenging for the first-generation college graduate who may not have family and/or friends to rely upon for discussing options and receiving other support. This challenge is compounded if the position is a tenure-track academic appointment because of the many responsibilities for teaching, research, and service that come with this career path. Thus, employment might be difficult to obtain and then secure, requiring not only years of education and training but also years of developing an academic-centered resume in order to retain the position and, hopefully, eventually be promoted for increased job security.

This publication is critically important for several reasons. First, it illustrates a librarian publisher's commitment to supporting publication and writing in the area of diversity: this volume is published as a monograph in a Library Juice series on Critical Multiculturalism in Information Studies. Second, this volume offers a valuable opportunity for contributors to enrich the published record while expanding their professional experiences and resumes. Third, the editors and contributors have provided readers with several different perspectives on the topic. Some essays are literature reviews and introduce key writings or theory, such as Critical Race Theory. Others present initiatives as case studies or mention efforts such as the Discovering Librarianship Program, Spectrum, ALA's Emerging Leaders program, the Minnesota Institute for Early Career Librarians, Miami University's Minority Residence Program within the university libraries, and the Association of Research Libraries' Leadership and Career Development Program. Other chapters are autobiographical statements wherein the authors share their personal career choices. In addition, writers employ several methods in presenting their findings, including survey results, narration, and storytelling.

Finally, *Where Are All the Librarians of Color?* is not the final word on this topic. There are still several gaps in relevant content areas, with much work yet to be accomplished before the successful tenured academic librarian is an option for every librarian's career and the librarian of color is a reality in each college/university student's daily experience. For example, it might be useful to compare how other disciplinary areas, such as social work and education, have responded to the need to increase diversity among their workers. Another contribution could compare diversity initiatives within the existing programs in LIS, providing details on their selection process, amount of support, requirements, and impact. Researchers might additionally consider the potential for creating a retention and promotion initiative that would mirror the Spectrum Initiative in terms of its level of direct support to the selected librarian and in the visibility and formation of a long-standing, supportive peer cohort. This project might be the focus of a grant proposal or be work conducted through a professional organization. Lastly, the life stories of librarians of color might be tracked over time in order to monitor career progression, identify potential critical points where intervention is needed, and highlight career paths.

INTRODUCTION

Rebecca Hankins and Miguel Juárez

When we initially started this book we wanted our ideas to be fresh and new, but we began to hear from a number of colleagues that there were already articles and books that addressed these issues. Why write another book on the same subject, we were often asked? We quickly realized there were two important views we needed to keep in mind before we proceeded; one was that yes, a review of the literature was in order and two, no one ever says there are too many books on information literacy, digitization, Shakespeare, or a myriad of other concerns in the field of librarianship, so why should there not be as many books and articles about diversity? There is a stark need for a corpus of research on the subjects of diversity/multiculturalism: the professional, informational, and digital divide within the library/archival profession. These ideas must also be tested, revised, discussed widely, debated often, and made accessible in as many venues and resources as possible. Diversity is not a settled issue that we can move on from to other concerns; diversity and the consequences of it to the profession, and dare we say the world, are the most consequential and important issue of our time. W.E.B. DuBois said "the color-line is the most important issue of the 20th century" and he was dealing with some powerful issues of racism, Jim Crow institutions, American Nativism, and other systemic and racialized policies of the state when he made his statement. In the

1

21st century there have been some changes, but many of the gains of the 20th century are being systematically eroded in subtle and more sophisticated efforts. So we say a firm "No!"—diversity has not been addressed enough and this tome will tackle some of these serious issues, with the hope that this work will add to the discussion of these challenges facing the informational fields.

There have been several recent texts devoted to an examination of people of color in academic professions, most notably Gabriella Gutierrez y Muhs recent text *Presumed Incompetent: The Intersections of Race and Class for Women in Academia* (2012), Brett C. Stockdill's *Transforming the Ivory Tower: Challenging Racism, Sexism, and Homophobia in the Academy* (2012), Christine Stanley's *Faculty of Color: Teaching in Predominantly White Colleges and Universities* (2006), as well as a few titles that are more specific to the library profession such as Raquel V. Cogell's *Diversity in Libraries: Academic Residency Programs* (2001), Barbara I. Dewey's *Achieving Diversity: a How-to-Do-It Manual for Librarians* (2006) and Gregory L. Reese's *Stop Talking Start Doing! Attracting People of Color to the Library Profession* (1999). The library-related titles focus on the recruitment of librarians of color rather than their experiences after the hiring is over. There have been journal articles that examine various aspects of the experiences of Black librarians such as Joyce Thornton's 2000 and 2001 articles that looked at job satisfaction for African American female librarians and librarians of African descent respectively. There have also been a few texts that address diversity in the archives profession with the most recent by Mary A. Caldera and Kathryn M. Neal titled *Through the Archival Looking Glass: A Reader on Diversity and Inclusion* (2014) and many others that address issues regarding diversification of the historical records and archives. However, there is no single text that addresses the shared experiences of academic librarians or archivists of color, i.e. Hispanics, African Americans, and Asians. These experiences are very similar and offer a narrative that explains the dearth of librarians of color in academia, especially those librarians who have experienced the daunting academic tenure process.

Drawing on the work of the previously mentioned authors, research in this monograph offers a look at the experiences of people of color after the recruitment is over, the diversity box is checked, and the stats are reported. What *is* the retention, job satisfaction, and tenure experience of these librarians of color? We review the literature and look at the history of librarians of color in academia, as well as the obstacles, roles, leadership opportunities, and tenure process for those who endure. What are the recruitment and retention methods employed to create a diverse workforce, and what are the successes and failures? How do we incorporate Critical Race Theory, racial realism, and intersectionality in the experiences of librarians and archivists of color? How does one's performance of their identity and all of its multiple ways, impact their experiences in the information world? These are often difficult concepts to express or explain, but we wanted to address a wide spectrum of experiences for an expected audience that includes public and private academic librarians and archivists, as well as the larger academic community. We see this monograph as an important addition to the scholarship on the experiences of people of color in and outside of the academy.

We chose to divide this book into three sections. In Section One: Setting the Stage for Diversity in the Profession, these crucial essays explore the fundamental issues that must be addressed when we speak about diversity. These essays take a real world approach to resolving issues related to recruitment and retention, mentoring, and strengthening the pipeline. In their essay "Discovering Librarianship: Personalizing the Recruitment Process for Underrepresented Students," **Emily K. Chan, Jovanni Lota, Holly A. Smith** and **Steven D. Booth** focus on four professionals' experiences in an ALA Office for Diversity IMLS funded Discovering Librarianship Program as it relates to strengthening the pipeline, mentoring others, and dealing with community expectations for librarians of color. **Tarida Anantachai, Latrice Booker, Althea Lazzaro** and **Martha Parker**'s essay, "Establishing a Communal Network for Professional Advancement among Librarians of Color," examines the ways in which collaborative partnerships among librarians of color, within and even across institutions, can greatly assist in job satisfaction, retention of professionals, and bolstering librarians' sense of support throughout their careers. The essay also provides specific examples and models in which these collaborations have occurred, including those that the authors have experienced and, in many cases, initiated. **Melody Royster, David Schwieder, Ava Iuliano Brillat,** and **Lori Driver**'s essay, "Mentoring and Retention of Minority Librarians," uses qualitative and quantitative data to explore the ways in which mentoring programs succeed and fail minority librarians, in order to uncover potential strategies for more effective mentorship. By sharing and analyzing the impact that mentoring or the lack thereof has on minority librarians, the authors hope that readers will be more informed and empowered to create and improve mentoring programs to truly support the librarians they seek to serve. **Jason Kelly Alston's** insightful essay looks at how the use of the term *interns* for diversity resident librarians affects their treatment within host institutions. His essay resonates very strongly with our experiences as library residents, as well as with the experiences of a number of our colleagues of color. We conclude Section One with **Agnes Bradshaw**'s essay "Strengthening the Pipeline—Talent Management for Libraries: A Human Resources Perspective," which addresses the concept of talent management practices for developing the people who will be needed by the profession, to ensure that the profession is seen as desirable for those from all groups, not just those from one group. Her essay further examines the representation of people of color within the profession and assesses how talent management strategies can be utilized to ensure that librarians of color are included, while ensuring that all groups of the user population are represented in the professional ranks.

We titled Section Two: How Diversity Benefits the Profession because we have all heard the statement, "diversity promotes excellence." These essays seek to address these ideals by detailing tangible ways that statement is proven, but also how, despite tremendous odds, the library and archival professions fall short of acknowledging those benefits. **Shaundra Walker**'s essay titled "Critical Race Theory and the Recruitment and Retention of a Librarian of Color: A Counterstory" uses

Critical Race Theory (CRT) as a theoretical framework for recruitment and retention experience of academic librarians of color. She examines the themes of white privilege, interest convergence, and counter-stories to understand the issues of library education for people of color and the history of higher education in America. In **Akilah Nosakhere**'s essay "Serving with a Sense of Purpose: A Black Woman Librarian in Rural New Mexico" we learn how an African America woman is able to overcome the reality of deep seated racial and gender biases to create a learning center for students, faculty, and the Carlsbad community at large. She writes about the challenges of being one of very few Black professionals in a predominantly white academic environment and what her presence says about her commitment to the philosophy of service to others. **Vince Lee**'s essay, titled "Like a Fish Out of Water, but Forging My Own Path," is one of two essays by archivists. Lee's essay discusses his career from a unique perspective as a Chinese American man who has worked with African American and now women's collections. Lee discusses how working in these two environments gave him an opportunity to reflect not only on preconceived notions and stereotypes of what archivists should serve in which institutions and roles, but also the self-imposed biases and discrimination we have in regards to how we see ourselves and how we fit in to the profession. The last essay in this section is by the co-editor **Rebecca Hankins** and is titled "Racial Realism or Foolish Optimism: An African American Muslim Woman in the Field." It discusses a number of identity issues related to what people of color experience in American society, with a particular focus on Derrick Bell's concept of racial realism. Although this concept could be considered very pessimistic, the author discusses how it really permits people of color the freedom to work from a platform of self-empowerment.

The final section, Section Three: Diverse Personal Stories explores how people have used their diverse experiences to push back against the system, work to build bridges, seek to find equity within their spaces, and tackle the need to go beyond our understanding of diversity. The first essay, titled "The Veteran and the Rookie: Our Story, Our Experience" written by **Rhonda E. Fowler** and **Karen Rogers-Collins**, is the shared experiences of two African American librarians at a mid-size Midwestern university; one who has spent her career working primarily in academia, the other who has spent her career working in special libraries and is new to academic libraries. **Stacy Brinkman, Jacqueline Johnson, Kwabena Sekyere,** and **Elías Tzoc**'s essay, "DiVeRsItY at Miami University Libraries: Four Unique and Similar Experiences," relates the experiences of five librarians recruited via Miami University Libraries' Minority Residency program in order to increase diversity among its staff and to encourage librarians of color to enter the profession. This essay traces their experiences through this residency program and what has occurred since, including their experiences of moving into permanent positions within the library, receiving promotion and tenure, and one who has moved into the position of Dean and University Librarian. "Building Dialogic Bridges to Diversity: Are We There Yet?" by **Roland Barksdale-Hall** is written from the perspective of an African American culture keeper, library educator, and academic library administrator. He looks at the professional literature, oral histories of African Americans in academia, librarian practitioner journals, case studies, and leadership theory. And if the struggles, trials and tribulations are not enough to dampen the spirit, sometimes librarians need to change direction and do something else, while not totally giving up on the profession. Our final essay, "Making Diversity Work in Academic Libraries" by co-editor **Miguel Juárez**, furthers the dialogue about diversity by focusing on what is not being discussed and how we can broaden the conversation.

The voices presented here expand the dialogue of diversity in academic and public libraries to places diversity has not ventured before. We encourage you to read and re-read these essays and sections; we hope to hear from you as you ponder, analyze, and engage with our stories.

References

Caldera, Mary A. and Kathryn M. Neal, eds. *Through the Archival Looking Glass: A Reader on Diversity and Inclusion.* Chicago, IL: Society of American Archivists, 2014.

Cogell, Raquel V. and Cindy A. Gruwell, eds. *Diversity in Libraries: Academic Residency Programs.* Westport, CO: Greenwood Press, 2001.

Dewey, Barbara I. and Loretta Parham, eds. Achieving *Diversity: A How-to-Do-It Manual for Librarians.* New York, NY: Neal-Schuman Publishers, 2006.

Muhs, Gabriella Gutiérrez y, Yolanda Flores Niemann, Carmen G. González, Angela P. Harris. *Presumed Incompetent: The Intersections of Race and Class for Women in Academia.* Logan: Utah State University Press, 2012.

Reese, Gregory L. and Ernestine L. Hawkins. *Stop Talking, Start Doing!: Attracting People of Color to the Library Profession.* Chicago, IL: American Library Association, 1999.

Stanley, Christine A. ed. *Faculty of Color: Teaching in Predominantly White Colleges and Universities.* Bolton, MA: Anker Publication, 2006.

Stockdill, Brett C. *Transforming the Ivory Tower: Challenging Racism, Sexism, and Homophobia in the Academy.* Honolulu: University of Hawaii Press, 2012.

SECTION ONE:

SETTING THE STAGE FOR DIVERSITY

IN THE PROFESSION

Chapter 1

DISCOVERING LIBRARIANSHIP: PERSONALIZING THE RECRUITMENT PROCESS FOR UNDER-REPRESENTED STUDENTS

Emily K. Chan, Jovanni Lota, Holly A. Smith, and Steven D. Booth

When Jovanni Lota recently read the *Huffington Post*'s November 2013 article "UCLA Has More NCAA Championships [109] Than Black Male Freshman [45],"[1] she mused that not much had changed. The poor numbers cited in the article mirrored her experience as an African American woman and alumna of the Graduate School of Education and Information Studies at the University of California at Los Angeles (UCLA). For Fall Quarter 2013, the African American student population at UCLA was approximately 3.8 percent.[2] However, when Lota was entering library school in Fall 2007, the African American student population was even less, at 1.9 percent of the total student population.[3]

---

1. "UCLA Has More NCAA Championships Than Black Male Freshmen," *Huffingtonpost.com*, last modified November 8, 2013, http://www.huffingtonpost.com/2013/11/08/ucla-black-enrollment-freshmen_n_4242213.html.

2. University of California – Los Angeles. "Quick Facts about UCLA," UCLA Undergraduate Admission, accessed June 18, 2014, https://www.admissions.ucla.edu/campusprofile.htm.

3. Elaine Korry, "Black Student Enrollment at UCLA Plunges," *NPR.org*, last modified July 24, 2006, http://www.npr.org/templates/story/story.php?storyId=5563891.

In fact, Lota was one of three African American students in her library science cohort.

Lota and her few Latino classmates often felt isolated. They also encountered high levels of cultural insensitivity. After reading the 2007 *Diversity Counts* report, which clearly shed light on the disproportionate number of librarians of color in America, Lota realized that diversity was a serious problem in the profession and that her experience in library school might just be a microcosm and foreshadowing of life as a librarian. As a result of reading this report and reflecting on her own experience in library school, she concluded that she needed to become an advocate for representation, equity, and inclusion. Lota decided to be the change she wanted to see in the profession, which meant getting involved in a way to make an impact. Lota applied, was accepted, and participated in the Discovering Librarianship initiative, which enlisted ethnically diverse, early career librarians to strengthen the pipeline and mentor prospective Master of Library and Information Science (MLIS) students of color. This chapter will focus on the experiences of four Discovering Librarianship participants: Jovanni Lota, Information Literacy Coordinator Librarian at University of Houston-Downtown; Emily K. Chan, Academic Liaison Librarian at San José State University; Holly A. Smith, College Archivist of Spelman College; and Steven D. Booth, Archivist in the Presidential Materials Division of the National Archives and Records Administration. Their involvement and work with the Discovering Librarianship initiative reflect some of the challenges to the recruitment and retention of underrepresented groups in librarianship and the American Library Association's response to these challenges and attempts to promote greater parity between the demographics of the profession and the communities that libraries serve. The program's impact on the recruiters' individual and professional practice will also be discussed.

Needs Assessment

In 2001, racial and ethnic minorities comprised 12% (504) of the 4,953 graduates receiving accredited MLIS degrees.[4] In 2011, they accounted for 1,117 (14%) of the 8,227 MLIS degrees awarded.[5] These numbers indicate little gains in diversifying the library professional workforce. Incoming numbers of diverse library professionals have largely remained stagnant, despite widespread acknowledgment of the severity of the issue.

In the 2012 update to the *Diversity Counts* report, a broad study on the library profession's demographics, the ethnic/racial breakdown of credentialed librarians in higher education was 86.1% White, followed by 5.4% African American,4.8% Asian or Pacific Islander, 2.6% Latino, 0.9% Two or more races, and 0.2% Native American (including Alaskan Native).[6] When contrasting these statistics to census numbers, it is evident that more needs to be done in order to attain greater parity between the profession and the communities that libraries serve.

The Discovering Librarianship Initiative and Training

To address these types of statistics, the Discovering Librarianship: The Future is Overdue program was proposed in 2011 by the American Library Association (ALA) Office of Diversity.[7] This Institute of

4. Association for Library and Information Science Education, "Library and Information Science Education Statistical Report 2002," accessed June 30, 2014, http://ils.unc.edu/ALISE/2002/Contents.htm.

5. Danny P. Wallace, ed., Library and Information Science Education Statistical Report 2012, (Chicago, IL: ALISE, 2012), 119.

6. American Library Association, "Diversity Counts," accessed June 30, 2014, http://www.ala.org/offices/sites/ala.org.offices/files/content/diversity/diversitycounts/diversitycountstables2012.pdf.

7. American Library Association, "Discovering Librarianship: The Future is Overdue," accessed June 18, 2014, http://www.ala.org/offices/diversity/imls.

Museum and Library Services (IMLS)-funded, multi-year initiative would
bring together a group of early career librarians to develop marketing
and recruitment materials; identify regional and national career, education, and cultural events; and serve as ambassadors for the profession.
Unlike other industries and professions such as science and business,
librarianship is generally passive in terms of recruiting minorities to
graduate school. Very few of the fifty-eight ALA-accredited graduate
library science programs across the United States and Canada actively
recruit at educational and professional fairs. Targeting these types of
events, recruiters would meet prospective students and publicize the
potential and merits of careers in libraries to ethnically diverse high
school and college students. Thus, the Discovering Librarianship program would promote librarianship to a new generation and offer the
information and support to assist these students in their future library
education and career endeavors.

The Discovering Librarianship program had several key goals,
including:

- Engaging a cohort of early career librarians from traditionally
  underrepresented groups, including past recipients from national
  diversity initiatives, to develop and deliver relevant and persuasive
  messages about the value of librarianship,
- Deploying the field recruiters to communicate with ethnically
  diverse prospective students at various regional and national
  events,
- Develop a database and system to continue contact with potential
  library students after a recruitment event,
- Foster early mentorship by connecting high school and undergraduate college students to recruiters, and
- Provide the cohort of early career librarians, some of whom
  were past participants of national diversity recruitment initiatives, a new avenue for professional development, training, and
  leadership.[8]

---

8. Ibid.

At the conclusion of the Discovering Librarianship program, there would be an increased capacity to attract students to the library and information science field using relevant recruitment materials. Greater professional visibility would strengthen the educational and career pipeline, while simultaneously changing existing stereotypical images of librarians. These efforts would increase the diversity of the library workforce so that it would more accurately reflect the communities that libraries serve.[9]

Proper development of a relevant and persuasive recruitment message required a thorough review and analysis of the profession. A two-day training session ensured that the participants were well versed in a variety of topics, including the current demographic trends of librarianship and the future labor market. Knowing the most recent numbers of individuals of color in the field through the Diversity Counts reports helped to emphasize how significant the recruiters' efforts could be in changing the professional landscape. Recruiters were also given information about scholarships, funding, and grant opportunities for prospective students and the myriad positions available in both library and non-library settings for holders of an ALA-accredited MLIS degree. This information is significant, as Kim and Sin note in their 2008 article that financing graduate education and discerning career options are among some of the most important recruitment and retention strategies for increasing ethnic diversity in library and information science.[10]

Recruiters were invited to provide personal narratives of how they were introduced to librarianship. These accounts solidified the fact that there are a wide variety of entry points to library and information science as a first, second, or even third career. Because recruiters were early career professionals, sharing work trajectories demonstrated the various motivations for entering, remaining, and thriving within the field as individuals of color. In numerous cases, the recruiters themselves

---

9. Ibid.

10. Kyung-Sun Kim and Sei-Ching Joanna Sin, "Increasing Ethnic Diversity in LIS: Strategies Suggested by Librarians of Color," *Library Quarterly* 78, no. 2 (2008): 163-164.

had not considered librarianship as a prospective career. Holly A. Smith reported the small number of librarians of color she had encountered from elementary school to graduate school. She remembered positive interactions with librarians, but rarely saw one that looked like her. Smith admitted to being guilty of stereotyping all librarians as older white women, complete with the glasses, sweaters, and "shushing" fingers.

Many recruiters spoke of how influential one person could be. Smith stated that she learned about library science directly from her mentor Dr. Tywanna Whorley, a young African American professor at Simmons College who was not much older than her. Smith had majored in History and Black Studies as an undergraduate, but was unsure how to translate those academic interests into a career. In 2005 she met Dr. Whorley, who encouraged her to sit in on her archival management course at Simmons. Since graduating from Simmons in 2008, Smith has looked upon that fortuitous meeting knowing that she probably would have never considered a career in academic librarianship if Dr. Whorley had not encouraged her to do so. Steven D. Booth was also urged to pursue library and information science. He stated that although he had worked at a public library in high school and served as a library assistant for several performing arts ensembles in college, he had never contemplated obtaining a degree in library science until a professor recommended it.

It was incredibly helpful to hear the recruitment stories of the other participants during the initial training at the 2011 ALA Midwinter meeting. It provided participants with other recruiters' stories and their career paths, many of which could be used to answer questions and inspire and educate potential students about the broad range of opportunities in the field. Due to the wide array of professional backgrounds, recruiters could identify the ones most closely aligned to students' interests and academic training. With the subsequent development of the Knowledge Alliance brand and website (http://knowledgealliance.org/), students could connect with recruiters for additional career information and/or even seek guidance and mentoring.

The recruiters also composed elevator speeches to assist with future presentations at college and career fairs. Emily K. Chan stated that this made her aware of how she wanted to present herself, her work, and librarianship as a career. Given that librarianship is burdened by stereotypes and misconceptions about the types of individuals involved in the profession, as well as the type of work being done, an elevator speech had the potential, for example, to dispel the popular idea that librarians' sole responsibility is to read books. Actively working on her elevator speech made Chan identify the essential functions of her job as an academic liaison librarian, characterize how these duties could be of interest to a new generation of students, and verbalize how significant these skills were in a 21st century knowledge economy. Being savvy information searchers and evaluators could resonate with high school and undergraduate students who often employed these competencies during the course of their studies.

Strengthening the Pipeline

After the initial training to develop the recruitment materials and Knowledge Alliance branding and message, the recruiters embarked across the United States and Canada to discuss the value and merits of library and information science careers. In the past three years, Smith attended three career fairs with two fellow recruiters – two at Howard University and one at American University. She commented that it was particularly exciting to be at Howard, a historically black college. Since 1926, there have been approximately four ALA-accredited programs at historically black colleges and universities (HBCU).[11] These programs helped strengthen the pipeline of diverse professionals by training and preparing African Americans for careers in librarianship with a focus on serving their own communities. Today, only one such program remains. Through grant-funded recruitment initiatives, a number of schools have

---

11. American Library Association "Accredited Library and Information Studies Master's Programs from 1925 through Present,", accessed June 21, 2014, http://www.ala.org/accreditedprograms/directory/historicallist. These institutions include Hampton Institute (1926-1940), Clark Atlanta University (1941-2005), Alabama Agricultural and Mechanical University (1973-1982), and North Carolina Central University (1973-present).

made efforts to remedy the lack of representation of students of color. Most recently, Wayne State University School of Library and Information Science and the HBCU Library Alliance received financial support from the IMLS Laura Bush 21st Century Librarian Program to "recruit, mentor, and provide an online Master of Library and Information Science degree to 10 students from underrepresented groups in order to achieve greater diversity among practicing library professionals."[12]

At Smith's career fair events, students were ethnically and racially diverse. There were Caucasian, Asian and Asian American, Latino, and African American students at American University and primarily African American students at Howard University. Nearly all were undergraduates looking for work experience or internships. These undergraduates represented a variety of majors: economics, history, computer science, psychology, and education. Students had seldom considered librarianship as a career option. This was not surprising, as many recruiters themselves had recounted that they had rarely encountered librarians from underrepresented racial and ethnic backgrounds in public and academic institutions. Students also possessed a limited understanding about the profession and libraries, due to the stereotypes and outdated images often portrayed in the media. After conversing with the Knowledge Alliance recruiters, many students were genuinely intrigued to hear about LIS graduate education and career options. Most students were unaware and shocked to learn that librarianship is a real and legitimate profession, requiring the MLIS as a terminal degree and, in some cases, necessitating additional subject master degrees. Even fewer students were familiar with the breadth of the job opportunities in the field. Despite having to educate students about librarianship job prospects, Smith felt that academic institutions bred intellectual curiosity, fostered collaboration, and were fertile grounds for planting the seed of librarianship.

---

12. Wayne State University, "Project IDOL (Increasing Diversity of Librarians) -- Wayne State University & Historically Black Colleges and Universities Library Alliance," accessed June 18, 2014, http://slis.wayne.edu/diversity/projectidol.php.

At these college and career fairs, recruiters could share unique aspects about their positions. Smith shared how exciting it was to work as an archivist with African American-related collections at University of North Carolina at Chapel Hill. Her work dovetailed with her advocacy efforts and interests, demonstrating how library and information science work, particularly within diverse communities, could be inspiring, passion-felt, and deeply personal. The students asked intelligent and insightful questions about how their own pursuits could relate to librarianship. At the end of each fair, Smith felt that the recruiters had generated genuine respect for the profession and dispelled some librarian stereotypes. After meeting almost a hundred students over the course of the three career fairs, Smith and her fellow recruiters had connected with numerous individuals who wanted to learn more about the profession. A number of students created profiles on the Knowledge Alliance website, where Smith was able to remain in contact with several of them. She was happy to serve as a resource as they investigated the prospect of library and information science as a career choice.

Chan also noted that speaking to prospective students reminded her of the reasons why she had entered the profession—to connect with and teach others, to assist in finding information, and to continually learn. She realized that at every event, she was serving as an ambassador for the profession. For those who were interested in possibly pursuing library and information science studies, Chan could mentor and assist them through the education, application, and funding processes. For everyone else, she could enlighten them about the importance and role of libraries and archives, as well as change their ideas about who could become a librarian. In that respect, it was incredibly fruitful to be able to speak to a variety of individuals and influence their perceptions of the library field and its workforce, regardless of whether or not they pursued LIS studies. While the majority of the individuals Chan spoke to may not enter the field of librarianship, those who desired more information became connected to the Knowledge Alliance network and its representation of the diversity of library work. The Knowledge

Alliance website enables students to communicate with field recruiters and continue their contemplation of librarianship as a career.

Attracting a diverse workforce extended beyond recruiters' scheduled visits to career, education, and cultural events. In many cases, recruiters targeted individuals within their workplace who would be good candidates for the MLIS. Chan recognized that every non-librarian in the organization could benefit from a greater awareness of the work that librarians perform and the opportunities that await ethnically diverse individuals who are seeking LIS education and careers. Smith affirmed that while she had positive experiences interning at different academic institutions, she was always disappointed and troubled at the lack of diversity among the library staff, particularly at the professional level. It was her firm belief that it is extremely beneficial and crucial to have a diverse staff to engage the equally varied campus and larger community. Thus, she has taken every opportunity she could to encourage library student workers to consider a graduate degree in the field. Using the Knowledge Alliance recruiting materials in her new position in the Spelman College Archives, she has connected with a number of students, including several young women who have expressed interest in learning more about archives and the LIS profession in general. She shared Knowledge Alliance brochures with them, connected them with other professionals in the Knowledge Alliance, and continued to meet with them. Lota also has made it her mission to target student workers and non-librarian staff members. She has made three connections with staff members in her current institution; one is currently enrolled in library school. Like other recruiters, Lota continues to send scholarship information and other resources through the Knowledge Alliance website. Fostering and maintaining these mentoring relationships will be critical in developing the next generation of academic library professionals. The Knowledge Alliance program has prepared these recruiters to be better representatives for their respective institutions and the LIS field.

Targeting individuals who already work in libraries for advanced LIS studies and careers in librarianship is a sound strategy. In Kim and

Sin's 2008 article about librarian-suggested approaches for increasing ethnic diversity in LIS programs, the most influential factor for pursuing LIS studies was previous library work experience, followed by recommendations by librarians.[13] This is quite understandable as many of the recruiters themselves, like the students attending the college/career fairs, were unaware of librarianship as a viable and available profession prior to someone's recommendation. Individuals who are already working in a library environment will have greater exposure to the myriad of positions that facilitate the operation of a library, including librarianship. Furthermore, current library employees may recognize that future advancement or greater job responsibilities could require the MLIS degree. To promote earlier LIS recruitment, Davis-Kendrick recommends LIS counseling at the high school level. In her study, she found that awareness of librarianship as a single factor was not enough to pursue LIS studies. Encouragement by a librarian, trusted individual, or mentor to pursue the MLIS and a career in librarianship initiated these efforts.[14]

Mentoring, Retention, and Community Expectations of Librarians of Color

After Lota, Chan, Smith, and Booth and their fellow recruiters attended and connected with students at various career, educational, and cultural events, they began to guide and mentor students through the LIS informational, application, and financial processes. Additionally, Lota, Smith, and Booth were able to share their experiences as former Spectrum Scholarship recipients with students. Booth shared with students

---

13. Kim and Sin, "Increasing Ethnic Diversity in LIS: Strategies Suggested by Librarians of Color," 167.

14. Kaetrena D. Davis-Kendrick, "The African-American Male Librarian: Motivational Factors in Choosing a Career in Library and Information Science," *Behavioral & Social Sciences Librarian* 28, no. 1-2 (2009): 44.

that after having received the Spectrum Scholarship, while attending graduate school at Simmons College, the Office for Diversity of the American Library Association (ALA) provided extensive resources and benefits for graduate students and early career professionals of color. He felt that the initiatives of this program office were integral to the development and success of many and played a vital role in helping to improve and foster a diversified workforce. Through the Spectrum Program, Booth was provided with the opportunity to connect with peers and learn firsthand from veteran librarians who looked like him. This experience opened his eyes and mind to the endless opportunities librarianship had to offer and gave him basic strategies and new skillsets to assist with his professional development and career goals. Considering the positive influence this program had on him, Booth thought it was only appropriate to reach out, inspire, and mentor a new generation of undergraduate students to the profession.

Smith emphasized the network building and inspiration that Spectrum could provide. When attending the Spectrum Scholar Institute at ALA Annual in 2006, Smith was gladdened to connect with a wide array of ethnically and professionally diverse library professionals. It was the first time she had encountered a large group of librarians of color, and she was heartened to have such an amazing experience at her first professional conference. Moreover, her experience with other Spectrum scholars and alumni greatly influenced her decision to pursue working in academic libraries. Smith perceived many benefits of working in an academic environment: being a part of an intellectual community, having access to invaluable primary and secondary research sources, and connecting with dedicated faculty, staff, and community members.

It has been observed that mentoring significantly contributes to retention, promotion, and success in the work environment.[15] Mentors can provide protégés with advice and guidance on difficult situations that

---

15. Peggy Johnson, "Retaining and Advancing Librarians of Color," *College & Research Libraries* 68, no. 5 (2007): 412-414.

require nuanced approaches, serve as a confidant when protégés worry and/or misstep, and offer insight into the cultural, political, and social subtleties of the work environment. The mentoring relationship can impart confidence, motivation, and career opportunities to protégés.[16] Moore, Miller, Pitchford, and Jeng indicate that mentoring is even more critical for librarians of color, who may encounter tokenism, racism, and isolation from their colleagues. Having a mentor who has faced similar challenges and may have coping strategies to share can ease the protégés' difficulties.[17]

Iuliano, Royster, Johnson, Larrivee, and Driver observed on an anecdotal level that mentoring relationships could improve a librarian's bond with his/her workplace. Mentoring appeared to assist in fostering protégés' sense of belonging and inclusion in the library community.[18] This is exceedingly important in an organization where there are few librarians of color and those lone individuals may feel disconnected from the larger employee group. Mentoring, which could improve the sense of attachment and rapport that an ethnically diverse librarian may have to the institution, can ultimately influence retention. Ragins and Scandura found that serving as a mentor or being a protégé in a mentoring relationship significantly affected one's likelihood of being a mentor in the future.[19] Those who had prior experience in a mentoring relationship reported that these relationships reaped positive dividends, such as satisfaction and fulfillment, while those without these experiences

---

16. Joan Howland, "Beyond Recruitment: Retention and Promotion Strategies to Ensure Diversity and Success," *Library Administration and Management* 13, no. 1 (1999): 12.

17. Alanna Aiko Moore et al., "Mentoring in the Millennium: New Views, Climate and Actions," *New Library World* 109, no. 1/2 (2008): 80.

18. Ava Iuliano et al., "Reaching Out to Minority Librarians: Overcoming Diversity Challenges through Mentorship," *ACRL 2013 Conference Proceedings*, accessed June 10, 2014. http://www.ala.org/acrl/sites/ala.org.acrl/files/content/conferences/confsandpreconfs/2013/papers/Iuliano_Reaching.pdf.

19. Belle Rose Ragins and Terri A. Scandura, "Burden or Blessing? Expected Costs and Benefits of Being a Mentor," *Journal of Organizational Behavior* 20 (1999): 506.

anticipated negatives, like extensive time commitments. Ragins and Scandura suggest that individuals who have been on the receiving end of a mentoring relationship are more likely to serve as mentors in the future. After becoming mentors, these former protégés have a greater propensity to continue to serve as mentors.[20] When applying this paradigm into one's own organization, this can help to create a community of practice focused on mentoring and support, leading to greater retention among librarians of color. This can strengthen the pipeline for the further recruitment and retention of diverse employees.

Given the paucity of librarians of color in LIS studies and the profession, mentoring relationships can be the difference between success and failure. Lota notes that her career has paralleled her library school experience in the matter of diversity. When she examines every job or internship she has worked at since being enrolled in library school, she has seen a similar pattern. In both of Lota's internships, she was one of three persons of color in a professional position. When she became a full-time librarian in her first professional position, she was one of two African American librarians. There were no other librarians of color in that environment. One year later, Lota moved to another academic institution and found herself to be the only librarian of color. She recounts that it is a frustrating and sometimes very isolating feeling to be the lone librarian of color. However, Lota credits mentorship for her continued presence in the profession and success. She states that she has had mentors who have supported her journey to librarianship from day one: mentors who kindly paid for her applications to library school, mentors who have driven her five hours across the state of California to make sure she was present at an important award ceremony, and mentors who pushed her to stay in library school when the cultural insensitivity and the loneliness were becoming too heavy. Lota is well aware that she did not walk down this road of success alone. She was guided down this path by mentors every step of the way and she has been fortunate to receive scholarships, awards, and opportunities like

---

20. Ibid.

the Spectrum Scholarship and being named an Emerging Leader. Lota confirms that the experiences she has encountered while being a librarian of color in academia, while solitary at times, have prepared her to be an advocate, mentor, and role model to those who are seeking a career in the information profession.

Chan agrees, stating that as a beneficiary of a mentoring relationship, she has been able to leverage her participation in the Knowledge Alliance to directly contribute by mentoring individuals who she meets at college and career fairs. Her recruitment endeavors extend outside of these events, targeting co-workers, friends, and acquaintances who have the aptitude, skills, and drive to contribute to librarianship. In her article "Your Worries Ain't Like Mine," Deborah Curry raises the conundrum that many librarians of color face—how to "sell academic librarianship or librarianship in general, as a positive career choice when they themselves are pondering their own rationales for staying in this profession."[21] In contrast, Chan's recruitment and mentoring activities have aided her feelings of connection to librarianship, the American Library Association, and current and prospective librarians of color. The American Management Association identified the most commonly utilized retention strategies as: "mentoring, networking, career and learning opportunities, interesting work, good benefits, and balance between work and home life."[22] Chan's involvement with Knowledge Alliance has provided her with mentoring, networking, learning, and professional development opportunities. As she seeks to recruit and help diversify the profession, her actions are reinforcing her own commitment to the field of librarianship.

These strong sentiments for the profession's workforce and its diversification are important. Echevarria emphasizes that librarianship, like any other profession, requires its own members to recruit new members

---

21. Deborah A. Curry, "Your Worries Ain't Like Mine: African American Librarians and the Pervasiveness of Racism, Prejudice and Discrimination in Academe," *Reference Librarian* 21, no. 45-46 (1994): 305.

22. Linda R. Musser, "Effective Retention Strategies for Diverse Employees," *Journal of Library Administration* 33, no. 1-2 (2001): 65-66.

to aid in its perpetuation.[23] Howland notes that experienced and senior librarians may unwittingly seek mentoring relationships with individuals who have similar cultural, ethnic, or racial backgrounds.[24] This can be unfavorable to librarians of color, especially given the potentially low numbers of librarians of color in any institution. Moore, Miller, Pitchford, and Jeng issue the professional charge to seasoned librarians to contact and connect with new librarians. As protégés have benefited from mentoring relationships, it is imperative that these individuals contribute in turn to the mentoring enterprise.[25] This professional obligation to participate in recruitment has been taken very seriously by the majority of the Discovering Librarianship program members who have used the tools, stories, and resources to connect with a new generation of students.

Lota states that when she attends Knowledge Alliance recruitment events, her love for librarianship speaks louder than her voice. She is emboldened and impassioned by the work and efforts of library luminaries, like E. J. Josey, who faced segregated libraries and changed the way the profession regarded librarians of color. When she attends Knowledge Alliance recruitment events, her commitment to become a mentor is reinforced by the sheer gratitude she feels and of a desire to pay it forward. Being a recruiter with the Discovering Librarianship program has given her the opportunity to strengthen the pipeline and plant seeds that will produce an amazing harvest, one recruitment event at a time.

Diversity initiatives can work in tandem to produce large gains. Booth believes that the Spectrum Program, along with other diversity programs, served as a feeder to Discovering Librarianship and its accompanying

---

23. Tami Echevarria, "Recruiting Latinos to Librarianship: A Continuing Need" in *Library Services to Latinos*, ed. Salvador Guerena (Jefferson, North Carolina: McFarland, 2000), 20.

24. Joan Howland, "Beyond Recruitment: Retention and Promotion Strategies to Ensure Diversity and Success," *Library Administration and Management* 13, no. 1 (1999): 13.

25. Moore et al., "Mentoring in the Millennium: New Views, Climate and Actions," 85.

Knowledge Alliance brand by enlisting the services of former scholars to develop and implement an assertive agenda that actively exposed high school and undergraduate students to the field of library and information science and educated them concerning career options. Presenting at educational and professional fairs enabled recruiters to personally connect with students. This benefited both the students and the recruiters. Recruiters were able to heighten their awareness of the profession and debunk librarian stereotypes. As librarians of color, the recruiters took responsibility for the issue and made a concerted effort to be a part of the solution, in order to remedy the problem. Being involved with Knowledge Alliance taught Booth that recruitment is an interactive and engaging endeavor—a personal calling that requires professionals to meet students where they are and share the necessary information and resources they need in order to be successful. Booth observed that these activities gave him a voice to speak out and advocate for a profession where he is often overlooked and declare, "Here I am. I do exist." Recognizing the need to actively inform, recruit, and support prospective librarians is important to the growth of diversity in graduate programs and the workforce.

In a short assessment of the efficacy of the Discovering Librarianship program, all of the responding recruiters (n=12) affirmed that the initiative's training sessions helped to 1) articulate the reasons for becoming an information professional and the merits of the profession, 2) discuss available LIS grant and scholarship opportunities, 3) speak to individuals interested in careers in LIS, and 4) serve as an effective recruiter for LIS studies. Recruiters also identified the following benefits to having participated in the program:

- the ability to provide tangible, professionally developed informational/recruitment materials to interested individuals,
- greater willingness to network and engage with students to promote librarianship,
- using one's participation as a way to introduce diversity issues and topics to colleagues and the work environment,

- remaining conversant in the initiatives and opportunities targeting students and newer librarians, and
- reaffirming one's commitment to the profession.

The Discovering Librarianship program is very special because the in-field recruiters are making connections to ethnically diverse students on a personal level, much like a grassroots movement. Recruiters are in their communities building a knowledge alliance, motivating and inspiring, and introducing new generations to information studies in a way that has not quite been done before. In conjunction with existing recruitment and retention strategies, the Discovering Librarianship program and its accompanying website Knowledge Alliance will continue to build momentum in long-term and sustainable recruiting efforts. As this program enlists more librarians who are interested in actively changing the demographics of the profession, the pipeline of students of color to librarianship will improve and strengthen. Early career librarians who mentor colleagues will create communities of practice, which will also assist retention. In addition to developing marketing materials to attract underrepresented groups to the field of librarianship, this program has trained and empowered early career librarians to articulate and share their professional work, passions, and experiences with new populations of prospective library students. The participatory and volunteer nature of this program, including its key features of building relationships and mentoring, offer greater capacity in the ongoing movement to diversify the library workforce.

References

American Library Association. "Accredited Library and Information Studies Master's Programs from 1925 through Present." Accessed June 21, 2014, http://www.ala.org/accreditedprograms/directory/historicallist.

American Library Association. "Discovering Librarianship: The Future is Overdue." Accessed June 18, 2014, http://www.ala.org/offices/diversity/imls.

American Library Association. "Diversity Counts 2012 Tables," Accessed January 27, 2014, http://www.ala.org/offices/sites/ala.org.offices/files/content/diversity/diversitycounts/diversitycountstables2012.pdf.

Association for Library and Information Science Education. "Library and Information Science Education Statistical Report 2002," Accessed June 30, 2014, http://ils.unc.edu/ALISE/2002/Contents.htm.

Curry, Deborah A. "Your Worries Ain't Like Mine: African American Librarians and the Pervasiveness of Racism, Prejudice and Discrimination in Academe." *Reference Librarian* 21, no. 45-46 (1994): 299-311.

Davis-Kendrick, Kaetrena D. "The African American Male Librarian: Motivational Factors in Choosing a Career in Library and Information Science." *Behavioral & Social Sciences Librarian* 28, no. 1-2 (2009): 23-52.

Echevarria, Tami. "Recruiting Latinos to Librarianship: A Continuing Need." In *Library Services to Latinos*, edited by Salvador Guerena, 18-27. Jefferson, NC: McFarland, 2000.

Howland, Joan. "Beyond Recruitment: Retention and Promotion Strategies to Ensure Diversity and Success." *Library Administration and Management* 13, no. 1 (1999): 4-14.

Iuliano, Ava, Melody Royster, Margeaux Johnson, Anne Larrivee, and Lori Driver. "Reaching Out to Minority Librarians: Overcoming Diversity Challenges through Mentorship." *ACRL 2013 Conference Proceedings*. Accessed June 10, 2014. http://www.ala.org/acrl/sites/ala.org.acrl/files/content/conferences/confsandpreconfs/2013/papers/Iuliano_Reaching.pdf.

Johnson, Peggy. "Retaining and Advancing Librarians of Color." *College & Research Libraries* 68, no. 5 (2007): 405-417.

Kim, Kyung-Sun, and Sei-Ching Joanna Sin. "Increasing Ethnic Diversity in LIS: Strategies Suggested by Librarians of Color." *Library Quarterly* 78, no. 2 (2008).

Korry, Elaine. "Black Student Enrollment at UCLA Plunges." NPR. org. Last modified July 24, 2006, http://www.npr.org/templates/story/story.php?storyId=5563891.

Moore, Alanna Aiko, Michael J. Miller, Veronda J. Pitchford, and Ling Hwey Jeng. "Mentoring in the Millennium: New Views, Climate and Actions." *New Library World* 109, no. 1/2 (2008): 75-86.

Musser, Linda R. "Effective Retention Strategies for Diverse Employees." *Journal of Library Administration* 33, no. 1-2 (2001): 63-72.

University of California – Los Angeles. "Quick Facts about UCLA." UCLA Undergraduate Admission, accessed June 18, 2014, https://www.admissions.ucla.edu/campusprofile.htm.

Ragins, Belle Rose, and Terri A. Scandura. "Burden or Blessing? Expected Costs and Benefits of Being a Mentor." *Journal of Organizational Behavior* 20, no. 4 (1999): 493-509.

"UCLA Has More NCAA Championships Than Black Male Freshmen," *Huffingtonpost.com*. Last modified November 8, 2013, http://www.huffingtonpost.com/2013/11/08/ucla-black-enrollment-freshmen_n_4242213.html.

Wallace, Danny P., ed. *Library and Information Science Education Statistical Report 2012*. Chicago, IL: ALISE, 2012.

Wayne State University. "Project IDOL (Increasing Diversity of Librarians)—Wayne State University & Historically Black Colleges and Universities Library Alliance," Accessed June 10, 2014, http://slis.wayne.edu/diversity/projectidol.php.

Chapter 2

ESTABLISHING A COMMUNAL NETWORK FOR PROFESSIONAL ADVANCEMENT AMONG LIBRARIANS OF COLOR

Tarida Anantachai, Latrice Booker, Althea Lazzaro, and Martha Parker

Introduction

As a demographic that is statistically and historically underrepresented in the profession, it is not uncommon for librarians of color to find themselves as one of the few professionals of color within their home libraries, if not the only one. The 2009-2010 update to the American Library Association's (ALA) *Diversity Counts* report—a comprehensive study of diversity within the library profession, incorporating data from the American Community Survey—found that, while there have been some minor increases over the past few years, there still remains a striking lack of diversity in the field. For instance, African American constitute 5.1 percent of credentialed librarians, with Asian and Pacific Islander constituting 2.7 percent, Latinos constituting 3.1 percent, and Native American constituting .2 percent.[1] While much has already been written about the largely homogenous nature of the library profession

---

1. American Library Association, "Diversity Counts 2009-2010 Update," last modified September 2012, http://www.ala.org/offices/diversity/diversitycounts/divcounts..

and the general need to recruit and retain librarians of color,[2] there is still also a paucity of literature regarding how institutions can effectively support their librarians of color to better serve the diverse communities for whom they aim to advocate.[3] This is not to say that there is no related research on this topic; rather, much of what has been written has focused more on diversity programs and scholarships that have been established to recruit potential students of color to graduate library school programs (some of which will be addressed later in this chapter). These recruitment efforts are an incredibly important and necessary step towards increasing diversity among future generations of librarians. Yet more must be done to ensure that these librarians continue to receive ongoing support even after they have earned their degrees and assumed their subsequent professional positions.

As libraries remain predominantly staffed and structured by the majority White culture, the few librarians of color often find themselves feeling marginalized and without access to a supportive group of similarly diverse-minded colleagues to whom they can relate and confide. This in turn can also affect their own advancement in the profession, as professionals are generally better equipped to grow and to succeed when they have such collegial group environments and networks at their disposal. Bearing this in mind, it is perhaps unsurprising that issues related to a lack of job satisfaction, advancement, and retention are also so prevalent among this group.[4]

---

2. Paul T. Jaeger, John Carlo Bertot, and Renee E. Franklin, "Diversity, Inclusion, and Underrepresented Populations in LIS Research," *Library Quarterly* 80, no. 2 (April 2010): 176, doi: 10.1086/651053.

3. Teresa Y. Neely and Lorna Peterson, "Achieving Racial and Ethnic Diversity among Academic and Research Librarians: The Recruitment, Retention, and Advancement of Librarians of Color: A White Paper by the ACRL Board of Directors Diversity Task Force," Association of College & Research Libraries, last modified June 2007, http://www.ala.org/acrl/sites/ala.org.acrl/files/content/publications/whitepapers/ACRL_AchievingRacial.pdf.

4. Peggy Johnson, "Retaining and Advancing Librarians of Color," *College & Research Libraries* 68, no. 5 (September 2007): 407-408, accessed April 30, 2014, http://crl.acrl.org/content/68/5/405.full.pdf+html.

One common observation is that supportive networks and mentorship are some of the key components in retaining librarians of color.[5] Connecting such librarians with both senior professionals and peers who share their backgrounds and experiences can help to alleviate these feelings of isolation.[6] These connections are especially valuable when they develop into or from active communities of practice, as they simultaneously help to bolster interpersonal relationships and professional growth.[7] Ideally, such partnerships should exist within librarians' own workplaces, yet again, because there are such limited numbers of librarians of color in the profession, it is often necessary for them to reach beyond their immediate environments to locate and cultivate such collaborative work groups.

As part of their work on the Association of College and Research Libraries (ACRL)'s Diversity Committee, the authors of this chapter have themselves been active in participating in and advocating for a number of these types of collaborations. What follows are several examples and models of these, including: diversity-related initiatives that have been internal to their own libraries or institutions, collaborations that have been externally sought and established with other institutions or professional association committees, and those that have emerged out of mentoring and other diversity-focused development programs. The outcomes of such partnerships are mutually supportive, providing librarians of color with invaluable opportunities to connect with a supportive, communal network of colleagues from across the profession, while also encouraging their own professional development and sustainability in the profession. This in turn has also led to a greater awareness within the wider library profession of the unique challenges

---

5. Johnson, "Retaining and Advancing Librarians of Color," 407-408; Neely and Peterson, "Achieving Racial and Ethnic Diversity among Academic and Research Librarians."

6. Joan Howland, "Beyond Recruitment: Retention and Promotion Strategies to Ensure Diversity and Success," *Library Administration & Management* 13, no. 1 (Winter 1999): 4-14.

7. Johnson, "Retaining and Advancing Librarians of Color," 406-407.

facing librarians of color and how to best support them on both the local and national level.

Internal Collaborations

In any profession, building relationships and a professional network of colleagues can greatly enhance one's advancement and growth. The question that many minority librarians face early in their careers is how to cope with a lack of networking opportunities when working within a mono-cultural, silo organization. In response to this question, librarians of color have developed a number of strategies that facilitate the development of supportive, nurturing environments within their own libraries and institutions. What follows is a summary of some of these internal collaborative efforts, with special emphasis on designated diversity positions and diversity committees.

Designated diversity positions, like library residency programs or related diversity internships, tend to have both positive and negative consequences for the library and the librarian. These positions can serve to create an environment where members of a library feel that they will be heard when they share ideas openly or ask questions. They also offer a great opportunity for the librarian of color to introduce staff to the most recent diversity research, and to reinforce the fact that the input from and contributions of all types of staff members are needed for an organization to produce the best service to its users.

Unfortunately, these positions can also be mistakenly considered by some staff as "charity," which serves to indirectly undermine the value of the program, the resident and diversity librarians themselves, and the strategic goal the library is attempting to achieve in creating such a program or position. Running an effective library goes beyond just doing a "good thing" for a particular minority group; in other words, doing the best work with all of the staff involved is, at a fundamental level, an ethical, inclusive organizational practice to which libraries should aspire. Broadly diversifying libraries serves both colleagues and users alike, as a recent full page ad run in the *New York Times* by The Association of American Universities recently reasoned: "Since graduates will be entering a diverse world, they will be well served if they are exposed to faculty of diverse cultures using varying research perspectives and teaching methods within varying or diverse curricula."[8]

Additionally, demographic changes and trends in the community are often problematically perceived as something unrelated to the strategic goal of serving all library users. In many organizations, changing that notion frequently becomes the responsibility of the librarians of color. Although this may sound simple and strategic, such tasks can be difficult to accomplish initially and puts additional pressures and duties upon the librarian, particularly when he or she is new to the organization and lacks the necessary connections and the networking partners to launch such a program. An alternative to asking a single librarian to instigate such an important institutional change is establishing a diversity committee within the library or reenergizing an existing one; this can help to create a supportive space for library workers who feel marginalized (as well as for their allies) to find community and raise awareness in the library about issues related to diversity.

The University of Arkansas Libraries' Diversity Committee is one example of a committee that has produced creative ways of contributing to a thriving work environment for new library staff and for introducing diversity-focused research and activities to all users. The committee developed a Diversity LibGuide to provide essential resources and services to students, faculty, and library staff.[9] The committee is also highly involved in campus-wide events such as iConnect, a program that introduces freshman from underrepresented backgrounds to the university and the libraries and its resources. As a reward, the library staff gains a great opportunity to interact with and support first year students,

---

8. Fred Piercy et al., "Improving Campus Climate to Support Faculty Diversity and Retention: A Pilot Program for New Faculty," *Innovative Higher Education* 30, no. 1 (January 2005): 54.

9. University of Arkansas, "Diversity Resources LibGuide," last modified June 2, 2014, http://uark.libguides.com/content.php?pid=302086&sid=2475833.

which in turn provides the students with lively diversity programming and dynamic exposure to the new demographic changes in the local area.

The committee also maintains a library diversity website that serves as a gateway for anyone interested in knowing where diversity resources are located throughout the campus, and guides users to diversity events held within the library, the university, and the local community.[10] The committee proudly welcomes all users to review its extensive network of resources and services. Some of the university's diversity resources provided within the website include: access to the Diversity Office, the Multicultural Center, the International Students Office, and the World, Literatures, and Cultures Department. An example of an event promoted through this website is Juneteenth, also known as Freedom or Emancipation Day. For this event, the University of Arkansas Libraries and its Multicultural Center collaborate with the neighboring city of Springdale and its local vendors to celebrate this holiday and its Arkansan roots. This highly attended program provides a fun, shared way for the surrounding community to learn about Arkansas' rich cultural history. During the Juneteenth celebration vendors provide music, food, and games for everyone to enjoy, to learn, and especially to connect with fellow residents.

At the University of Washington's Bothell/Cascadia Community College Campus, the Library's Diversity Team has chosen to pursue staff training, brown bag discussions, and workshops to increase awareness of diversity on campus and build cultural competency among its staff.[11] Though initially the team was composed solely of white library workers (this is no longer the case), they put race and racism at the center of their first two years of work, and have conducted training on topics ranging from intersectionality to micro-aggressions, to variations in ethnic discourse styles in the information literacy classroom. Essential to this

---

10. University of Arkansas, "Diversity and the Libraries," accessed June 1, 2014, http://libinfo.uark.edu/diversity.

11. For a more detailed description of the team's work, see Althea Eannace Lazzaro et al., "Cultural Competency on Campus: Applying ACRL's Diversity Standards," *College & Research Libraries News*, 75, no. 4 (2014): 332-335.

work was relationship building with librarians at other UW libraries, and faculty, staff, and students across their two campuses. In addition to developing the teams' understanding of culture, discrimination, and power, this relationship building demonstrated the connection between the library's priorities and those of the institutions that they served; as a result, the library increased its visibility and its relevancy to its communities. Through several iterations of assessment, the team has received overwhelmingly positive feedback about the impact this work has had on staff competency and well-being. Inspired by the University of Arkansas Libraries' work, as of this writing, the team is developing a public LibGuide that contains artifacts of their work, copies of their training, and a bibliography of readings and videos that were particularly influential for their cultural competency growth. This will serve the dual purposes of sharing material with other libraries, while demonstrating accountability and transparency to their larger community.

Cross-campus programs can provide another opportunity for collaborations within an institution. An example of this is a "Human Library" program, an event designed to "promote dialogue, reduce prejudices and encourage understanding"[12] by inviting people of differing backgrounds and experiences to engage in intimate conversations on a given topic. In the spring of 2014, the Syracuse University Libraries, in conjunction with the Office of Multicultural Affairs and School of Information Studies, organized just such an event under the general theme of "cultural diversity." The "human books" were recruited from various campus offices and programs, including the library—and each provided a brief synopsis of a story they would be interested in sharing. These stories included tales of migrating between cultures of experiences, working with local indigenous groups, and overcoming various discriminatory hardships, among others. Through this event, patrons were able to approach and "check out" a "human book" to both listen to their personal stories as well as ask them questions they might not

---

12. The Human Library Organisation, "Human Library," accessed May 27, 2014, http://humanlibrary.org.

normally feel comfortable bringing up in their everyday lives. Students and staff alike enjoyed the opportunity to serve as human books and open access to their cultures, while "readers" appreciated being in a safe zone where they could learn about new cultures and experiences, or just confide in someone who shared a story similar to their own. At the same time, it helped to establish the library and its staff as being open and supportive, and further encouraged opportunities between librarians, staff, and students of color to develop additional cross-cultural and cross-campus collaborations.

Diversity programs such as these not only provide important resources to a library's patron community, but also serve as a welcoming, culturally responsive space for those patrons who might not otherwise feel comfortable there. Diversity programs also provide the library staff with an empowering opportunity to make a difference and to interact with students of color, who may also be adjusting to the unexpected demographic makeup in their new campus environment. This fact alone highlights the importance of embracing and advocating for diversity within a library organization—that is, doing so can also help to better reflect, address, and relate to the increasingly diverse patron communities they intend to serve. At the same time, they also support the library workers themselves who run them; in fact, the authors of this chapter have themselves experienced a great sense of accomplishment while actively participating in these events. Indeed, the overall job satisfaction of minority librarians is markedly improved and productivity is increased within the organization.

External Collaborations

Yet a librarian of color might not always have the proper connections within his or her home institution to drive and to promote such diversity-related initiatives and support systems. This could be due to several factors, including a lack of diverse colleagues among the current library staff with whom the librarian can relate, a lack of awareness of the importance of supporting diversity within the context of the library, or even their tenuous state of being a newly hired librarian of color within a mono-cultural institution. The topic of diversity can sometimes be controversial and some staff may be unaware of the importance of diversity because they may not have previously had the opportunity to engage with colleagues who have backgrounds and experiences that are significantly different from their own. In institutions that suffer from this lack of awareness, diversity research can often be viewed as "unofficial work" that is not recognized as fitting into a traditional scholarly paradigm. In some instances, staff may even perceive that their organization is doing "enough" by implementing a diversity program or simply by employing an underrepresented librarian, once again putting the onus of responsibility on librarians marked out as being "different." This can make it difficult for engaged librarians of color to locate partners at their institution who are genuinely invested in the librarian of color's experience at the library. With limited internal options for connecting with other librarians of color, it can be useful for these librarians to seek out partners and collaborations outside of their respective institutions.

While these can sometimes be more challenging to initially locate, there are many options for identifying potential partners and collaborators outside of one's organization. This chapter alone, compiled by librarians at several institutions, is just one example of an external collaboration among diverse librarians who have grown into mutual allies and peer mentors. The authors have created relationships during the past three years through attending and contributing to virtual conferences, participating in physical conferences throughout the country, and by serving on various national committees together. For instance, library professional associations, also recognizing the need to bring to light issues related to diversity and professional support, have established a number of related committees and working groups addressing this.

One of these national groups is the Diversity Committee of the Association of College & Research Libraries (ACRL); in addition to providing opportunities to connect with other diversity-focused librarians, it also aims to disseminate and address new trends and initiatives related to diversity, such as the recently released ACRL Diversity Standards for Academic Libraries.[13] As noted earlier, the authors of this chapter are active members of this committee, headed by current chair Martha Parker, and together have promoted the application of these standards for academic libraries through different venues, including Library 2.013 (an international virtual conference), the San Jose State University 2013 Spring Colloquia Conference, the 2013 ALA Annual Conference, and regional library conferences in Washington State. Like ACRL, ALA has a Diversity Committee that annually calls for diversity research papers through its ALA Annual Diversity Research Grant Program. The grant proposals are intended to address any diversity topic that speaks to critical gaps in the knowledge of diversity issues within library and information science.[14]

A group particularly designed for newer librarians of color is ACRL's Residency Interest Group (RIG),[15] a professional community of practice established to support resident librarians and other early career librarians. As many library residency programs themselves are initiated with the goal of supporting entry-level librarians of color, RIG is just one example of a cross-institutional opportunity dedicated to advancing diversity-related programs within the profession as a whole, and to creating a community of practice of like-minded colleagues. Primarily (but not exclusively) made up of former and current residents, as well as residency coordinators directly involved with or looking to launch such programs within their respective institutions, RIG is one of many groups that have helped newer librarians of color build their professional networks—oftentimes leading to the establishment of long-standing professional relationships, presentations and other such career enhancement opportunities, and

13. Association of College & Research Libraries, "Diversity Standards: Cultural Competency for Academic Libraries (2012)," accessed May 29, 2014, http://www.ala.org/acrl/standards/diversity.

14. American Library Association, "ALA Annual Diversity Research Grant Program," accessed April 30, 2014, http://www.ala.org/advocacy/diversity/diversityresearchstatistics/diversityresearch.

15. Association of College & Research Libraries, "Residency Interest Group," accessed June 19, 2014, http://acrl.ala.org/residency.

an overall sense of advocacy for other types of initiatives supporting diversity in the field.

Getting involved in professional organizations such as these is a major way in which librarians have been able to successfully connect with and collaborate with colleagues at different institutions, and ultimately to find support and validation. ALA also provides avenues to various affiliate organizations of interest, including, most notably, five ethnic caucuses that offer expert sources for more specialized support groups and related research for particular populations. AILA (American Indian Library Association), APALA (Asian Pacific American Librarians Association), BCALA (Black Caucus of the American Library Association), CALA (Chinese Americans Library Association), and REFORMA (The National Association to Promote Library & Information Services to Latinos and the Spanish Speaking) offer various orientation committees for new members, as well as mentoring committees to guide new librarians in understanding the nature of their organization's work and its contributions to diversity.[16] Most of these caucuses also host their own programs and discussion groups at the major professional library conferences (and some even organize their own caucus conferences entirely). These caucuses also notably convened to help support JCLC (Joint Conference of Librarians of Color), an impressive conference (most recently held in 2012) in which attendees were able to interact jointly, grow, and exchange knowledge on a range of diversity-related topics within the field of librarianship as a whole.

While these provide a number of potential opportunities, this is by no means an exhaustive list; in fact, other library professional organizations offer their own related committees as well. For instance, the Society of American Archivists (SAA) also has its own Diversity Committee, which itself is also divided into a number of special interest roundtables, including the Latin American and Caribbean Cultural Heritage Archive

---

16. American Library Association, "Associations of Ethnic Librarians," accessed June 19, 2014, http://www.ala.org/offices/diversity/ethniclibrariansassociations.

Roundtable and the Native Archives Roundtable, among others.[17] Some state- and regional-level organizations also offer their own diversity-related committees, allowing librarians of color to connect with an external support network that is somewhat closer to their own home institutions.

Networking and collaborating at conferences and through committee work can go a long way to redress the isolation that many librarians of color experience at their home institutions. Finding a community of like-minded colleagues validates an individual's experience, and can help to encourage that individual to move from being a listener to an active contributor to the profession. By promoting diversity within their organizations and with the connections made at the national level, underrepresented librarians greatly assist the profession in creating awareness of diversity issues and an understanding of diversity work and its academic value to the profession. These acts in turn can greatly help to empower librarians of color, expanding their collegial networks across the profession as a whole, and encouraging them to bolster others like them who may also be in need of support. The importance of these collaborations makes it absolutely essential for institutions to support travel and professional development, especially for librarians who are in the minority at their home institutions.[18]

---

17. Society of American Archivists, "Diversity Committee," last modified February 2010, http://www2.archivists.org/governance/handbook/section7/groups/Diversity.

18. In recognition of this, librarian-in-residence programs usually carry a statement that ensures that new hires will be able to travel and to attend these conferences, opening doors to committee work and collaboration. For example, the University of Arkansas at Fayetteville's Librarian-In-Residence position description states: "…other prerequisites, such as an allowance for professional travel and assigned time for scholarship, will give the Resident a competitive advantage in the search for a successive professional position." University of Arkansas Libraries, "Librarian-In-Residence Program," accessed June 19, 2014, http://libinfo.uark.edu/diversity/residency/overview.asp.

Mentoring

Mentoring, often an implicit part of internal and external collaboration, is perhaps one of the most critical ways in which librarians of color can create a communal network of support. Mentoring relationships, whether informally or formally established, can help librarians of color leverage opportunities at every phase of their careers. Informal mentorships can develop in a number of ways, such as through networking and getting involved in meeting people through the professional opportunities discussed above. Networking is an excellent opportunity for librarians of color to connect with and learn from experienced and knowledgeable colleagues. This may initially be an intimidating prospect, but oftentimes, others are more than happy to share their experiences and advice, especially to up-and-coming librarians.

The authors of this chapter themselves have informally gained mentors by attending conferences and volunteering for professional committees. By volunteering on the ACRL Diversity Committee, for example, they have established a support network and have become informal yet valuable peer mentors for each other. The trust built by working together on a national committee has led to further advantages, such as collaborative publications and presentations and other forms of professional engagement and portfolio-building. Through these collaborations, invaluable relationships and support systems can be formed, even if the term "mentor" is not officially uttered between colleagues.

Formal mentorship opportunities can also present themselves in a multitude of ways. Some organizations have created their own internal mentorship programs to help librarians advance within their respective organizations and successfully make it through the promotion and tenure process. The Indiana University (IU) Libraries Mentor Program serves eight IU campuses across the state to help tenure-track librarians successfully achieve tenure and promotion. Direct supervisors still have a role in assisting their librarians in the process and focusing their mentoring on the librarian's performance, yet the primary objective of the IU Mentor Program is to give tenure-track librarians an additional resource to consult when seeking advice on professional development, research, and service.[19]

It is worth noting that having a formal mentor program as part of an organization has its strengths and weaknesses. New librarians who are assigned a formal mentor can experience a very different dynamic than those who acquire one more naturally or serendipitously. It is important that new librarians are placed with a mentor who has knowledge in their area of librarianship. Also, mentors within the same organization must be strategically placed and must be mindful of potential work conflicts that may arise. For instance, one of the authors of this chapter was paired with a library dean who had previously guided eleven librarians through the entire promotion process during her own tenure. In doing so, the relationship auspiciously developed, with terms set at the beginning. The mentor asked what the mentee needed and made herself available. Open and honest communication was essential to the relationship for both parties; for instance, the mentee followed the recommendation that she "should be clear and specific in communicating [her] immediate needs," goals, and what she was looking for in a mentor.[20] The pressures of being new in a career and organization can sometimes be daunting, but having a mentor who understands the pressures, and the particular organization itself, can help remove potential roadblocks that may occur.

While this specific program is not exclusive to librarians of color (that is, it serves to aid all new librarians), having such support networks can greatly assist librarians of color in obtaining a much needed sense of support and advocacy in their career advancement. There are, however, examples of similar programs that are more targeted to supporting the specialized needs of librarians from underrepresented groups. In 2001,

19. Indiana University Faculty Council (IULFC), "Mentor Program," accessed May 20, 2014, http://www.iu.edu/~iulfc/mentor/mentorprogram.shtml.

20. Alanna Aiko Moore et al., "Mentoring in the Millennium: New Views, Climate and Actions," *New Library World* 109, no. 1/2 (2008): 78.

Camila Alire wrote an article about Colorado State University's New Beginnings program for junior faculty of color. This particular program differs from Indiana University Libraries' Mentor Program because it exclusively serves the needs of faculty of color, offering them tips on how to "network with senior faculty," how to write annual reviews, and tips for research and publishing, among other areas.[21] Colorado State University is another institution that implemented a similar program to connect junior faculty with senior faculty of color who were successful in publishing and grant writing, and were knowledgeable to the formalities of the organization; this completely volunteer-based program, made up of senior faculty who strongly believed in recruiting and retaining multicultural faculty, is an example of an initiative that identified the specialized needs of underrepresented faculty and then worked to fulfill those specific needs. Indeed, the implementation of these types of programs can give librarians of color a supportive environment that may otherwise be lacking, due to the simultaneous pressures of the tenure process and the marginalization and micro-aggressions (whether intentional or not) they may face in their everyday work. Ideally, more programs like these should be implemented to better ensure the career advancement and advocacy of librarians of color in the profession. After all, the goal of every library should be to assist in making each member of their organization successful, to find out what their librarians need in order to succeed and to then attend to those needs.

Formal mentoring programs targeted at librarians of color are also offered through various professional organizations. The ALA ethnic caucuses described above offer varying degrees of mentorships, from those providing a mentor and listing specific conditions of the mentorship relationship, to those that mostly serve to initiate introductions between mentors and mentees and then allow the relationship to grow more organically. One of the authors of this chapter informally experienced

---

21. Camila A. Alire, "The New Beginnings Program: A Retention Program for Junior Faculty of Color," *Journal of Library Administration* 33, no. 1-2 (2001): 26.

the benefits of BCALA's mentorship program through a colleague who was more officially affiliated with the program. After first being invited to join the mentor at a casual dinner meeting and then building the relationship through continued informal get-togethers at subsequent conferences, the author was able to learn more about BCALA and how to get involved, in addition to gaining personal insights about ALA and what steps to take to get more involved nationally. The BCALA mentorship program gave her both a valuable colleague for future consultation and advice, and, through the collaboration that followed, a potential professional reference for future career endeavors.

The ALA Emerging Leaders (EL) program is another well-established opportunity worthy of consideration. The EL program was established to, among other things, cultivate leadership and collaborative skills, and serve as a fast track for direct involvement within ALA itself. Participants engage in two all-day workshops at the ALA Midwinter Meeting and the following ALA Annual Conference, and continue to engage with each other in between the conferences through various webinars and virtual group discussions. The focus of this training ranges from an orientation to the organizational structure of ALA, to leadership development, to learning about micro-aggressions in the workplace. Participants are also sorted into collaborative work groups and have chances to further develop their leadership skills by networking with peers, as well as by problem solving an actual ALA-sponsored project over the course of the several months between the two conferences. Although the EL program is not limited to librarians of color, the program does assert the importance of many levels of diversity in its selection process, stating that it "seeks diversity based on geography, gender, ethnicity and type of library,"[22] and it has in recent years addressed diversity-related topics in its webinar training. This program has provided some of the authors of this chapter with invaluable opportunities to participate on initiatives and committees at a national level, opened doors to connect

---

22. American Library Association, "ALA Emerging Leaders Program," accessed May 20, 2014, http://www.ala.org/educationcareers/leadership/emergingleaders.

with peers of many backgrounds from across the nation. Career boosting opportunities such as these need to be further advertised and encouraged, especially for librarians of color looking to advance their professional development and support systems.

Other diversity related programs are also available for librarians seeking to bolster their careers. As alluded to earlier, for those from minority populations who are considering entering the field of librarianship, ALA offers its Spectrum Scholarship Program. This program helps to provide not only library school scholarships, but also opportunities to connect with fellow Spectrum Scholars through mentorships, virtual discussion lists, and invitations to attend, or even present at, various conference programs of interest. Similarly, the Association of Research Libraries (ARL) also offers several diversity programs to recruit librarians and students from ethnic populations, including its Initiative to Recruit a Diverse Workforce and Career Enhancement Program, to those geared more towards underrepresented librarians interested in the fields of music librarianship or archives.[23] Again, while these programs are focused on the actual recruitment of would-be librarians of color to the profession, they have sought to further embed within them ongoing supportive networks that these library school students can then potentially carry with them and turn to throughout their careers.

Other opportunities include the Minnesota Institute for Early Career Librarians from Traditionally Underrepresented Groups, a biennial program intended for librarians of color with no more than three years of professional library experience.[24] Over the course of a week, this institute provides a varied slate of workshops, which have included topics such as leadership and organizational dynamics, program management and assessment, and grant writing. The intensive, cohort nature of the institute helps to establish and encourage a sense of camaraderie, enabling the participants to connect meaningfully with each other, and

23. Association of Research Libraries, "Diversity Recruitment," accessed June 8, 2014, http://www.arl.org/leadership-recruitment/diversity-recruitment.

24 . University of Minnesota, "Minnesota Institute for Early Career Librarians," accessed June 8, 2014, https://www.lib.umn.edu/sed/institute.

establish a peer network of diverse librarians who are also at the start of their careers. At the same time, recognizing that ongoing mentorship can greatly help to supplement what is learned over the course of the week, the Institute asks participants to self-select a mentor within their own institutions to serve as an additional resource. Mentors and mentees engage both before the Institute by discussing short assigned readings, and afterwards to reflect upon how to apply what the mentee learned actively as he or she moves forward in their work and their future career goals.[25]

The International Librarians Network (ILN) is another, somewhat recent and independently created peer mentoring program. The ILN pairs librarians at all stages of their careers and from all types of libraries with those from other countries. These mentorships are more formally supported through the facilitation of various online discussions—both between the individual paired partnerships as well as with other participating members of the program. Each program cycle lasts for four months, after which the participants are welcome to continue their working relationships more informally, or even to sign up to engage in an additional partnership in the following cycle. Run by volunteer coordinators from around the world, the ILN provides a unique opportunity for librarians to connect with and learn from a global network of colleagues who share their own widely diverse backgrounds and experiences.[26]

Also for international librarians, the International Relations Roundtable (IRRT) is an ALA unit established in 1949 to promote library issues and librarianship worldwide. Some of the initiatives related to this group include creating welcoming presentations and receptions for international librarians at the major ALA conferences.[27] The IRRT also consistently hosts the International Visitor's Center (IVC) at both ALA conferences every year, as well as a table within the vendors pavilion

---

25. Johnson, "Retaining and Advancing Librarians of Color," 410.

26. International Librarians Network, "International Librarians Network," accessed June 8, 2014, http://ilnetwork.wordpress.com.

27. American Library Association, "International Relations Round Table (IRRT)," accessed June 18, 2014, http://www.ala.org/irrt/front.

to inform members of benefits and to share information about trending library issues worldwide. It also pairs international librarians with national librarians at other various conferences with the idea of assisting international visitors while touring American cities and establishments.

Regardless of how librarians of color identify, finding a mentor who can thoughtfully guide them through their career can prove to be an invaluable professional and emotional experience. While they offer the same types of support and guidance as other programs, mentoring programs that focus on the specific challenges of being from a marginalized racial and ethnic group in a predominantly white profession offer another level of support that the mentee may not get elsewhere. Librarians of color may have concerns that are not shared by their white colleagues, and a mentor who is not able to grasp the complexity of their mentee's situation may not always be able to offer advice that is as pertinent to the mentee's diverse circumstances. Being able to share concerns with someone who understands one's own personal experiences is a refreshing and comforting aspect to the best mentoring relationships, and can relieve many of the pressures that librarians of color typically face.

Conclusion

Due to a history of marginalization and underrepresentation in the profession, it is essential for librarians of color to develop support networks that will allow them to advance, grow, and contribute within the historically mono-cultural field of librarianship. The efforts to recruit library students of color are tremendous, but recruitment efforts alone will not lead to retention unless librarians of color are given the continued support that they need to flourish. Students partaking in opportunities such as the ALA Spectrum Scholarship and ALA Doctoral Fellowship Programs aid in bringing diversity into librarianship in part because they assist students in creating networks with future librarians who will have similar experiences, understanding, and qualms as themselves. While these initiatives are undoubtedly a great start, supportive networks, committees, colleagues, and friends must infuse the profession as a whole in order to ensure the ongoing representation, development, and retention of librarians of color in the profession.

Coming together, librarians of color can accomplish a number of things simultaneously: they can validate each other's experiences; lend essential emotional support through times of discrimination and isolation; share the demanding work of time-consuming presentations, papers, articles, and projects; offer advice during moments of change and promotion; and help each other find positions in institutions and professional associations that will support them. Librarians of color may often take the more difficult road simply because they do not know that another road exists. Yet through collective work, they can share the wisdom and experiences that they gain individually to ultimately create a sense of belonging and possibility together. Collaboration can help librarians to help each other, and ensure that the diversity that is so essential to the future of librarianship will continue to grow within the field.

References

Alire, Camila A. "The New Beginnings Program: A Retention Program for Junior Faculty of Color." *Journal of Library Administration* 33, no. 1-2 (2001): 21-30.

American Library Association. "ALA Annual Diversity Research Grant Program." Accessed April 30, 2014. http://www.ala.org/advocacy/diversity/diversityresearchstatistics/diversity-research.

American Library Association. "ALA Emerging Leaders Program." Accessed May 20, 2014. http://www.ala.org/educationcareers/leadership/emergingleaders.

American Library Association. "Associations of Ethnic Librarians." Accessed June 19, 2014. http://www.ala.org/offices/diversity/ethniclibrariansassociations.

American Library Association. "Diversity Counts 2009-2010 Update." Last modified September 2012. http://www.ala.org/offices/diversity/diversitycounts/divcounts.

American Library Association. "International Relations Round Table (IRRT)." Accessed June 18, 2014. http://www.ala.org/irrt/front.

Association of College & Research Libraries. "Residency Interest Group." Accessed June 19, 2014. http://acrl.ala.org/residency.

Association of Research Libraries. "Diversity Recruitment." Accessed June 8, 2014. http://www.arl.org/leadership-recruitment/diversity-recruitment.

Association of College & Research Libraries. "Diversity Standards: Cultural Competency for Academic Libraries (2012)." Accessed May 29, 2014. http://www.ala.org/acrl/standards/diversity.

Howland, Joan. "Beyond Recruitment: Retention and Promotion Strategies to Ensure Diversity and Success." *Library Administration & Management* 13, no. 1 (Winter 1999): 4-14.

Human Library Organisation, The. "Human Library." Accessed May 27, 2014. http://humanlibrary.org.

Indiana University Libraries Faculty Council (IULFC). "Mentor Program." Accessed May 20, 2014. http://www.iu.edu/~iulfc/mentor/mentorprogram.shtml.

International Librarians Network. "International Librarians Network." Accessed June 8, 2014. http://ilnetwork.wordpress.com.

Jaeger, Paul. T., John Carlo Bertot, and Renee E. Franklin. "Diversity, Inclusion, and Underrepresented Populations in LIS Research." *Library Quarterly* 80, no. 2 (April 2010): 175-181. doi: 10.1086/651053.

Johnson, Peggy. "Retaining and Advancing Librarians of Color." *College & Research Libraries* 68, no. 5 (September 2007): 405-417. Accessed April 30, 2014. http://crl.acrl.org/content/68/5/405.full.pdf+html.

Lazzaro, Althea Eannace, Shardé Mills, Tami Garrard, Emily Ferguson, Megan Watson, and Dave Ellenwood. "Cultural Competency on Campus: Applying ACRL's Diversity Standards." *College & Research Libraries News*, 75, no. 4 (2014): 332-335.

Moore, Alanna Aiko, Michael J. Miller, Veronda J. Pitchford, and Ling Hwey Jeng. "Mentoring in the Millennium: New Views, Climate and Actions." *New Library World* 109, no. 1/2 (2008): 75-86.

Neely, Teresa Y. and Lorna Peterson. *Achieving Racial and Ethnic Diversity among Academic and Research Librarians: The Recruitment, Retention, and Advancement of Librarians of Color: A White Paper.* Association of College & Research Libraries, 2007. http://www.ala.org/acrl/files/publications/whitepapers/ACRL_AchievingRacial.pdf.

Piercy, Fred, Valerie Giddings, Katherine Allen, Benjamin Meszaros, Peggy Dixon, and Karen Joest. "Improving Campus Climate to Support Faculty Diversity and Retention: A Pilot Program for New Faculty." *Innovative Higher Education* 30, no. 1 (January 2005): 53-66.

Society of American Archivists. "Diversity Committee." Last modified February 2010. http://www2.archivists.org/governance/handbook/section7/groups/Diversity.

University of Arkansas. "Diversity Resources LibGuide." Last modified June 2, 2014. http://uark.libguides.com/content.php?pid=302086&sid=2475833.

University of Arkansas. "Librarian-In-Residence Program." Accessed April 30, 2014. http://libinfo.uark.edu/diversity/residency/overview.asp.

University of Arkansas. "Diversity and the Libraries." Accessed June 1, 2014. http://libinfo.uark.edu/diversity.

University of Minnesota. "Minnesota Institute for Early Career Librarians." Accessed June 8, 2014. https://www.lib.umn.edu/sed/institute

Chapter 3

MENTORING AND RETENTION OF MINORITY LIBRARIANS

Melody Royster, David Schwieder, Ava Iuliano Brillat, and Lori Driver

Academic librarianship employs comparatively few faculty and staff members of color. It has long been apparent that the proportion of Black, Hispanic and Native American librarians is substantially lower than in the U.S. working population. Numerous librarianship studies have documented this persistent pattern of minority under-representation. A variety of reasons have been cited, including a limited candidate pool, the nature of library recruitment and hiring practices, and low retention rates for minority librarians. Recognizing these issues, numerous academic libraries, and library professional associations such as the American Library Association (ALA) and the Association of College & Research Libraries (ACRL), have created programs designed to attract and retain more minority librarians and staff.

While recruitment of minority librarians is essential, retention may represent the most serious challenge to establishing librarians of color within the field. One survey found that minority librarians believe their biggest professional problem is "not discrimination in hiring, but lack of career development or advancement strategies for minorities."[1]

---

1. Ashley E. Bonnette, "Mentoring Minority Librarians Up the Career Ladder," *Library Administration and Management* 18, no. 3 (2004): 134.

Minorities who are uncomfortable in their positions, or who face uncertain prospects for promotion or tenure, may feel little motivation to remain at their library. Failure at the retention stage may be particularly problematic, and costly, involving the loss of a substantial investment of time and resources from both the library and librarian. This failure leaves the library back with its original lack of diversity, and it leaves future minority librarians lacking mentors who have experience with the same unique set of challenges. Thus the culture and demographics of librarianship remain unchanged.

Many types of retention efforts have been proposed, including salary inducements for librarians of color, or cultural sensitivity training programs for library faculty and staff, but one key strategy involves mentoring of librarians new to the library environment.[2] Mentoring can bolster retention by helping junior faculty and staff to master work tasks, manage time, and adapt to a library's organizational culture, all of which can lead to greater success and satisfaction in the workplace.[3] But while the general effects of mentoring in libraries have been identified, quantitative and cross-institutional analyses remain rare. This chapter addresses this gap by reporting results from a cross-institutional survey designed to provide quantifiable insights on two key topics: the effects of mentoring on minority librarians, and the factors that determine mentoring effectiveness for these librarians.

Literature Review

Effective mentorship can be an efficient and useful strategy for retaining employees from underrepresented communities in professional positions within academic institutions. Mentoring is a widely-accepted practice for nurturing and acclimatizing beginning professionals, where required, to the rigors of the tenure and promotion process. The

2. Mark D. Winston and Haipeng Li, "Managing Diversity in Liberal Arts College Libraries," *College & Research Libraries* 61, no. 3 (2000): 205-215.

3. Kathy E. Kram, *Mentoring at Work: Developmental Relationships in Organizational Life* (Lanham, MD: University Press of America, 1988).

professional socialization provided by mentoring allows new professionals to become more ingrained in their communities.[4] These connections greatly assist in establishing essential networks within home institutions and the profession as a whole.

Literature in human resources research and librarianship support the positive effects of mentoring on new employees. Mentored employees—i.e. protégés—find that a connection with a more experienced, more senior mentor can help with matters like mastering work tasks, managing time, and adapting to an organizational culture.[5] In addition to the general challenges of navigating the early- and mid-stages of a career, librarians of color can also face unique difficulties and barriers. Majority-dominated workplace cultures can be unfamiliar or confusing, and colleagues' stereotypes and expectations can be problematic, even if they fall short of actual discrimination. Women and racial minorities may also find themselves excluded from male- or majority-dominated social and professional networks. Given these problems, some studies have found that mentoring can be especially important for members of traditionally under-represented groups. In a study of ARL libraries, Black and Leysen found that librarians of color valued mentoring relationships and diversity in the library more than their counterparts, and that entry level librarians felt that mentoring was essential for having a clearer understanding of promotion and institutional politics.[6] Indeed, one business-oriented study identified mentoring as the single most common characteristic shared by successfully advancing minorities.[7]

At first glance, the link between mentoring and retention may not be obvious but research clarifies the connection. Protégés rely on mentors for socialization and professional development. In successful mentoring

---

4. William Black and Joan M. Leysen, "Fostering Success: The Socialization of Entry-Level Librarians in ARL Libraries," *Journal of Library Administration* 36, no. 4 (2002): 12.

5. Kram,"Mentoring at Work."

6. Black and Leysen, "Fostering Success," 3-27.

7. David A. Thomas, "The Truth about Mentoring Minorities," *Harvard Business Review* 79, no. 4 (2001): 98-107.

relationships, today's protégés eventually become tomorrow's mentors, assuming protégés are successfully retained in the work environment. Mentoring provides a number of psychosocial benefits that are significant factors in retaining protégés at their current place of work. Mentors provide assistance and advocacy for their protégés, helping them create essential network connections.[8]

Mentoring produces positive effects by providing vocational and psychosocial support.[9] More experienced librarians training and guiding protégés through work responsibilities fall into the vocational support experienced by protégés. More senior co-workers can convey relevant information, career advice, and strategies for effective job performance. They can also serve as advocates for their protégés. 'Psychosocial' will refer to the combination of psychological and social needs which are required for the individual to develop, similar to the concept of Erik Erikson's theory of development through psychological tasks, but made specific to the psychological and social needs of an employee to develop effectively in the library workplace.[10] Psychosocial benefits involve relational and emotional aspects. An established mentor can help a protégé feel accepted and included, both directly and through interaction with other co-workers. A trusted mentor can be an important element in acclimatizing new librarians to their work environment. Studies have found that the psychosocial component may be more important than vocational support.[11] Librarians new to their libraries have the same needs as any new employees. They look for vocational and psychosocial

8. Alanna Aiko Moore, Michael J. Miller, Veronda J. Pitchford, and Ling Hwey Jeng, "Mentoring in the Millennium: New Views, Climate and Actions," *New Library World* 109 nos. 1/2 (2008): 75-86.

9. Kram, "Mentoring at Work"; Melanie R. Schockett and Marilyn Haring-Hidore, "Factor Analytic Support for Psychological and Vocational Mentoring Functions," *Psychological Reports* 57, (1985): 627-630.

10. Joseph Sclafani, "Psychosocial Development," in *Encyclopedia of Human Development*, ed. Neil Salkind. (Thousand Oaks, CA: Sage Publications, 2005).

11. Marilyn Haring, "Foreword from the field," in *New Directions in Mentoring: Creating a Culture of Synergy*, ed. Carol A. Mullen and Dale W. Lick (New York: Falmer Press, 1990).

support in order to more effectively engage in their work environments and become part of their institution. Ultimately, mentoring can help to foster greater success in libraries, as in any other workplace environment.

Data and Methods

In the fall of 2012, we created and administered a survey designed to explore if and how mentoring impacts new librarians' attitudes towards retention. Survey respondents were solicited in several ways. First, human resources representatives at ARL institutions were asked to distribute the survey to their faculties. Second, notices were posted on several minority-oriented American Library Association-hosted electronic lists, including those for the Chinese American Librarians Association and the Black Caucus of the ALA. The survey generated a total of 445 responses, with 48 of these respondents self-identifying as minorities.

The survey is a composite of a mentor survey tool created by Ensher and a teacher mentoring survey tool created by Tepper, later modified by Reiman and Edelfelt.[12] Both of the original tools include blocks of questions on vocational guidance and psychosocial support. In our survey, the largest set of questions asked protégés about the conduct and behaviors of their mentors in order to examine vocational and psychosocial support. Respondents were asked to assess the degree to which they identify with their mentor(s) to provide insight on the effectiveness of the psychosocial support they are receiving. Finally, respondents were asked to express their general feelings about working conditions and the library work experience. Retention was addressed with two questions. One question asked respondents if they expected

---

12. Ellen Ensher, "Effects of Perceived Attitudinal and Demographic Similarity on Protégés' Support and Satisfaction Gained from their Mentoring Relationships," *Journal of Applied Social Psychology* 32, no. 7 (2002): 1407-1430; Kelly Tepper, "Latent Structure of Mentoring Function Scales," *Educational and Psychological Measurement* 56, no. 5 (1996): 848-857; and Alan J. Reiman and Roy A. Edelfelt. *The Opinions of Mentors and Beginning Teachers: What Do They Say about Induction?* ERIC Research Report 91-1, (1991), accessed September 23, 2013, http://files.eric.ed.gov/fulltext/ED329519.pdf.

to still be working in their current library in five years' time while the other item asked if they expected to still be employed in the library field at that point. A small set of demographic items was also included.

The survey asked respondents to explore their relationships with their current mentor(s) by reporting the support they receive from their mentors as well as how they perceive their library work environments. Respondents were also asked to report work place satisfaction and their perspective on whether or not they would remain at their current library.

Results: Effects of Mentoring

Given our interest in the value and effects of mentoring, we began with a direct measure of mentoring's effects on minority retention. Two of our survey questions capture retention most directly; 1) respondents' expectation that they will still be working in the library field in five years' time, and more specifically, 2) if they expected to still be working in their current library at that point. **Table 1** compares mean scores on these variables for minority librarians, based on whether they are participating in a formal library mentoring program.

Table 1. Respondents' Expected Retention (Mean Scores, 1-6 Scale)

	Still Working in Library Field	Still Working at Same Library
Mentored Librarians	4.46	4.15
Non-Mentored Librarians	4.42	3.10

Interestingly, participation in a mentoring program did not increase minority librarians' expectation to remain in the library field, however, involvement in a mentoring relationship did affect these librarians' desire to remain at their current library. On a 1-6 scale, mentored librarians were slightly over one point more likely to indicate an expectation to remain at their current institution. This substantively significant finding, roughly equivalent to the move from "sometimes" to "often" on the scale, suggests that mentoring affects retention at one's own library, but not within the field as a whole.

What factors contribute to this difference? To assess this, we turned to a set of variables focused on respondents' feelings about work. One of these variables measured overall work satisfaction, and thus indicates respondents' overall satisfaction with librarianship (**Table 2**).

Table 2. Satisfaction with Librarianship (Mean Scores, 1-6 Scale)

Mentored Librarians	4.69
Non-Mentored Librarians	4.45

This result suggests that mentoring may have a slight effect on overall work satisfaction, but hardly a strong influence. A finer-grained examination allows us to evaluate this satisfaction more precisely. This set of variables included items measuring both vocational and psychosocial factors. Results revealed that mentored and un-mentored librarians gave similar answers across most of these questions, but they differed on four items. **Table 3** shows the four variables that differed by at least .33 points (one third of a scale point) between the mentored and un-mentored groups, along with the actual size of the differences.

Table 3. Feelings About Work (Mean Scores, 1-6 Scale)

	Have Gotten Help from Colleague	Have Chance to Talk to Others	Feel Part of the Community	Have Adequate Time to Do Assignments
Mentored	4.31	4.77	4.62	4.69
Non-Mentored	3.95	4.20	4.25	4.10

Mentored librarians, regardless of race, were more likely to report feeling like part of the community and having more opportunities to ask for and receive help from colleagues. Mentoring provides psychosocial support needed for junior librarians to feel included, which in turn feeds into the commitment to the current library work place. Mentors advocate for their protégés and provide much needed career assistance and networking. For librarians of color, mentors with a common background serve as positive role models to establish rapport and connections, resulting in a higher probability of retaining new librarians.[13]

Determinants of Mentoring Effectiveness

Having found evidence suggesting that mentoring has an effect, we return to a logically prior question: what makes for effective mentoring? While we lack direct protégé evaluations of their mentor's performance, we do have a useful alternative. Mentoring research commonly finds that the protégé's identification with their mentor is important to the success of the relationship, and to realizing benefits from it. Accordingly, factors that facilitate such identification could arguably be expected to facilitate mentoring effectiveness.

To examine this—that is, to determine the factors that facilitate mentoring effectiveness—we conducted a factor analysis on the variables measuring protégés' evaluations of their mentors. This factor analysis produced four interpretable factors, which we labeled (in order of extraction): general vocational assistance, psychosocial factors, skill development, and association and communication. We then combined four identification-with-mentor variables into a summary index of protégé identification.

Following this, we conducted a linear regression analysis to determine how these factors affected protégés' identification with their mentors. This regression procedure produced a model with an adjusted R2 of

---

13. Moore, et al., "Mentoring in the Millennium."

.642, indicating that these four factors explained almost two-thirds of the variance in the protégés' identification with their mentors. The regression slope coefficients were as follows (**Table 4**):

Table 4. Factor Effects on Identification with Mentors

	Beta	**Sig.**
Vocational Assistance	.271	.000
Psychosocial Factors	.539	.000
Skill Development	.465	.000
Association and Communication	.058	.351

Several aspects of these results are of interest here. First, the model as a whole performed well, with the vocational, psychosocial, skill and communication factors explaining almost two-thirds of the variance in respondents' sense of identification with their mentors. Clearly, as we had hypothesized, there is a strong association between individual evaluative items and overall identification. Second, consistent with the earlier-cited argument that psychosocial factors matter most for protégés, the beta coefficients show that psychosocial factor had the strongest effect here. Third, our factors broke vocational skills into two meaningful sub-scales—general assistance and skill development—and, interestingly, while both mattered, the latter had the strongest effect on the protégés' evaluations of their mentors.

Open-Ended Comments

To augment the quantitative data analysis, the survey included an open-ended question; "Do you have any other comments about your experiences as a mentee (or as a librarian without mentorship)?" Of the 48 respondents of color, 29 (60.4%) offered some kind of comment. These comments were not classified with a formal coding scheme, but some patterns did emerge.

While the survey focused on formal mentoring programs, some respondents had found informal mentoring relationships, generally by necessity. "Our mentoring program is not strong. I have developed my own mentors..." One librarian saw a useful division of labor here. "Formal mentors are ... to guide us through the tenure and publication process, whereas I bring my personal and work problems to my informal mentor..."

Respondents expressed divergent views on other aspects of mentoring. Some preferred mentors from outside their own library, while others had established an outside relationship by necessity, despite an apparent wish for an in-house mentor: "My current mentor is very nice and I love having a relationship with her, but I feel that having a mentor in my community would have a significant impact on my life." "I've rarely had mentors within the same institutions ...which put me in a difficult situation..." "My mentor is at another university but she has been a great assistance to me while I am in school and looking for jobs." Another respondent had found an outside relationship via a program offered by a professional association "I had to seek library mentorship outside my state via BCALA."

Most respondents saw value in mentoring. "I think it is highly recommended to have a mentee relationship...we all need advice and someone to discuss ideas and issues with." "I've benefited from having mentors who have been open to discussing all issues related to my jobs." And most directly, "I am more successful as a librarian because I have the support of my mentor(s)." One respondent emphasized mentoring's value at the hiring stage. "Having a mentor was crucial to me getting the kind of experience I need to get my first professional position...." Others expressed such support for mentoring upon feeling its absence; "Without a mentor relationship, I have found it extremely difficult to find my place within the field." Only one respondent was distinctly negative; "Mentorship is a waste of time, as adults you should know what you want to do and go after it."

Whatever the nature of the mentoring relationship, two respondents tied mentoring directly or indirectly to retention. "Without a mentor relationship, I have found it extremely difficult to find my place within the field. As a result, I often find myself thinking about leaving my current institution (or just completely leaving the profession.)." "I think often about how my career would have blossomed much earlier had I been in a more supportive, mentoring environment. On several occasions I've felt that I hated librarianship but realized with the right environment I probably would enjoy it."

Several of the librarians of color hinted at dissatisfaction with their workplace treatment or situation as a racial minority. Given the focus of the survey, these sentiments emerged in a mentoring context; "… there is very little attention paid to mentoring librarians of color…" "As a minority librarian, it is very difficult to find mentor opportunities at the college I am employed at" and "My position has caused me to seek more experienced librarians that are part of my ethnic, economic and educational background." As is evident, several of these comments also suggest an interest in a demographically similar mentor. Interestingly, the last cited comment widened the definition of demographic similarity by including class and education.

Discussion

The survey results reveal some interesting points about the retention of minority librarians in academic libraries. First, at least as measured by librarians' future expectations, mentoring seems to have a stronger effect on retention within a particular library rather than on retention within the library profession as a whole. Librarians not engaged in mentoring relationships were no less likely to plan to remain in librarianship than were their mentored peers. However, un-mentored librarians were substantially less likely to expect to remain at their current library than were their counterparts involved in a formal mentoring relationship. With an average of 3.10 on a 6 point scale, un-mentored librarians had little expectation to remain in their current library of employment (Table 1).

Secondly, in order to determine what aspects of mentorship impact feelings of retention, we deconstructed mentoring into its composite factors; general vocational assistance, psychosocial support, skill development and association/communication. Of these factors, general vocational assistance, psychosocial support in the forms of receiving social support, and skill development are the most important from the perspective of protégés. In order to support protégé satisfaction, academic libraries must make an effort to create mentoring programs that specifically include vocational assistance, psychosocial support and opportunities for skill development in order to increase the likelihood of retaining new librarians of color.

Limitations

Consistent with general practice, it is also useful to identify the limitations of this research. As with many library studies, our use of a non-randomly selected sample suggests that we need to be cautious about generalizing our findings. Another limitation involves both the survey and in the broader reality it addresses. Minority librarians are under-represented in the field, and thus while our overall sample of 445 seems adequate; our minority sample of 48 is smaller than we would like. This aspect of the sample generates a bit of additional concern about generalization.

Our minority sample also has an additional issue, one we might call the "generic minority" problem. The small size of this sample forced us to treat minority librarians as a single group, rather than as members of distinct communities, which could blur or obscure important differences between the mentoring experiences for members of different minority groups. While we obviously would have preferred to report more specific results by group, this is simply another result of our small sample size of librarians of color.

Finally, our results may understate the effectiveness of mentoring for minority protégés. Previous research suggests that perceived similarity between mentors and protégés can play an important role in facilitating a productive mentoring relationship, and that a shared racial or ethnic identity may contribute to such similarity.[14] Unfortunately, however, the scarcity of minorities in senior librarian ranks means that relatively few minority protégés will have a minority mentor. While our survey did not record the race or ethnicity of mentors, it likely that most minority protégés in our survey had a White mentor. Had our minority protégés been matched with racially or ethnically similar mentors, then participation in a mentoring relationship might have produced stronger beneficial effects. Accordingly, the results reported here may understate the potential effectiveness of mentoring for minority librarians.

Most of these limitations involve an unfortunate irony—the very minority under-representation that we are seeking to study makes effective analysis of minority mentorship difficult. The obvious solution would involve collecting a larger sample, ideally one that is randomly selected. It would also be highly useful to gather longitudinal data, indicating actual librarian retention patterns, rather than relying on minority librarians' predictions about their future behaviors.

Conclusion

Issues of diversity and minority under-representation have long been a concern in academic libraries, and in the professional as a whole. While there are a number of possible avenues to address these concerns, focusing on retention of working minority librarians may be a particularly useful approach. Mentoring acts as a strategy to improve retention. Librarians of color—whether library students, new hires, or experienced professionals—can benefit from effective mentoring programs. Protégé librarians, regardless of racial identity, value the psychosocial benefits and opportunities for skill development that are provided by mentoring. Mentors help protégés meet their psychological and social needs in their work environment and provide vocational guidance. Many formal mentoring programs are focused on vocational guidance and may not

---

14. Ensher, E. "Attitudinal and Demographic Similarity."

emphasize the psychosocial benefits of mentoring relationships. For academic libraries concerned with retaining new librarians of color, it is clear that mentoring can help meet the psychosocial needs of new librarians while supporting their skill development. Through making connections with their mentors, librarians of color are more likely to view their current library work environments more favorably and to have their vocational needs met. Today's novice librarians are tomorrow's mentors. Through proper mentoring that includes emphasis on psychosocial and vocational needs, academic libraries are better poised to change the culture of academic librarianship. It is imperative that academic libraries work to retain librarians of color in order to invest in a diverse future.

References

Black, William, and Joan M. Leyson. "Fostering Success the Socialization of Entry-Level Librarians in ARL Libraries." *Journal of Library Administration* 36 (2002): 3-27.

Bonnette, Ashley E. "Mentoring Minority Librarians Up the Career Ladder." *Library Administration and Management* 18 (2004): 134-139.

Ensher, Ellen. "Effects of Perceived Attitudinal and Demographic Similarity on Protégés' Support and Satisfaction Gained from their Mentoring Relationships." *Journal of Applied Social Psychology* 32 (2002): 1407-1430.

Haring, M. "Foreword from the Field." In *New Directions in Mentoring: Creating a Culture of Synergy,* edited by Carol A. Mullen and Dale W. Lick. New York: Falmer Press, 1999.

Iuliano, Ava, Melody Royster, Margeaux Johnson, Anne Larrivee, and Lori Driver. "Reaching Out to Minority Librarians: Overcoming Diversity Challenges Through Mentorship." In *Imagine, Innovate, Inspire: The Proceedings of the ACRL 2013 Conference,* edited by Dawn M. Mueller, 483-490. Chicago: American Library Association, 2013.

Kram, Kathy E. *Mentoring at Work: Developmental Relationships in Organizational Life.* Lanham, MD: University Press of America, 1988.

Moore, Alanna Aiko, Michael J. Miller, Veronda J. Pitchford, and Ling Hwey Jeng. "Mentoring in the Millennium: New Views, Climate and Actions." *New Library World* 109, no. 1/2 (2008): 75-86.

Reiman, Alan J., and Roy A. Edelfelt. *The Opinions of Mentors and Beginning Teachers: What Do They Say about Induction?* ERIC Research Report 91-1 (1991). Accessed November 14, 2013. http://files.eric.ed.gov/fulltext/ED329519.pdf

Schockett, Melanie R., and Marilyn Haring-Hidore. "Factor Analytic Support for Psychological and Vocational Mentoring Functions." *Psychological Reports* 57 (1985): 627-630.

Sclafani, Joseph. "Psychosocial Development." In *Encyclopedia of Human Development,* edited by Neil Salkind, 1048-51. Thousand Oaks, CA: Sage, 2005.

Tepper, K. "Latent Structure of Mentoring Function Scales." *Educational and Psychological Measurement* 56, no. 5 (1996): 848-857.

Thomas, David A. "The Truth about Mentoring Minorities: Race Matters." *Harvard Business Review* 79 (2001): 99-107.

Winston, Mark D. and Haipeng Li. "Managing Diversity in Liberal Arts College Libraries." *College & Research Libraries* 61 (2000): 205-215.

Chapter 4

Interns or Professionals? A Common Misnomer Applied to Diversity Resident Librarians Can Potentially Degrade and Divide

Jason K. Alston

Abstract

Diversity resident librarians are entry-level professional librarians who are often branded "interns" by other personnel at their hosting institutions despite holding a position requiring a professional degree. This study sought to determine whether this misidentification truly is common, and how residents respond to the misidentification, both emotionally and professionally. Twenty-six usable questionnaires from current and past diversity residents were collected, and results revealed that mislabeling had been common among the participating residents, and that residents responded to the mislabeling in a variety of ways. Most participants reported being able to continue with their duties as a diversity resident librarian undeterred, though a few reported that the mislabeling did negatively impact their performance. The concluding determination is that hosting institutions should foster environments where residents are not subjected to being called interns or being seen as interns.

Introduction

Diversity residency programs have become a popular way for academic libraries to demonstrate a commitment to diversity initiatives and to recruit and retain practitioners of color. Informal rumblings, however, suggest that some past and present diversity resident librarians do not feel as though residents are respected as professionals. While many diversity residents have been mislabeled as "interns," nothing previously written explores whether this is a mere confusion of terms, or whether misidentifying residents by colleagues is meant to be malicious, or whether it stems from failure by the institutions to assign the residents professional responsibilities and duties that an intern would not have.

This article explores the experiences of past and present diversity resident librarians to determine if they felt they were respected as professionals, if they were given professional responsibilities, and if and how they may have responded to marginalizing situations. Respecting diversity residents and holding them professionally accountable are key to ensuring future employability for the resident after the residency.

Literature Review

The Association for Library and Information Science Education (ALISE) defines a residency as, "The post degree work experience designed as an entry level program for professionals who have recently received the MLS degree from a program accredited by the American Library Association.[1] Diversity residency programs generally offer a newly-graduated librarian a multitude of varied experiences, usually by rotating them through various departments within the library. Residencies usually last between one to three years and allow new professionals a chance to gain practical experience in a variety of areas so that they

---

1. Quoted in Jason K. Alston, "Minerva's First Born: My Experiences as UNCG's First Diversity Resident Librarian," *North Carolina Libraries* 68 (2010), 16.

are more aware of what area of librarianship they wish to pursue. There are nuanced differences between individual diversity residency programs, but they generally work towards similar goals.

Since the establishment of the first post-MLS diversity resident librarian program at the University of Delaware in 1984,[2] diversity residencies have become a popular tactic for supporting diversity initiatives at multiple academic libraries throughout the country. Diversity residency programs have been lauded for their ability to not only increase faculty diversity, but also to help institutions demonstrate their commitments to diversity and counter environmental and cultural factors that limit employment opportunities for early-career librarians.[3]

The true intentions of residency programs have been called into question. Hu & Patrick (2006) reported feeling at times that their presence at their host institution was more about politics than recruiting and retaining minorities; further, they stressed that residents should not be pigeonholed into handling diversity and multicultural-related issues.[4] Hankins, Saunders & Situ (2003) asserted that residency programs are often responses to accreditation threats and that they, "take newly graduated students, insert them into often hostile environments, and expect them to address all problems of diversity that continue to simmer and stew among faculty."[5]

The labeling of residents as "interns" by coworkers at their host institutions has been subject for informal conversation among current and former residents, and was discussed during a residency workshop

---

2. University of Delaware Library, "Pauline A. Young Residency," accessed June 8, 2014, http://www2.lib.udel.edu/personnel/residency/history.html.

3. Julie Brewer, "Understanding the Organizational Value of Post–Master's Degree Residency Programs" *Research Library Issues* 272 (2010): 23-27.

4. Sylvia S. Hu and Demetria E. Patrick, "Our Experience as Minority Residents: Benefits, Drawbacks, and Suggestions," *C&RL News* 67, no. 5 (2006), 299.

5. Rebecca Hankins, Michele Saunders, and Ping Situ, "Diversity Initiatives vs. Residency Programs Agents of change?" *C&RL News* 64, no. 5 (2003), 309.

at the 2008 National Diversity in Libraries conference in Louisville, Kentucky.[6] It is not covered much, however, in professional literature. Hu & Patrick (2006) discussed being addressed as interns while serving as diversity residents at Miami University in Oxford, Ohio, even when other entry-level librarians were not; they later discovered that the residency grew out of internship positions at the school and decided to educate others on the differences between interns and residents.[7] Alston (2010) discussed personal experiences with being labeled as an intern and suggested the burden was on the host institution to provide residents with experiences that truly differentiated them from interns.[8]

The University of Notre Dame has gone on record differentiating their residency from an internship, noting that residents have masters degrees and enjoy full benefits packages. In contrast, internships are for students who have yet to graduate and need resume enhancers.[9] In earlier years, there were institutions that deemed "internships" as what could be called diversity residencies today; the University of Minnesota in 1991 hosted the "Affirmative Action Internship Program."[10] The 2001 book *Diversity in Libraries: Academic Residency Programs* has a "Directory of Programs" section where multiple institutions, including the University of Massachusetts-Worcester, the University of California-Santa Barbara, Vanderbilt, and Ithaca College, list their programs as "internships."[11]

---

6. Alston, "Minerva's First Born," 16.

7. Hu & Patrick, "Our Experience as Minority Residents," 299.

8. Alston, "Minerva's First Born," 16.

9. Laura Bayard, "Notre Dame's Librarian-in-Residence Program," *Indiana Libraries* 28, no. 2 (2009), 16.

10. Karen Beavers, "Becoming the Institution: The Residency Experience," in *Diversity in Libraries: Academic Residency Programs*, ed. Raquel V. Cogell and Cindy A. Gruwell. (Westport, CT: Greenwood Press, 2001), 113-118.

11. Raquel V. Cogell and Cindy A. Gruwell, *Diversity in Libraries: Academic Residency Programs* (Westport, CT: Greenwood Press, 2001), 165-170.

Method

This study was conducted through an online questionnaire distributed through email, listservs, and social media. Because the participants needed to be current or past diversity resident librarians, past residents associated with ACRL's diversity residency interest group and current residents listed in academic library staff directories were emailed.

The survey instrument featured both multiple choice and open-ended questions. Multiple choice questions collected demographic data as well as more basic data on the experiences of the residents (i.e. "Were you ever referred to as an 'intern' while in your residency?"). There were seven open-ended questions that requested more substantive responses about specific experiences and emotions experienced by the resident (i.e. "If you were referred to as an intern, how did this make you feel? Did you find the use of this term demeaning, insulting, or otherwise offensive?").

While there was originally concern that participants would not offer detailed responses to online open-ended questions, these responses were sufficiently detailed, and thus planned phone interviews with random participants did not take place. Each participant was assigned a coded name by the researcher to protect confidentiality.

For demographic questions and basic closed-ended questions, simple tallies were recorded and compared. When appropriate, response subsets for some questions were treated as independent variables and crossed with responses for other questions as dependent variables. For example, in addition to tallying how many participants were referred to as "interns" during their residencies, it was also determined how many participants who were their institution's first resident or in the institution's first resident cohort were called "intern"; the hope was to determine if those who served in new residency programs were more likely to be labeled as such. For open-ended questions, trends and patterns within responses were noted, and responses were combed for similar experiences or emotional outcomes.

Results

Twenty-eight participants began the online questionnaire, with 26 identifying as current or former diversity residents. The responses of two participants who had never been diversity residents were discarded. Four participants were current diversity residents, while 22 were former residents. Twelve participants were Black/African-American (46%), six were Hispanic/Latino (23%), five multi-ethnic or other (19%), two Asian/Pacific Islander (8%), and one American Indian (4%). Twenty-one participants were female (81%) and five were male (19%).

Thirteen participants were 25-34 years old when their residencies began (50%). Six were 35-45 years old (23%), four were 46 or older (15%), and three were 18-24 (12%). All 26 completed their residencies at academic libraries. Nine participants finished their residencies over seven years before completing the questionnaire (35%), seven finished their residencies 4-7 years before completing the questionnaire (27%), seven finished their residencies three or fewer years before completing the questionnaire (27%), and three were current residents (12%). Sixteen participants were not their institution's first resident or in the first residency cohort (62%), while 10 were either the first resident or in the first cohort (38%). Nineteen residents were not the only resident employed when they served (73%), while seven were (27%).

Despite holding residency, or entry-level professional positions, 17 participants (65%) said they were referred to as "interns" during their residencies, and an additional three (12%) said they were unsure if they had been or not. Only three participants said they believed referral to them as "interns" was meant to be malicious (16% of the 19 who answered this question), while eight said they were not sure and eight said they did not believe the intern label was meant maliciously or as an insult. Thirteen participants (50%) said they felt they were respected as professionals versus mere "interns" while they were residents; six said they did not feel they were respected as professionals (23%) and seven were unsure (27%).

Whether a resident was an institution's first resident or part of the first residency group appears to have little bearing on whether they were referred to as "interns" during the residency. Seven out of 10 first residents or first-cohort residents were referred to as "interns" at some point in the residency (70%), while 10 of 16 residents who were not their library's first resident or in their library's first cohort were referred to as "interns" (63%). Two of the 16 who were not the first resident or in the first cohort were unsure if they were referred to as interns. Two of the first/first-cohort residents (20%) however felt they were respected as professionals, while 11 of the residents who were not first/first-cohort residents (69%) felt they were respected as professionals. None of the residents who were not first/first-cohort felt they were not respected as professionals while five (31%) said they were unsure if they felt they were respected as professionals; six first/first-cohort residents felt they were not respected as professionals (60%) and two said they were unsure (20%).

Six residents who served more than seven years ago were referred to as interns at some point (67%), while one was not and two were unsure. Five residents who served more than seven years ago feel they were respected as professionals (56%), while two felt they were not and two were unsure. Five residents who served four to seven years ago were referred to as interns at some point (71%), while two were not. Three residents who served four to seven years ago felt they were respected as professionals versus interns (43%), while two felt they were not respected as professionals and two were unsure. Three residents who served 0-3 years ago were referred to as interns at some point (43%), while three were not and one was unsure. Four residents who served 0-3 years ago felt they were respected as professionals (57%), while two did not feel they were respected as professionals and one was unsure. All three current residents reported being described as "interns" in their residencies, and one of the three current residents felt s/he was respected as a professional while the other two were unsure.

Nineteen residents served simultaneously with other residents at their institution (73%) while seven were the only resident during their residency term (27%). Fourteen of the nineteen residents who served in cohorts reported being called an intern during their residency (74%) while four reported they were not called interns and one was unsure. Ten of the 19 residents who served in a cohort felt they were respected as professionals (53%) while three felt they were not (16%) and six were unsure (32%). Seven residents served as the only resident at their institution at the time, and of those seven, three said they were referred to as "interns" (43%), while two said they were not (29%) and two were unsure (29%). Three residents who were the only resident at their library during their term felt they were respected as professionals (43%), three felt they were not respected as professionals (43%), and one was unsure.

Job Duties

In order to be respected as a professional versus an intern, residents would need duties, expectations and other responsibilities that separated them from mere interns. Twenty-four of the participants provided feedback on what, if anything, separated them from an intern at their institution. Four residents' experiences suggest their institutions did not assign duties and responsibilities to clearly separate them from interns. SPRINTER said she performed, "Circulations, shelving and finally copy cataloging," and that, "These duties separated me from the regular intern at the time who was allowed to pretty much be a show piece. She went to meetings and gatherings while I worked." AZALEA said, "The staff there wasn't told I had an MLIS. So that was a surprise. I was told later the responsibilities were selected based on what the other librarians did not want to do." PHOENIX said, "I was responsible for instruction, developing research and projects, expectation for conference attendance and project development (sic)," and added, "I felt like I was treated by Admin as a professional, but staff and students did not fully understand what I did. And faculty usually asked whether my fellowship was a part of a graduate program." NAPPA said, "Despite attempts to inform other staff that we (the first two in the then-new residency program) were indeed professional librarians, many were stuck on the term 'intern' wondering if we were in school, or, working as community or university service. We were expected to perform and handle responsibilities of a regular professional librarian and were evaluated on the same criteria as the full time librarians."

INDEPENDENCE had a unique take on the question, saying, "My library didn't employ interns. I remember having this sense that many librarians and staff didn't realize that I was a librarian with an MLIS degree who just happened to have gained employment as a resident." She continued, "What I found interesting during the first year of my residency was that many of my colleagues assumed that this was my first time working for a living and that I had no academic work experience. My confidence in my abilities to get the work done was interpreted as being too assertive or aggressive. Clearly, I worked in an institution that was very homogenous; additionally in race and socio-economic status. It cause(d) me not to engage colleagues in social situations as a result. I managed to get what I needed to take my career to the next level. I learned a lot, and I'm glad that I have created a body of work beyond my residency." INDEPENDENCE was one of three participants whose libraries did not employ interns.

The remaining participants did share experiences that on some level differentiated them as professionals from mere interns. Four participants specifically identified professional development as a critical factor sepa-rating them from an intern, including LAUGHTER who said, "I was strongly encouraged to participate in professional development, both on a local and national level. I was given opportunities to chair library committees, work on committees on a university level, and coordinate projects/events."

Most residents recalled duties they had in their residency that would not be entrusted to an intern. COLLEEN reported having a high level of responsibility and said, "(I) oversaw acquisitions processes, negoti-ated licenses, served on committees and task forces. Status as a resident was also Visiting Faculty, which also allowed for acceptance within the library and university faculty community. People who were interns in the department that I worked in were current graduate students at the local library school, so (they) did not yet have an MLS degree." Several residents identified duties in the reference and instruction department, committee work, collection development, annual reports, research and assessment work as factors separating them from interns, saying that interns at their institutions did not perform these duties. One respondent noted that her position in the residency generated more interdepartmental communication and collaboration for her than possibly any other faculty member. Three participants noted pay and benefits as factors that distinguished them from interns.

Informing Staff

The responsibility for educating faculty and staff about why residents are hired and what roles they will serve likely falls on the committee at the hosting institution which was responsible for implementing the residency program and/or hiring the resident. Failing to educate the faculty and staff about the resident's role may foster misunderstanding about the position and spawn anger, jealousy, and other forms of discontent towards the resident. Fifteen of 25 participants to respond to a question asking what the hosting institution did to inform faculty and staff on the purpose, expectations, and duties of the resident, gave responses indicating that the hosting institution adequately informed faculty and staff in this area.

Four of the residents whose responses indicated that their host institutions had done a sufficient job informing staff about the purpose of the residents stated explicitly that they were not the first resident or part of the first residency cohort. WAITING said, "I participated in the second iteration of the residency on the campus. There was a robust communication strategy in place for the program and about the mission and expectations. Department heads, in particular, were well versed about roles and expectations as many of them were vying to host residents for rotations." MOUNTED said, "The staff and faculty were invited to our in-person interviews. During the first few weeks, we were introduced to every department. At that time, we were informed about potential projects in those areas. The majority of faculty and staff were very welcoming and continued to be supportive throughout the residency." Residents who felt their faculty and staff were sufficiently knowledgeable about the residents said this knowledge came through such steps as including faculty and staff on the planning and hiring processes, detailed introductions of residents to faculty and staff, providing descriptive job vacancy announcements, distributing clarifications through department heads, and inviting staff to in-person interviews.

Five participants said their institutions failed to communicate the purpose, expectations, and duties of the resident with the rest of the faculty and staff. SPRINTER said, "They did not, I was sheltered in a basement office. The only time I spoke directly with anyone was when they were applying for a Lumina Grant." A current resident, MILLIE, said, "They did not inform library faculty and staff. They think I am a glorified intern of sorts. Other than those who were on my search committee, the rest of the library is unaware of what a resident/fellow does." HOLDING said, "That was the problem. They did very little if any PR in that respect. People wondered who we were and why were we there. It was a total of three (3) of us. In fact, both the professional and paraprofessionals seemed to hate us. They constructed us as affirmative action cases and thus dismissed us. The library was more or less all white Americans. We were the only people of color in positions of power."

Four participants were unsure if the hosting institution adequately informed faculty and staff on the resident's purpose and duties. MARCHER said, "I am unsure if this ever happened, based on the reception from the library faculty and staff. A few later stated that they were informed by the Dean that the library would be getting a resident, but no one was sure of the responsibilities of the resident. Also some library faculty were resistant to give up certain duties or responsibilities because they did not see the resident as a permanent position." There was one response that did not descriptively convey whether the respondent believed the faculty and staff were sufficiently informed on the resident's purpose.

Marginalizing Experiences

Twenty-five of the participants answered the question: "What were some experiences, if any, that made you feel as though you were perceived or treated as a glorified and overpaid intern in your residency?" Twelve reported having at least some experience that made them feel as they were perceived as a glorified or overpaid intern, while twelve participants reported never encountering such a feeling. One respondent was uncertain.

SPRINTER said, "When the janitor called in sick they asked me to clean the toilets on all three floors. No student or intern that I ever met was ever called on in that capacity, ever." NORTHSTAR said, "In general labeling was an extreme issue. It placed the residents on the outside of the mainstream so that we constantly had to prove ourselves. We had administrative support so major issues were minimal." CLARITY said, "Sometimes, people would pass off tasks to residents that they didn't want to do themselves. We are professionals too with our own agenda due to our limited time so we quickly had to say 'no' to projects that people wanted to pawn off to us." MITTENS said, "A few people commented that we shouldn't be allowed to move between departments, that the position was not professional enough."

Three participants who reported that there were times when they were made to feel like overpaid interns noted that duties and tasks were assigned to them that no one else wanted. One example was MARCHER, who said, "The lack of cohesive responsibilities. A lot of the instruction and collection development areas, were areas no one wanted to do. I was often approached for overflow duties, when someone did not have time for a task." WESTSKY had a different but possibly related experience, saying, "(One librarian) and a few other librarians would also make comments when my supervisor would assign tasks/responsibilities to me instead of to the continuing appointment librarian in my department."

INDEPENDENCE expounded the most about experiences she found marginalizing, saying, "Whenever the job presented opportunities to engage librarians and staff in work-related social situations, I found it annoying that employees felt it was okay to touch my hair and invade my space. As a person of multi-racial background, (it was) challenging sometimes to ignore the ignorance. I am not the spokesperson for my race, nor do I ever intend to be. During the presidential election of Obama, I was confronted with 'bleeding-heart liberal' mentality of which many apologized for not wanting to vote for John McCain, and especially not voting for Obama. It was ridiculousness at its best. Working in libraries has the same issues and concerns of racial, sexual identity, etc. as most corporations have. The only difference is that corporate is front and center with its issues, and libraries are a passive-aggressive dichotomy of angry people who won't move on to let new diverse energy take libraries to the next level. To speak more plainly, I readily took the residency, I was extremely successful at it, and then I moved on to another institution with great success. In other words, I played the game and won."

Other recurrent themes from participants who experienced marginalizing experiences were insensitive statements from coworkers, rumblings that the residents received too much professional development support, and apparent amazement from coworkers when the residents actually managed to accomplish something. The one respondent who struggled to answer this question was HOLDING, who said, "This is hard to answer. Because of the lack of education of library staff and faculty, they did not really (know) what to make of us. I was in a position where the person training me had not completed her MLS, yet she was someone I "reported" to at least in part, but (I) made much more money than she did. For the first 2-3 months I did very little work, but (would) just sit at my desk. I was given nothing to do. Again no PR, I just sort of showed up. The library Dean had started this program then retired so."

Does It Feel Demeaning?

Twenty-two participants provided a response to the prompt: "If you were referred to as an intern, how did this make you feel? Did you find the use of this term demeaning, insulting, or otherwise offensive?" There was a virtual even split on feelings about this, with eight participants indicating on some level that they felt demeaned or insulted by the mislabeling. Seven participants indicated that they did not feel demeaned or insulted by the "intern" label, and seven participants either responded "N/A" or otherwise indicated that the question was not applicable to their experiences.

MILLIE felt demeaned by the label and said of it, "Yes, it was offensive because then it made others (outside of the institution) treat me as a student and not a professional. I would get questions like so 'when do you finish school?' Or 'what do you want to do next?' Then, if time allowed, I would have to explain that I was/am a resident/fellow and what that meant." NOTABLE felt the mislabeling was an innocent mistake and said, "Yes, I little hurt, but I think it was because the person wasn't really familiar with the program and was rather new to the institution themselves." CAPABLE believed the mislabeling could have been a failure to recognize the difference, stating, "I don't think the users of this term understood the difference and used the terms interchangeably. It felt like micro-aggressive behavior." NORTHSTAR also felt marginalized, saying, "I felt that I was thought of as less than a professional, when I was indeed a colleague."

WAITING took only limited offense to being called an intern, saying, "Only to the extent that I knew there was an intentional effort to discern the terms by library administration, and some within the library (and many outside of the library) either didn't comprehend those differences or, in the case of library staff, didn't care enough to know it might have been demeaning or devaluing to refer to us as 'interns.'" CLARITY said she did not find usage of the term malicious, but, "I know it was never used in an offensive way but it's hard not to take offense to it. It's like people think we're completely inexperienced professionals when really all the residents have worked in libraries previous to the program and we're all very capable and contributing very heavily. The only distinction is that we are early in our careers but not oblivious."

Not taking any genuine offense was INDEPENDENCE , who said, "I laughed and walked away many times. It was meant to be demeaning, but being the type of person I am, I 'kept it moving.' If I were a new professional to the working world, I would not have finished my residency and librarianship, because I don't have time for other people's perceptions and values they want to impede on me." MITTENS spun such misclassifications into teachable moments, saying, "I usually corrected the person who made the mistake (and they were often outside of the Libraries), and explained what the residency program was designed to do. So, I didn't take offense at the use of the term - instead I used it as a teaching/learning opportunity." EASTHILLS understood the mislabeling to be a product of past procedures, saying, "I didn't (take offense), as I understood that that had been a prior title -- it was changed to resident because of the negative connotation some might read into it. I never felt slighted or insulted on the few occasions when it came up."

NAIL, whose residency ended over a decade ago, said the question was not applicable to her, but speculated on how she would handle it. She said, "As I mentioned, I do not believe that this happened to me while I was actively employed as a resident. If it did, I would have corrected it and moved on as it did recently when it came up, 15 years later! Given that I had a lot of experience working in academic libraries as a student at a prestigious university with a top library program, it would have been hard for anyone to make me feel inferior, to be honest!"

Misnomers and Performance

Twenty-one participants provided some sort of response to a question asking if the misnomer affected their job performance in any way. Only three participants said that being called an "intern" had any effect on their job performance. Eleven participants said this misnomer did not affect them while the remaining seven who responded to the question said the question was not applicable to them.

Two of the three participants who said their job performances were impacted by the misnomer reported that the impact was negative. SPRINTER said, "My self-confidence and self-esteem are still to this day damaged." HULL said, "It made me feel apathetic, as if all of my work would be viewed through a tainted lens." However, NORTHSTAR responded positively to the labeling, saying, "I did even more than other professionals and excelled in all areas."

Most participants , however, seemed to cope with the misnomer. MITTENS said, "It did not, though it was pretty common knowledge that whether we were called interns, residents, or anything else, we had to work twice as hard to prove that the program was relevant and worth continued funding." Many who were not affected gave responses similar to MARCHER who said, "It didn't (affect me), I knew I was a degreed professional." INDEPENDENCE appeared to recognize the misnomer as a sign of discontent and disregarded it, saying, "Again, I laughed because another angry white person got mad because I got confidence and experience in my ability to connect to people."

Correcting a Misnomer

When asked if they corrected people who labeled them interns, or if coworkers corrected people who used the term, eight of 21 participants who answered the question said they would be able to described situations in which someone had been corrected. Six participants indicated that they could recall no situation in which they or a coworker corrected someone who referred to them as an intern. Seven participants responded "not applicable."

Among those who could recall examples of when they themselves corrected someone was NAPPA, who said, "If referred to that way I would remind people that we did have both an undergraduate and graduate degree." MARCHER recalled actually correcting a former administrator, saying, "Once the former dean came by and introduced himself. He asked was I the new intern, I said, 'Yes, I'm the resident.' He said, 'Oh, we called them interns when I was here.' I did know that the library did have interns previously, but they were MLS students."

In other instances, other faculty spoke up on behalf of the residents if anyone did at all; this may be due to the fact that the residents were new professionals and generally were newer professionals in the company of library vets. EASTHILLS said, "I didn't bother to correct people when they called me an intern, though the organizers of the residency program immediately corrected people that used the term. It happened a few times early on, and the organizers said something to the effect of 'He's a diversity resident.'" WAITING recalled other faculty correcting those in error, saying, "I can't provide any detailed description as it was so long ago, but I do have a vague recollection of both of those scenarios. They were usually (if I'm remembering correctly) in more casual contexts. Our supervisors and the residency coordinator (an associate dean) were adamant about the nomenclature."

NAIL shared a unique experience, in that she is still combating the misnomer and having to correct someone years after her residency ended. She said, "Again, this happened recently and not while I was in the residency program, but when my experience was referred to as an 'internship' in a group setting. I made sure to correct what was said and to re-state my actual credentials and experience in a matter of fact way that was unapologetic, yet polite and non-defensive."

It appeared though that a significant number of residents chose not to correct people. A current resident, MILLIE said, "I did not correct the person using the word 'intern', in fact, he still uses the word. When he introduces me to community members as an intern, I also use the opportunity to explain the situation. Also, having business cards that say otherwise makes a world of difference. After all, what kind of interns are given business cards?" NORTHSTAR said, "I left well enough alone. I don't remember correcting anyone personally. It looked bad on them.

Not all librarians were on board with the program and they used that type of negative reference to show displeasure." INDEPENDENCE said that attempting to correct someone would have been, "a waste of time."

Broader Implications for Failure to Distinguish

Twenty participants provided responses to the question, "How do you think failure to distinguish interns from residents may negatively impact the organizational culture at the hosting library?" Few actual patterns surfaced from the responses to this question, though most responding to this question provided thoughtful and thorough feedback.

NAIL voiced concern that failure to distinguish interns from residents furthers ignorance regarding the purpose of residency programs. She said, "Many white librarians are unaware of these programs as they are generally marketed to underrepresented groups, and when they do learn about them, they are often confused by them or not sure why there is a need. They may even feel that it is unfair that we have access to these programs and the additional resources and support that comes with them, when it is difficult for new grads to find jobs overall. In some cases, I do feel that it is ignorance on the part of some colleagues, in an attempt to diminish any programs directed at people of color as inferior, remedial, paraprofessional, or not merit-based. This definitely can set a tone at the hosting library that the residents are in a separate and unequal class, but this was not my experience, at least not from what I noticed or allowed to impact me. It helps that I was not their first resident and that there was another resident at the same time, and one of our colleagues that was hired into a permanent position had also been a resident."

MARCHER also believed that failure to distinguish could lead to devaluation, saying, "For me it made me think that the library faculty and staff did not know what a residency was or that it was not valuable to them."

INDEPENDENCE suspected that word of mistreatment or devaluation of residents could spread and harm the hosting institution's reputation. She said, "Here's the thing, if a resident librarian experiences enough passive-aggressive attempts that negatively impact their employment/learning experience of being a resident librarian, the word will get out via various social and professional networks about that organization."

EASTHILLS perceived that there could be problems if there were actual interns at the host institution whose responsibilities were comparable to that of the resident, but otherwise did not perceive potential issues. MITTENS suggested that responsibilities of a resident should be visibly distinguishable, saying, "If you have a large number of interns and the interns are doing the same level of work as the residents, then you run the risk of creating a rift between the interns and the residents. And also of creating a negative image of the residents for the other professional librarians (who may associate the interns and residents as being the same if they do the same activities)."

MILLIE believed that problems could go beyond the walls of the library and affect the whole institution by minimizing the relevance of the residency program to a university's commitment to diversity. LAUGHTER also invoked the larger institution, and said that failure to recognize a distinction between residents and interns could lower a resident's morale and leave the resident with a negative opinion of the institution.

There were those who believed that there were no broader implications for the hosting institution if the misnomer of intern is persistent. NAPPA said, "Any word use can be interpreted in many ways by the reader or listener to the word, I do not think there was an impact upon the organizational culture." MINIROSE said, "Not really. I think it's par for the course. As previously mentioned, I think in my instance there was enough preparation for (and experience with) the program, that the library community was aware of the roles and expectations. They seemed to be cognizant of the fact that even though these were temporary positions that they were professional positions." Finally, NORTHSTAR dismissed the question, saying, "I think they got over it because subsequent cohorts had better experiences."

Discussion

This study's aim was to capture the experiences of current and former diversity resident librarians in regards to whether they were labeled as "interns," and whether broader effects such as perceived lack of professionalism stemmed from such labeling. While the results from this study are not generalizable to the entire population of past and current diversity resident librarians, that roughly two-thirds of the 26 participants in this study recalled being labeled "intern" while serving as residents may indicate that this mislabeling is common, if not prevalent. To create a welcoming and encouraging environment for the resident, host institutions should strive to ensure that all faculty and staff know the difference between a resident and an intern and avoid calling the resident an intern. This may also prevent the resident from feeling as though the host institution is only paying lip service to diversity initiatives, but are not respectful of and buying into such initiatives in day-to-day practice.

Along with ensuring that faculty and staff know the difference between a resident and an intern, the host institution must make certain that there are occupational differences between a resident and an intern. These differences should not be mere differences of salary, benefits, and hours, as this does invite criticism of residents as being "overpaid interns." Instead, there should be levels of expectations and responsibilities for residents that equate to those of a professional and are beyond those of an intern. Capstone projects and expectations to publish, present, and serve on committees may supply residents with professional experience.

While most of the study participants encountered the "intern" misnomer while serving as residents, responses to this—both in action and in emotion—varied. It should be remembered that these residents served at various institutions, so organizational cultures likely varied. The "intern" misnomer may have been meant maliciously at some institutions, but not at others. Correcting those who misidentified residents may have been acceptable at some institutions, but seen as aggressive, insubordinate, or nitpicky at others. Also, individuals may react to like situations in different ways. This study did not attempt to determine an appropriate response to being mislabeled an intern, and a universal appropriate response may not exist.

This study may inform the process of establishing or improving diversity residency programs by legitimizing this as an actual concern in the literature. The topic of mislabeling of residents as interns does not appear much in the professional literature, and residents may forget or be reluctant to bring up the issue during exit interviews. Hosting institutions should offer professional-level experience and address residents as professionals. Also, prospective and practicing residents may gain insight from this study concerning things to anticipate during their residencies and how they might react.

Limitations and Suggestions for Further Research

While the interview phase was scrapped for this study because the questionnaire alone yielded the needed data, actual interviews with past and current residents may be beneficial to gather richer qualitative data. This study also collects data only from the point of view of residents, past and current. It may be useful to conduct a study seeking data on how faculty and staff at diversity residency-hosting institutions perceive the host institution's residency program and residents; input from non-residents may be beneficial in ensuring that residents are receiving skills and experiences throughout their terms that make them appear hirable among tougher audiences. A study of residency coordinators requesting data on how they provide residents with actual professional opportunities may also be in order.

Conclusion

Residents are not interns. They are entry-level professionals. Residents, residency coordinators, faculty and staff at hosting institutions, and potential next-employers of diversity residents recognizing this distinction may avoid some of the negative experiences recounted by residents in this study. The goal of diversity residency programs is to recruit and retain talent, not alienate and stunt the growth of practitioners with potential. Though the resident versus intern terminology may seem like nuanced semantics to some, clearly there is enough concern here that hosting institutions should take care to ensure that residents are not referred to as or seen as mere interns, both within and beyond the hosting institution.

References

Alston, Jason K. "Minerva's First Born: My Experiences as UNCG's First Diversity Resident Librarian." *North Carolina Libraries* 68 (2010): 14-16.

Bayard, Laura. "Notre Dame's Librarian-in-Residence Program." *Indiana Libraries* 28, no. 2 (2009): 16-19.

Beavers, Karen. "Becoming the Institution: The Residency Experience." In *Diversity in Libraries: Academic Residency Programs*, edited by Raquel V. Cogell and Cindy A. Gruwell, 113-118. Westport, CT: Greenwood Press, 2001.

Brewer, Julie. "Understanding the Organizational Value of Post–Master's Degree Residency Programs." *Research Library Issues* 272 (2010): 23-27.

Cogell, Raquel V. and Cindy A. Gruwell, eds. *Diversity in Libraries: Academic Residency Programs*. Westport, CT: Greenwood Press, 2001.

Hankins, Rebecca, Michele Saunders, and Ping Situ. "Diversity Initiatives vs. Residency Programs: Agents of Change?" *C&RL News* 64, no. 5 (2003): 308-315.

Hu, Sylvia S. and Demetria E. Patrick. "Our Experience as Minority Residents: Benefits, Drawbacks, and Suggestions." *C&RL News* 67, no. 5 (2006): 297-300.

University of Delaware Library. "Pauline A. Young Residency." Accessed June 8, 2014. http://www2.lib.udel.edu/personnel/residency/history.html

Chapter 5

STRENGTHENING THE PIPELINE-TALENT MANAGEMENT FOR LIBRARIES: A HUMAN RESOURCES PERSPECTIVE

Agnes K. Bradshaw

Introduction

Within any profession, there is a need to have talent (skilled employees) currently working in the profession. In addition, there is also a need to have employees "in the pipeline;" those employees ready and able or in the process of developing and preparing for higher-level roles. A term that has been in use by the private sector for more than a decade is "talent management." The term originated from a 1997 report from McKinsey & Company which reported on the management consulting firm's study of more than 200 corporate executives. The term "talent management" is now used within the human resources profession when discussing the recruitment function. For purposes of this chapter, I will use the following definition of talent management: "Broadly defined as the implementation of an [sic] integrated strategies or systems designed to increase workplace productivity by developing improved processes for attracting, developing, retaining and utilizing people with the required skills and aptitude to meet current and future business needs.[1] If organizations outside librarianship are recognizing the need to compete for

---

1. Society for Human Resources Management Glossary, http://www.shrm.org/TemplatesTools/Glossaries/HRTerms/Pages/t.aspx.

the best talent, why isn't librarianship? This chapter will look at talent management practices for developing the people who will be needed by the profession to ensure that it is seen as desirable for those from all groups, not just those from one group. In addition, the next steps after recruitment include the development of those within the profession to assume managerial, executive, and leadership roles. We will look at the representation of people of color within the profession and assess how talent management strategies can be utilized to ensure that librarians of color are included as a part of the organizational need to recruit and retain the best people, while ensuring that all groups of the user population are represented in the professional ranks.

There are many segments of librarianship: school media, public, academic, and various types of what is considered to be special librarianship, such as art, legal, medical, and music. In addition, library professionals may also be academics, such as being an LIS (Library and Information Science) educator. This chapter will concentrate on librarianship outside of LIS educators, although the lack of diversity within LIS educators is also an area of note. However, the role of an LIS educator is different from that of a librarian. The primary work of LIS educators is academic; it is not that of a practitioner, although many will also have a master's degree in library and information science in addition to the doctoral degree. This chapter will also focus on libraries within the United States.

Talent Management - Why Do Libraries Need It?

Talent management is the process that an organization uses to attract, develop, and retain skilled and valuable employees. In many organizations, talent management is a prime responsibility of the human resources function. Human resources professionals work together with managers on talent management processes including: workforce planning, recruitment, succession planning, leadership development, career and professional development, and finally the rewards strategy (salaries and employee benefits.) Human resources professionals together with organizational leaders work to ensure that the organization has the talent it needs to meet the current and future demands of those who utilize the products and services of the organization. There is no universal definition of talent management, nor is there a universally acknowledged way to conduct it. However, even in a poor economy, employers are competing for employee talent. There may be greater availability of those positions at lower levels within the organization, but even for lower level positions, there are often more people than jobs. There are generally more jobs at the lower ends of the organizational chart, but this means that while employers may have a large selection from which to choose, all those applying for positions will not have the desired skills the employer is seeking, or will otherwise prove not to be suitable for a specific opening. For higher-level positions, there are usually fewer openings, but there are also fewer people with the skills and experience for those positions.

Although the research around talent management by McKinsey & Company focused on the private sector, the conclusions drawn from the private, for-profit sector workforce can also be applied to librarianship. Libraries are organizations that provide a service to their constituencies just like for-profit corporations: they must provide the products and services that the user wants; they must be prepared to adapt to the changes in external environment that set the stage for changes in the way those services are being delivered; they must cultivate a new generation of users to utilize their services and in doing so, embrace new technologies that provide the products that the new users want and need. Libraries, just like for-profit organizations, do these things—except at no direct cost to the user, and the organization is not charged with making a profit. Libraries must have the talent necessary to not only do the work that needs to be done for its current customer base, but must also be prepared to forecast and plan appropriately to staff for the future. They must have staff who can not only perform the core work that a library does but staff who have the skills (or are willing to acquire and develop the skills) necessary to move the organization to where it needs to be in order to meet the challenges of the future. Fifty years ago, if you wanted to know what materials were in the library, you had to look in the physical card catalog and you needed to be in the physical library. In less than fifty years, library catalogs are now online and accessible to anyone with an Internet connection and a computer. Users are obtaining information in a variety of sources, not just via printed documents. Electronic journal articles, e-books and e-readers, digital images, and streaming video—all methods of obtaining information that did not exist a few generations ago. Public libraries are valuable resources to many, from young children first learning to read, to recent immigrants longing for news in their native language, to those seeking employment and looking for guidance on how to apply for a job online, to those who want to check out the latest John Gresham thriller.

Academic libraries serve a different constituency—students needing to research a topic for an assignment, a faculty member needing to locate an obscure text for an article he or she is writing, a community member needing to interpret recent online census data. All of these needs must be met by those employees with a varied skill base, including instruction, information technology, classification and organization, and customer service, to name a few. K-12 librarians (often called school media specialists) provide instructional assistance to students throughout elementary and high school. School librarians are often the first teachers of information literacy to students, and school libraries are often where students first encounter formal researching skills. Special librarians have specialized knowledge and serve in a variety of arenas, including academia, government, and the private sector. Finding and retaining people for these roles are where the process of talent management plays a significant role.

The pipeline for talent would consist of those employees who have been identified as having leadership or management potential, and can eventually assume management or leadership roles within the organization. For purposes of this chapter we will consider pipeline development as the strategy for ensuring that an organization is developing the human capital for all levels within the organization. This could mean developing those who are new to the profession and preparing them to assume first level management roles, or developing those who are in management roles and preparing them to assume leadership roles such as director or dean. It could also mean preparing for those employees who will eventually leave their entry level positions and planning to fill those positions when they become vacant. Finally, it could mean attracting those to the profession who have not considered librarianship to be a career choice.

Does Librarianship Need to Compete for Talent?

For several years, the American Library Association (ALA), the largest professional organization for librarians, has been sounding an alarm about the "graying of the profession,"[2] when huge numbers of librarians would reach retirement age and stop working. According to the U.S. Bureau of Labor Statistics *Occupational Outlook Handbook* 2012 report, job growth for librarians was predicted at a 7% increase from 2012-2022. This growth was defined as "slower than average" for all occupations. In the "Job Outlook" section of the report "budget limitations especially in local and educational services may slow demand."[3] The report also predicts that fewer librarians will be needed as people become more proficient with using electronic resources and that libraries may concentrate on the hiring of library paraprofessionals to save costs. By contrast, the BLS report predicts a 12% growth increase (as fast as average) for the same period of time for library paraprofessionals.

As do many professional organizations, ALA maintains demographic information on its members. In 2006, ALA released a report, *Diversity Counts*, which was updated most recently in 2012. The study provided data on librarians in six library types: K-12, Academic, Public, Hospital, Legal, and Other. The study revealed data that should not be surprising to any librarian of color currently working in the profession, or who has worked in the profession in the past—that the profession is

---

2. Rachel Singer Gordon, "Get Over the 'Graying' Profession Hype," Library Journal, 129 (January 15, 2004): 62.

3. U.S. Department of Labor, Bureau of Labor Statistics, *Occupational Outlook Handbook, 2014*, http://www.bls.gov/ooh/education-training-and-library/librarians.htm (accessed July 15, 2015).

overwhelmingly comprised of white females who are over 45 years of age. The study also pointed out that although there are students in LIS programs who are under age 35, there is a failure to incorporate those students into the profession. The report looked at statistics from the 2000 United States Census and the National Center of Education Statistics (NCES) that reports on national, state and individual library statistics. The study revealed that "the 110,000 credentialed librarians in public, school and academic librarians are predominately white, regardless of age group or gender."[4] ALA keeps statistics on its membership and while all librarians do not belong to ALA, the figures compiled on its membership coincide with the figures of the 2000 Census estimates: White, 89%; African American, 5%; Latino, 2%; Native American (including Alaskan), less than 1%; Asian Pacific Islander, 3%; Two or more racial groups, 1%. The study also showed that the greatest percentage of all librarians by age was in the range of 45-54, although for this reporting on age groups there was a substantial difference between the ALA demographic responses and the 2000 census estimates. The study also revealed the distribution of the type of credentialed librarians. Most of the minority librarians work in public libraries.

A report from the ALA Office of Research and Statistics "Planning for 2015: The Recent History and Future Supply of Librarians" was prepared in 2009. The focus of this report was "credentialed librarians" defined as "persons who report their occupation in the Census of American Community Survey as librarians, and also report having at least a masters degree."[5] As with any strategic plan, there is no way for the writers to see into the future. In 2009, it would have been impossible to predict the lingering economic woes in the United States, and see the budget cuts that would impact municipalities, higher education,

---

4. American Library Association, Office for Research and Statistics; Office for Diversity, *Diversity Counts*, revised January, 2007, 9, http://www.ala.org/offices/sites/ala.org.offices/files/content/diversity/diversitycounts/diversitycounts_rev0.pdf.

5. American Library Association, Office of Research and Statistics, *Planning for 2015: The Recent History and Future Supply of Librarians*, June 2009, 5.

and the private sector which would impact the creation of new jobs, job eliminations and the delayed retirements. According to Michael Kelley in the 2012 Annual Budget Survey published in *Library Journal*, "many public libraries are, at best, furiously treading water."[6] Those same economic woes would be responsible for layoffs, the elimination of permanent positions, and more employers relying on hiring part-time and/or contingent workers (in many instances, so they would not be required to pay for employee benefit costs) to fill positions in attempts to save money. In addition, public libraries, as well as school systems, are reliant on tax revenues for funding. Municipalities throughout the United States have suffered from decreasing tax revenues which has resulted in cutbacks to municipal services, including library services.

In spite of these predictions of slow job growth, enrollment in graduate Library and Information Science (LIS) programs continue to increase. According to the Association for Library Science Education (ALISE) we are seeing (and have seen over the past several years) LIS programs enrolling and graduating students to an employment picture that does not look bright. BLS is predicting a change of 11,000 jobs for a 20-year period. **Table 1** shows the numbers of students library related programs in 2011 and **Table 2** shows the demographics of the graduates from library programs in 2011. While program enrollment does not guarantee program completion, the numbers of graduate students enrolled does seem to exceed the number of available jobs.

With an abundance of talent seeking employment, why is talent management needed by libraries? Even if supply exceeds the demand for available jobs, employers must still focus on recruitment, selection, employee development, and succession planning. It is not easier to recruit talent in a competitive environment. Even with high numbers of people entering and completing MLS programs, one must be mindful that the majority of those graduates will be seeking (and probably only qualified for) entry level positions. Annual salary surveys published by *Library Journal* conclude that most of the jobs that open up annually are

---

6. Michael Kelley, "The New Normal," *Library Journal* (January, 2012): 37.

Table 1. Student Enrollment in LIS Programs

(Wallace, Danny P. ed., *Library and Information Science Educational Statistical Report 2012*. Association for Library and Information Science Education, p. 67).

Program	Status	Male		Female		Total Number	Percent FT/PT
		Number	Percent	Number	Percent		
Bachelor's	Full-Time	1,369	67	673	33	2,042	78.3
	Part-Time	388	68.7	177	31.3	565	21.7
	Subtotal	1,757	37.4	850	32.6	2,607	
Master's – LIS (ALA Accredited)	Full-Time	1,615	22.80	5,474	77.20	7,089	38
	Part-Time	2,207	19.10	9,361	80.90	11,568	62
	Subtotal	3,822	20.50	14,835	79.50	18,657	
Master's-IS	Full-Time	240	32.9	489	67.1	729	59.8
	Part-Time	121	24.7	369	75.3	490	40.2
	Subtotal	361	29.6	858	70.4	1,219	
Master's - Other	Full-Time	407	50.4	401	49.6	808	59.4
	Part-Time	343	62.1	209	37.9	552	40.6
	Subtotal	750	55.1	610	44.9	1,360	
Post Master's	Full-Time	17	37.8	28	62.2	45	13.7
	Part-Time	77	27.2	206	72.8	283	86.3
	Subtotal	94	28.7	234	71.3	328	
Doctoral	Full-Time	257	43.0	340	57.0	597	58.1
	Part-Time	157	36.5	273	63.5	430	41.9
	Subtotal	414	40.3	613	59.7	1,027	
Other Undergraduate	Full-Time	131	49.8	132	50.2	263	16
	Part-Time	519	37.5	866	62.5	1,385	84
	Subtotal	650	39.4	998	60.6	1,648	
Other Graduate	Full-Time	10	41.7	14	58.3	24	8.6
	Part-Time	43	16.9	212	83.1	255	91.4
	Subtotal	53	19	226	81	279	
Total	Full-Time	4,046	34.9	7,551	65.1	11,597	42.8
	Part-Time	3,855	24.8	11,673	75.2	15,528	57.2
	Total	7,901	29.1	19,224	70.9	27,125	

Table 2. Degrees and Certificates Awarded by Gender, Ethnicity, and Race
(Wallace, Danny P. ed., Library and Information Science Educational Statistical Report 2012. Association for Library and Information Science Education, p. 119).

Degree	Gender	Hispanic of Any Race	American Indian or Alaska Native	Asian	Black or African American	Native Hawaiian or Pacific Islander	White	Two or More Races	International	Race or Ethnicity Unknown	Total
Bachelor's	Male	28	2	69	51	0	277	8	8	16	459
	Female	30	2	23	22	0	95	3	2	17	194
	Subtotal	58	4	92	73	0	372	11	10	33	653
Master's LIS (ALA Accredited)	Male	78	6	66	54	1	1217	16	47	273	1758
	Female	244	40	269	278	13	4492	52	132	949	6469
	Subtotal	322	46	335	332	14	5709	68	179	1222	8277
Master's – IS	Male	3	2	36	21	1	89	0	39	20	211
	Female	5	0	20	13	1	34	1	30	12	116
	Total	8	2	56	34	2	123	1	69	32	327
Master's – Other	Male	3	0	13	3	0	37	0	35	36	127
	Female	4	1	3	4	1	53	0	33	75	174
	Total	7	1	16	7	1	90	0	68	111	301
Post-Master's	Male	4	0	1	0	0	25	1	0	9	40
	Female	4	0	0	4	0	53	2	1	28	92
	Total	8	0	1	4	0	78	3	1	37	132
Doctoral	Male	1	0	5	2	0	12	0	12	4	36
	Female	0	0	5	1	0	64	0	15	4	89
	Total	1	0	10	2	0	76	0	27	8	124
Total	Male	117	10	190	130	2	1657	25	141	358	2630
	Female	287	43	320	322	15	4791	58	213	1085	7134
	Total	404	53	510	452	17	6448	83	354	1443	9764

not entry-level positions. Statistics from BLS do not include the types and levels of positions they expect to become available in the forecast, only the numbers of positions. While jobs are expected to be available, as in any profession, we should assume there will be a variety of skillsets and specializations needed, as well as depth and breadth of experience. An effective talent management strategy ensures that an organization is prepared to fill positions when they become vacant, allows the organization to provide career development practices for those employees currently working in the organization to prepare to assume supervisory or leadership roles when possible, and develop succession plans for those in key leadership positions. As a way to prepare for the future, that strategy will also include planning to incorporate recent MLS grads into the workforce,

Demographic Information

The lack of diversity within librarianship was discussed earlier in the chapter. While there is greater ethnic and gender diversity within the profession among those working as library clerks than those working as credentialed librarians, the profession as a whole is mainly comprised of white females. Some would not see this as an issue of concern. As seen in our most recent United States Census data, the demographics of the United States are changing. The greatest population growth is coming from the Latino/Hispanic and Asian populations. "The U.S. population will be considerably older and more racially and ethnically diverse by 2060, according to projections released today by the U.S. Census Bureau. These projections of the nation's population by age, sex, race and Hispanic origin, which cover the 2012-2060 period, are the first set of population projections based on the 2010 Census. 'The next half century marks key points in continuing trends — the U.S. will become a plurality nation, where the non-Hispanic white population remains the largest single group, but no group is in the majority,' said Acting Director

Thomas L. Mesenbourg."[7] As the racial and ethnic makeup of the nation changes, there are those that would argue that initiatives to make the profession "more diverse and inclusive" are unnecessary and perhaps unwanted. Reasons for reluctance and opposition are varied, including opposition to government intrusion into hiring and promotional practices by way of equal opportunity legislation and/or affirmative action requirements put in place as a remedy for previous acts of discrimination; the increasing outcries of "reverse discrimination" from certain groups and even the reluctance of those in groups that may be granted treatment that they do not feel they want or need. There may also be a need to preserve the status quo of the current demographics of the profession by those currently in positions who feel they would suffer if opportunities for those in the majority shift. An effective talent management strategy ensures recruitment and promotional opportunities are open to a wide segment of the available population. To assume that the best and most qualified talent comes only from a single group is to limit the possibilities of the organization to succeed.

Focus on Minorities or Underrepresented Populations

It is important to provide some historical background on the concept of minority groups and their representation in the workforce as a whole to better understand the concern about what may be termed the lack of adequate minority representation within librarianship. Over the last 50 years, there have been several instances of legislation enacted against discrimination in various forms. Probably the most sweeping legislation regarding civil rights in the United States was the Civil Rights Act of 1964, specifically Title VII, which made it illegal to discriminate in

7. United States Census Bureau, "U.S. Census Bureau Projections Show a Slower Growing, Older, More Diverse Nation a Half Century from Now," last modified December 12, 2012, https://www.census.gov/newsroom/releases/archives/population/cb12-243.html.

human resources activities such as hiring, pay, employee benefits, and promotional opportunities. Title VII "bars discrimination in all HR activities, including hiring, training, promotion, pay, employee benefits, and other conditions of employment. Discrimination is prohibited on the basis of race, color, religion, sex (also referred to as gender), or national origin."[8] While there have been several amendments to the original Act, as well as various litigation regarding how the Act should be interpreted, laws prohibiting employment discrimination are still in effect. In additional to the federal requirement, many, if not all states and municipalities have similar laws against discrimination. Under Title VII, the Equal Employment Opportunity Commission (EEOC) was created to enforce the provisions of the Civil Rights Act. The EEOC has responsibility for ensuring that "covered employers comply with the intent of this Act."[9] Another development impacting civil rights and equal opportunity employment issues was the signing of Executive Order 11246, which created the Office of Federal Contract Compliance Programs (OFCCP), which has the authority to ensure equal opportunity for federal procurement. Federal contractors or subcontractors with "contracts in excess of $50,000 must develop affirmative action plans."[10]

There is often confusion between affirmative action and equal employment opportunity. "Affirmative action – policy that goes beyond equal employment opportunity by requiring organizations to comply with the law and correct past discrimination practices by increasing the numbers minorities and women in specific positions."[11] "Affirmative action aggressively includes individuals from protected groups as candidates in search processes, whereas equal employment opportunity,

---

8. George Bolander and Scott Snell, *Managing Human Resources*, 13th ed. (Mason, OH: Thomson South-Western, 2004), 53-54.

9. Ibid., 73.

10. Ibid., 755.

11. Ibid.

in a more passive fashion, addresses the avoidance of discrimination based upon protected group members."[12] It should be noted that most colleges and universities in the US are federal contractors (as well as many municipalities), and thus are required to have an Affirmative Action plan in place. It is this requirement (and the perception that an individual was hired only to fill a quota, despite that person's qualifications) that is the source of much of the controversy surrounding hiring of members of minority groups.

The justification often used for increasing diversity within for-profit organizations is the "business case," which may be defined as the rationale for undertaking a strategy or a project. The hope is that the successful strategy or project will lead to greater profits, an increased customer base, higher sales, etc. Libraries are not profit-making organizations, so the argument for increasing diversity within the profession is not the drive to increase customers, etc. but to have the employees within the profession who are more reflective of the constituencies they serve. According to Howland, "an equally wide range of well-researched scholarship has been published addressing the concern that, as demographic indicators point to increasingly culturally and racially diverse communities, libraries need to recruit increasingly diverse professional staffs."[13] While the notion of "celebrating diversity" is quite common today, it is doubtful that there is a universal agreement on the definition of diversity. In fact, the application of the term "diversity" is not the same as legislative measures taken to redress prior instances of legalized discrimination. "Prior research has posited that diversity, as a term and a concept, is essentially a euphemism, designed to avoid the

---

12. Deetta Jones, "The Definition of Diversity," *Journal of Library Administration* 27, no. 1-2: (1999): 12.

13. Joan S. Howland, "Beyond Recruitment: Retention and Promotion Strategies to Ensure Diversity and Success." *Library Administration & Management* 13, no. 1 (1999).

complexity and emotion laded natures of terms, such as race, racism, sex and sexism."[14]

Librarianship is no different from any other profession such as law or accounting. There are various stages of employment within a profession: entry level, supervisory/management, and executives (deans/directors.) For librarianship, the first stage of recruitment may be the marketing of the profession, preparing those with an interest in library work (perhaps generated by library use as a child or by working in a library in high school or college). ALA has created a page on their website about librarianship as a career, and has also created a website about careers within librarianship (www.librarycareers.org). There is also a page on the careers website specifically addressing diversity, which makes mention of the ALA ethnic caucuses and scholarship programs directed at minority students (http://librarycareers.drupalgardens.com/content/diversity-libraries).

Winston's Recruitment Theory identifies factors that influence the career choice of individuals, and according to Winston the factor that stands out for many in recruitment for librarianship is the desire to make a contribution. Better marketing of the profession and the skills necessary might take the profession beyond the impression of the "lady with bun and glasses" telling patrons to shush, and would probably go a long way to enhance the profession's reputation. While some efforts have been made to change the perception of the profession, it is debatable as to success of those efforts.

Increasing Diversity – Educational Opportunities

Ask any librarian if they have spoken to someone who expressed surprise that being a librarian required a master's degree, they would probably say "Yes." Librarians are aware that many outside the profession

---

14. Mark Winston, Diversity in Librarianship: Is There a Color Line? in *The 21st Century Black Librarian in America: Issues and Challenges*, eds. Andrew P. Jackson, Julius Jackson, Julius Jefferson, Jr. and Akilah S. Nosakhere. (Lanham, MD: Scarecrow Press, 2012), 204. (Winston on p. 131 in original document.)

have no understanding of the work they do and the skills and knowledge needed to do that work. However, for those who wish to be a credentialed professional librarian, a master's degree is almost always required. Graduate school is an investment and a commitment of numerous resources including finances and personal time. There are also the opportunity costs associated with committing to a graduate program. In recent years, there have been several programs designed to increase minority representation within professional librarian ranks by providing financial assistance for graduate education.

In 1997, ALA created the Spectrum Scholarship Program, designed to provide assistance to members of ethnic minority groups (American Indian/Native American, Asian, African American, Hispanic/Latino, and Native Hawaiian or Other Pacific Islander) seeking a career in librarianship.[15] The Spectrum Scholarship provides financial assistance for use towards an ALA accredited master's program, as well as connection to library professionals by using methods such as mentoring, networking assistance, stipends for professional association (ALA) membership dues and financial assistance for professional conference attendance (the annual ALA conference). According to Cooke, the creation of the Spectrum Initiative was not without controversy.[16] As of 2009, there had been more than 600 graduates of the Spectrum Initiative. We have no way of knowing how many Spectrum Scholars (as they are known) would have entered LIS programs and become librarians without the assistance of the scholarship. However, if this program or others similar to it has had an impact on easing the entry barrier to the profession, we should celebrate the program and consider it to be a success.

Another initiative under the Spectrum program is the Spectrum Doctoral Fellowship, created to broaden diversity among those interested

---

15. American Library Association. "Spectrum – Scholarship Overview," http://www.ala.org/offices/diversity/spectrum/scholarshipinformation.

16. Nicole A. Cooke, "The Spectrum Doctoral Fellowship Program: Enhancing the LIS Professoriate," *InterActions: UCLA Journal of Education and Information Studies* 10, no. 1, (2014), http://escholarship.org/uc/item/7vb7v4p8.

in becoming LIS educators. The program was created in 2006 by ALA and the University of Pittsburgh, and was funded by the Institute of Museum and Library Services (IMLS), which was established in 1996 under the National Foundation for Arts and Humanities. As with the Spectrum Scholars at the master's level, Cooke indicates that there was also resistance to supporting a program directed at minority groups for doctoral studies. In addition to the Spectrum programs, there are other programs designed to increase representation of minority groups within the profession (see **Table 3**).

Table 3. LIS Diversity Programs

Program Name	Institution	Targeted Group	Professional Focus
Academic Cultural Enrichment (ACE)	University of North Carolina -Greensboro	Underrepresented Communities	Academic, Community College and Public Libraries
Association of Research Libraries (ARL)/Society of American Archivists MOSAIC Program	Various	Underrepresented Communities	Archives, Special Collections
Association of Research Libraries/Music Library Association Diversity and Inclusion Initiative (DII)	Various	Unrepresented Communities	Music and Performing Arts Librarianship
Circle of Learning	San Jose State University	Native Americans and Alaska Natives	Increase the number of Native librarians who understand tribal culture and are committed to addressing the challenges faced by libraries serving Native patrons.
LIS Across Midwest Program (LAMP)	Various schools in the Midwest United States	Underrepresented Communities	N/A
Knowledge River	University of Arizona	Native Americans and Latinos	Cultural heritage services to Latino and Native American cultures.
Project IDOL	Wayne State University	Underrepresented Communities	N/A

Increasing minority representation within a profession does not stop at education. The next step is professional recruitment. As with so many other areas of our lives, technology has had an impact on employment recruitment. Two generations ago, print advertisements in newspapers and professional association publications were probably the most common way of advertising for a job opening. Less common was college recruiting (usually used for entry level positions and for those in professional graduate programs such a law or business). For executive positions, a professional search firm may have been used. In a short period of time, employment recruitment has gone almost completely online. Employers advertise positions on their own websites, or advertise on online recruitment sites, including professional organization websites (ALA JobList, Special Librarians, etc.), or publications dedicated to a specific market, such as the *Chronicle of Higher Education*. There are also hundreds, perhaps thousands, of discussion lists dedicated to various branches of any profession and librarianship is no exception. Job postings are sent via email to members of a particular list and from the original email, the notice of the opening may be passed by the recipients to any number of other interested parties. Social media has also become a part of recruitment efforts, the most common probably being Facebook, LinkedIn, and Twitter. However, seeing an ad is not enough; the advertisement must be attractive enough to a sufficient candidate pool in order to generate applicants worthy of consideration for an interview. Talent management is a lengthy process and advertisement is only one step in the recruitment process.

A common refrain from employers concerning recruitment is that they are not getting the talent that they need. Moreover when it comes to minority recruitment, according to the Association of Research Libraries Minority Recruitment and Retention in ARL Libraries Systems and Procedures Exchange Center (SPEC) report, "while some libraries are getting results, none are experiencing significant success." [17] If an organization is having difficulty attracting qualified candidates, they should take a strong look at their recruitment practices and assess both what

---

17. Association of Research Libraries, "Minority Recruitment and Retention in ARL Libraries - SPEC Kit 167," (Washington, DC: Association of Research Libraries, 1990), Introduction.

they are doing and what they are not doing to attract candidates. Issues resulting in a less than satisfactory talent pool include a less than competitive compensation and benefits structure or geographical locations that people may consider less than desirable for any number of reasons.

Providing Steps on the Career Ladder

In recent years, it has become increasing difficult to find entry-level full-time professional librarian positions. *Library Journal* conducts an annual survey of library schools and their graduates. Participation is voluntary, and many LIS programs do not respond, nor do the graduates of the program. In the results published in 2013, data gathered from the 2012 graduates indicates that 30.7 percent of the approximate 1900 LIS graduates from that year responded to the survey.[18] According to Gordon, many LIS graduates are pursuing a second or third career."[19] So while the problem of finding an entry-level position may be problematic within the profession, since the numbers of non-white librarians are so small in comparison, it would appear that it would be even more difficult for librarians of color to find an entry-level position. One way that some academic and governmental libraries (specifically the National Library of Medicine and the Library of Congress) are providing increased opportunities for recent graduates is by offering a post-graduate residency program. Often these programs are geared towards members of underrepresented populations, as is the Diversity Residency programs. These residencies are usually not permanent positions; they normally last from one to two years and are designed to expose the resident to various segments of academic or specialized governmental librarianship.

Residency programs may have a generalist or a specialist focus. Other academic library residency programs that while not geared to minority populations (North Carolina State University, University of Pennsylvania,

---

18. Stephanie L. Maatta, "The Emerging Databrarian," *Library Journal* 138, no. 17 (2013): 26.

19. Gordon, 62.

and University of Illinois at Chicago) should certainly be considered by people of color as a way to gain entry to librarianship, and ultimately gain an advantage in the job market when seeking a permanent position.

Of course, diversity residency programs (and there are actually very few of them) can give members of minority groups valuable exposure to professional librarianship, but should not be viewed as an all-compassing solution to the lack of diverse representation. Concerns noted by former residents include: being considered "interns as opposed to professional librarians, being singled out for representation when the libraries needed assistance with a multicultural or diversity initiative or having their minority status emphasized" according to Hu and Patrick.[20] In addition to academic libraries, two of the country's largest library systems have programs similar to academic residencies: the New York Public Library and the Los Angeles County Public Library. While the residencies at the public libraries are not geared specifically towards underrepresented populations, public libraries, especially those in large urban areas like New York and Los Angeles, have very diverse populations. Such programs are a good way to attract librarians that mirror the communities in which they live and work, and perhaps more importantly, those who may be bilingual and have the language skills necessary to communicate with the patrons they are serving. Other initiatives to help retain and foster career development of minority librarians include the Association of Research Libraries (ARL) Leadership and Career Development Program and the Minnesota Institute for Early Career Librarians.

Is Recruitment Still Necessary?

Recruitment into a profession by an organization is a multi-step process and may take many routes. Although it is not possible to see into the future, organization executives (library directors, deans, etc.) must somehow be able to determine a way to estimate what kind of work will need to be done in the future and the skills needed to do that

---

20. Sylvia Hu and Demetria E. Patrick, "Our Experience as Minority Residents," *College & Research Libraries News* 67, no. 5 (2006): 297.

work. Workforce planning is a critical element of strategic planning, for which all library leaders will have at least partial responsibility. Elements that should be considered for workforce planning include, but are not limited to: economic factors (almost impossible to predict); competitive trends; technological changes; political and legislative issues; social concerns; and demographic trends. For some careers, recruitment is done at the college or graduate school level and begins while the potential recruit is still a student. To reach those who are no longer students, but actually working within the profession or desiring to work in the profession, recruitment involves making the job appear desirable to as many candidates as possible. Of course, all of this assumes that there is a vacant position that needs to be filled. In recent years, libraries have at best seen flat budgets, and at worst seen declining budgets. *Library Journal* reports that libraries have responded to these budget challenges in a variety of ways, including eliminating positions, personnel cross-training, using volunteers, hiring non-MLS holders to save salary dollars, outsourcing some professional tasks, and reducing hours and services.

Work conditions are another factor that can contribute to successful recruitment. For several years now we have seen a growth in part-time professional positions, and for many, part-time work is not desirable. It is probably safe to say that no one becomes a librarian because they want to be rich, but expecting to find a full-time job earning enough money to support oneself should be not unreachable.

We know that there are many new and recent LIS graduates looking for jobs and we know there are not enough jobs for all those who are looking for work. However, there are jobs openings within librarianship and those job openings include replacements for an employee who left the organization; a position that was reworked or reclassified based on some organizational change, such as a technological change; or a newly created position. How then, do you recruit for those jobs? More importantly, how do you attract people of color to those positions and get them to apply? This is especially important when you consider the barrier for entry to the profession (a master's degree) is higher than some other professions, such as teacher or nurse, which only require a bachelor's degree for an entry level professional.

Shifting Focus to Diversity

Over the years since the passing of the Civil Rights Act of 1964, there has been a shift from a focus on discrimination (perhaps by the mistaken belief that it no longer exists) to an emphasis on diversity. According to Kelly and Dobbin, "EEO/AA practices were soon recast as the diversity management component of the new human resources management paradigm. Practices designed to achieve legal compliance were re-theorized as efficient when the original impetus for adopting them was removed...." [21] Ensuring equal opportunity by law is not the same thing as embracing diversity. Rarely will someone on a hiring committee come out and specifically say that they are not going to hire someone because of their gender, race, ethnicity, or religion; or at least say it out loud. Cotton, O'Neill, and Griffin indicate that bias in the hiring or promotional practice is more difficult to detect, and may not be known to the decision maker(s). Bias may be defined as "intentional and unintentional, conscious and subconscious, attitudes, behaviors and actions that have a negative and differential impact on segments of the society or favor one segment of society." [22]

> These subtle forms of bias subtlety impact the hiring and promotion process. For example, when selecting between two 'equally qualified candidates,' raters often will select the candidate who matches their stereotypical picture of the "right fit" for the position. They will arrive at this decision by accentuating the positive attributes of the traditional

21. Erin Kelly and Frank Dobbin, "How Affirmative Action Became Diversity Management: Employer Response to Antidiscrimination Law, 1962 to 1996" *American Behavioral Scientist* 41, no. 7 (1998): 962.

22. William Shakelford, "The New Face of Bias in the Workplace – 2011, Part 1 – The Subtlety of Bias," Workforce Diversity Network, http://www.workforcediversitynetwork.com/res_articles_newfaceofbias_Shackelford.aspx.

candidate and, likewise, focusing on the negative attributes of the other candidate, or look for similar personal experiences to find common ground as justification for a hiring decision, experiences people of color may not have had. In addition, they may use the diversity characteristics of the candidates as strikes against them…Or, they may raise concerns about how customers (or employees) will respond if the person of color is hired/promoted.

Under these circumstances, the decision to hire/promote is not based solely on the qualifications of the candidates (objective criteria). It is greatly influenced by subjective criteria (their "fit"). When these subjective criteria relate to fixed diversity dimensions of candidates (race, gender, age, sexual orientation, etc.), the resulting decision is inherently bias. The organization may be blind to the biases and insist the process was fair and unbiased.[23]

We can't attribute to bias or overt discrimination every instance of a person of color not getting an interview or a job offer or not being promoted. There are almost always more applicants than jobs, and there is usually only one vacancy. In a promotion situation, only one person can receive the promotion.

In one study, Hodge and Spoor found that 70% of the respondents identified personality/attitude and institutional fit to be "very important" criteria for job selection.[24] The same study found that the top three character traits for selecting a candidate were: intelligence, enthusiasm, and cooperativeness. While very few people want to work with colleagues who are considered unintelligent, there is no objective measurement for enthusiasm or cooperativeness. Those in hiring positions or serving on hiring committees might want to review their personal definition of "enthusiasm" and "cooperativeness" to see how the group defines those terms. They should consider how a candidate whose first language is not English and is being careful to not to use jargon that native English speakers take for granted as "unenthusiastic" or "uncooperative" or even "unintelligent." Using "organizational fit" as an acceptable way to judge whether or not someone is qualified for a position may also

---

23. Ibid.

24. Megan Hodge and Nicole Spoor, "Congratulations! You've Landed an Interview," *New Library World* 113, no 3 (2012): 139-161.

be an excuse not to hire them because the candidate does not fit the preconceived notion of "qualified" by the selection committee. Care should also be taken to avoid making assumptions that a candidate who has an outgoing personality is a more appropriate person for a position than a person who does not.

In spite of ALA's diversity initiatives over the decades, the diversity of the profession has not increased significantly. Within all types of librarianship, but especially within academic libraries, the numbers of librarians of color have also not increased significantly in more than a decade. Academic librarians, especially those who are hired within a tenure/tenure track system, have additional hurdles such as the candidate being deemed qualified to do the scholarly work, research, and publishing that are necessary to obtain tenure. These are professional requirements not faced by librarians in non-academic settings. Publishing and service to the profession (and in some cases, service to the university) are important factors in order to obtain tenure; but perhaps more crucial is securing the votes of colleagues in support of your tenure candidacy. Types of research interests may also have an impact on tenure attainment. Tenured colleagues who have a vote on candidates' tenure may not value the research done by colleagues from underrepresented populations if the research interest is not seen as important or scholarly.

For librarians at academic institutions that offer tenure (including those institutions that offer rank and promotion) developing a support network is even more crucial. There are numerous publications about the daunting and often subjective process of obtaining tenure, some specifically targeted at academic faculty members of color. However, the literature on tenure and librarians of color is not as prolific. In spite of the limited amount of professional literature on librarians of color achieving tenure, there is enough to provide evidence that the percentage of those not receiving tenure is higher for people of color than those of the majority population, according to Damasco and Hodges.[25]

25. Ione T. Damasco and Dracine Hodges, "Tenure and Promotion Experiences of Academic Librarians of Color." *College & Research Libraries* 73, no. 4 (2012): 279-201.

Successful navigation of a career takes skills and acumen beyond just excelling at the job one was hired to do and librarianship is no different.

Beyond Recruitment: Retention

According to the *Diversity Counts* study, "that credentialed librarians under age 45 comprised almost a third, 30% of the total for that category in 2000, yet accounted for 44% of credentialed librarians leaving the work force, speaks not so much to an inability to effectively recruit individuals to LIS education and practice as an inability to effectively retain them."[26]

People make decisions to leave a job or a career for many reasons, some of which may be unrelated to work conditions. Over recent decades we have seen workforce trends such as the emphasis on work-life balance. Employers know that retention of employees is a part of a successful talent management strategy. It is expensive to replace an employee who leaves a job. Library budgets are already stretched; using resources as a result of staff turnover in response to circumstances that can be controlled is not a good use of resources. Hiring an employee is an expensive investment. When you consider the costs (actual cash expenditures of recruiting and hiring an employee including marketing costs, travel expenses for the candidates, and relocation expenses; and non-monetary expenses, such as search or hiring committee time for reviewing applicant pools), as well as the opportunity costs of those employees whose normal job responsibility is not recruitment, it is clear that recruitment is expensive.

While less has been written about retention and librarians of color, there is no reason to expect that librarianship is any different from any other profession that loses employees because of the lack of opportunity for advancement or the feeling that their achievements are not valued in

---

26. American Library Association, *Diversity Counts*, 11.

the same manner as their white counterparts. St. Lifer and Nelson note that professional librarianship is no different than other professions regarding the concerns about a diverse workforce and the diversity of those within the higher ranks.[27] However, professions such as law and engineering do attract larger numbers of minorities, perhaps due the higher compensation for those professions. Given that it appears that minority librarians are underrepresented within the profession, when they are able to get professional librarian positions, why don't they stay? Why don't they rise to senior positions within the organization? As with other professions, the reasons are many. However, while there has been less written in library literature about retention of minority professionals, there is plenty of literature within management literature about employee retention. Here again, retention, leadership development, and succession planning are key components of the talent management strategy. According to Sullivan, little to no turnover might be bad news.[28] However, high turnover or turnover of only of specific types of employees should generally be a cause for concern. Each time an employee makes a decision to leave, the organization must revamp its operations until a replacement employee is recruited, hired, and trained to be able to provide value to the organization. Within the profession, in today's economic climate, it is not unusual to have a position not replaced or replaced by a part-time position. The entire organization suffers when competent people leave because they feel their talents are not recognized.

According to Klein, Mendoza, and Allers "diversity initiatives put in place may have the best intentions, but there are studies to show that

27. Evan St. Lifer and Corinne O. Nelson, "Unequal Opportunities: Race Does Matter," *Library Journal* 122, (1997): 42-46.

28. John Sullivan, "A Low Turnover Rate Could Mean That You Have Ugly Employees," ERE.NET, last modified August 8, 2011, http://www.ere.net/2011/08/08/a-low-turnover-rate-could-mean-that-you-have-ugly-employees/.

such programs are not effective. For people of color, gay, lesbians and women of all backgrounds, hidden biases can become hidden barriers in three major areas: commitment of the leadership, career development and feedback, and an unwelcoming environment."[29]

Commitment of the Leadership

Commitment of the leadership to having a diverse staff at all levels is essential. That commitment must also be put in practice by lower levels within the organization. One possible way to increase minority representation within management and leadership ranks is a version of the National Football League (NFL) "Rooney Rule, which says for all coaching and general manager jobs openings there must be a minority candidate who had to at least get an interview."[30] While such a practice may be helpful, others may see the practice as offensive, as if the only qualification for the interview was race or ethnicity.

Mentoring

Mentoring is frequently cited as an important component to career success for all employees. For people of color, mentoring may be an even more crucial component, because "mentors help new employees understand the unwritten rules of the workplace such as the importance of socializing, the preferred organization style of communication, and the ins and outs of departmental politics."[31] These items are not written

29. Freada Kapor Klein, Martha Mendoza, and Kimberly Allers, *Giving Notice: Why the Best and the Brightest Leave the Workplace and How You Can Help Them Stay* (San Francisco: Jossey-Bass, 2008), 2-5.

30. Monte Burke, "Why the NFL's Rooney Rule Matters" Forbes, last modified January 26, 2013, http://www.forbes.com/sites/monteburke/2013/01/26/why-the-nfls-rooney-rule-matters/.

31. Joe Steele "Sharing the 'Unwritten Rules' Impacts Retention," *Cultural Diversity at Work* 9, no. 6 (July 1997): 6, quoted by Linda Musser, "Effective Retention Strategies for Diverse Employees," in *Diversity Now: People, Collections, and Services in Academic Libraries,* ed. Teresa Y. Neely and Kuang-Hwei (Janet) Lee-Smeltzer (New York: Haworth Press, 2002).

in a job description, but knowing how to successfully navigate them can mean the difference between job success or job failure. This is especially true for higher-level positions where the expectation is less on knowing how to do a job, but how to get work done through other people.

Mentoring may have many approaches, and having a mentor can help a new employee become acclimated to a new job. Mentoring can be also valuable to employees looking to advance their careers, make a career directional change (i.e. move from a public library to a special library), provide assistance with and for publication collaboration opportunities (crucial for many academic librarians), or ease the transition for an employee who has relocated to a new area.

While many mentoring relationships occur on an informal basis, professional organizations such as ALA and state library associations offer the opportunity for formal mentoring relationships for a variety of purposes such as new professionals, career progression, and peer mentoring. Librarians of color should not make the assumption that only people who look like them can be a mentor. First, since there are so few librarians of color, there are probably not enough to go around. Also, not all working professionals are interested in being a mentor. The mentoring relationship may have defined parameters for the purpose of the relationship according to the sponsoring organization, but a mentoring relationship is a highly personal and ultimately defined by the people in the relationship.

Career Development

Career development is something that organizations know they must focus on if they wish to retain quality employees. Career development is another tenant of a complete talent management strategy. Career development is something that every employee needs to think about, even if that employee does not aspire to be a manager or a leader. Rarely does an employee do the same job for their entire career or remain employed at the same institution. Even for those employed at the same institution, librarianship is constantly evolving so the acquisition of new skills is required in order to meet the demands of the patron base. Failure to provide career development opportunities can be a reason employees leave an organization for other opportunities, especially if other employees are given opportunities to develop their careers.

Conclusions

In order to both increase the pipeline of new librarians and develop "bench strength" (which is a human resources term used to refer to the capabilities and readiness of potential successors to move into key professional and leadership positions), librarians of color can work to form and develop strong, sustaining professional networks (in and outside the employing library) in order to help navigate the hiring process and to develop a support network that can be utilized throughout a professional career. Developing a professional network need not be limited to those whose ethnicity, race and/or gender mirrors your own. In fact limiting oneself to a single group for support may be just that, limiting. However, the support these networks can provide when jobs are not obtained or promotions are not received can be crucial when trying to overcome the presumption of incompetence towards people of color by many with hiring authority. The fallacy that the best-qualified person always gets the job (or only the best qualified person gets the job) is just that—a fallacy. Hiring is always a subjective practice. The definition of "best qualified" will often vary with the person making the decision. The belief that the reason that more people of color are not included in the profession due to inferior qualifications and skills is false. Incompetence comes in all colors.

While strides have been made in terms of education, there are still barriers to entry into professional librarianship, including having an advanced degree, and fewer job openings for those at the entry level. In addition, many of the positions in libraries have a need for skills that are not just utilized within librarianship, but could be utilized in a variety of professions. When you consider that some of those professions offer higher paying salaries, in professions that may have more flexibility in terms of experience, it is not surprising that many who could have gone into librarianship decided on another profession.

Studies have shown that in the resume evaluation process, those with ethnic sounding names are less likely to be called for an interview, yet alone hired.[32] Other studies have looked at the differences in how the labor market can prevent (intentionally or otherwise) people of color from being successful. "The whites among those DiTomaso interviewed found 70% of the jobs they held over their lifetimes through inside information shared by a family member, friend, or neighbor, a direct intervention (someone walking a resume into a hiring manager's office or a direct request that a family member or friend get an open job) or other means not open to the general public."[33] While none of these studies were directed specifically at librarianship, we can assume that librarianship hiring practices does not differ significantly from other professions.

Leaders must be willing to invest in talent at all levels of the organization and understand that all employees do not have the same career aspirations, but organizations must have policies in place to ensure that those who do are provided an equal opportunity to realize those aspirations.

There is a need for people of color within the profession, with various skills, backgrounds and interests. As our country becomes more diverse, it is important that libraries provide a welcoming and inclusive environment for all that use it. Having people of color represented in

32. See: John Cotton, Bonnie O'Neill and Andrea Griffin."The 'Name Game': Affective and Hiring Reactions to First Names," *Journal of Managerial Psychology* 23, no. 1 (2008): 18-39 and Marianne Bertrand and Sendhil Mullainathan, "Are Emily and Brendan More Employable than Lakisha and Jamal? A Field Experiment on Labor Market Discrimination." *American Economic Review* 94, no. 4 (2004): 991-1013.

33. Janell Ross, "For Black Kids in American, a Degree is No Guarantee," *Atlantic,* last modified May 27, 2014, http://www.theatlantic.com/education/archive/2014/05/when-a-degree-is-no-guarantee/371613/

the profession will ensure that libraries provide the services that mirror populations using them.

References

Adkins, Denice. "Latino Librarians on Becoming LIS Educators: An Exploratory Investigation of the Barriers in Recruiting Latino Faculty." *Journal of Education for Library & Information Science* 45, no. 2: (2004): 149-161.

American Library Association, Office for Research & Statistics. *Diversity Counts*. Last modified January, 2007. http://www.ala.org/offices/files/diversity/diversitycounts/diversitycounts_rev0.pdf

American Library Association. "Spectrum – Scholarship Overview," accessed June 2, 2014, http://www.ala.org/offices/diversity/spectrum/scholarshipinformation.

American Library Association. "Spectrum Scholarship Program," accessed June 2, 2014, http://www.ala.org/offices/diversity/spectrum.

Association of Research Libraries. "ARL/SAA Mosaic Program," accessed June 29, 2014, http://www.arl.org/leadership-recruitment/diversity-recruitment/arl-saa-mosaic-scholarship-program#.U8FtUbHxLgU.

Association of Research Libraries. "Minority Recruitment and Retention in ARL Libraries - SPEC Kit 167." Washington, DC: Association of Research Libraries, 1990.

Bolander, George and Scott Snell. *Managing Human Resources*. 13th ed. Mason, OH: Thomson South-Western, 2004.

Bertrand, Marianne and Sendhil Mullainathan. "Are Emily and Brendan More Employable than Lakisha and Jamal? A Field Experiment on Labor Market Discrimination." *American Economic Review* 94, no. 4 (2004): 991-1013.

Bonnette, Ashley E. "Mentoring Minority Librarians up the Career Ladder." *Library Administration & Management* 18, no. 3(2004): 134-139.

Bourg, Chris. "Working on the 'Pipeline Problem' in Librarianship," Feral Librarian Blog. March 1, 2014. http://chrisbourg.wordpress.com/2014/03/01/working-on-the-pipeline-problem-in-librarianship/.

Brewer, Julie. "Post-Master's Residency Programs: Enhancing the Development of New Professionals and Minority Recruitment in Academic and Research Libraries." *College & Research Libraries* 58, (November 1997): 528-537.

Bright, Kawanna, and Jayati Chaudhuri. "Seeding the Vision: Designing a Minority Librarian Residency Program—Part 2." *Southeastern Librarian* 53, no. 3 (2005): 6-10.

Burke, Monte. "Why the NFL's Rooney Rule Matters." *Forbes*. Last modified January 26, 2013. http://www.forbes.com/sites/monteburke/2013/01/26/why-the-nfls-rooney-rule-matters/.

Chambers, Elizabeth G., et al. "The War for Talent." *McKinsey Quarterly* no. 3 (September 1998): 44-57.

Cooke, Nicole A. "The Spectrum Doctoral Fellowship Program: Enhancing the LIS Professoriate" *InterActions: UCLA Journal of Education and Information Studies* 10, no. 1 (2014). http://escholarship.org/uc/item/7vb7v4p8

Cotton, John, Bonnie O'Neill and Andrea Griffin. "The 'Name Game': Affective and Hiring Reactions to First Names." *Journal of Managerial Psychology* 23, no. 1 (2008): 18-39. doi.org/10.1108/02683940810849648

Damasco, Ione T. and Dracine Hodges. "Tenure and Promotion Experiences of Academic Librarians of Color." *College & Research Libraries* 73, no. 3 (2012): 279-301.

Davis, Denise M., comp. *Planning for 2015: The Recent History and Future Supply of Librarians.* Chicago: American Library Association, 2009. http://www.ala.org/research/files/librarystaff-stats/recruitment/Librarians_supply_demog_analys.pdf.

Eckard, Max, Ashley Rosener, and Lindy Scripps-Hoekstra. "Factors that Increase the Probability of a Successful Academic Library Job Search." *Journal of Academic Librarianship* 40, no. 2 (2014): 107-117. doi: 10.1016/j.acalib.2014.02.001

Edwards, Eli, and William Fisher. "Trust, Teamwork, and Tokenism: Another Perspective on Diversity in Libraries." *Library Administration & Management* 17, no. 1 (December 15, 2003): 21-27.

Fine, Eva and Jo Handelsman. *Searching for Excellence & Diversity: A Guide for Search Committees.* Madison, WI: WISELI-University of Wisconsin –Madison, 2012.

Freeman, Rodney. "A Snapshot of Indiana's Librarians Leading in Diversity Fellowship Participants After the Program Has Concluded." *Indiana Libraries* 33, no. 1 (2014): 12-15.

Fujimoto, Eugene Oropeza. "Hiring Diverse Faculty Members in Community Colleges: A Case study in Ethical Decision Making." *Community College Review* 40, no. 3 (July 2012): 255-274.

Griffin, Karin L. 2013. "Pursuing Tenure and Promotion in the Academy: A Librarian's Cautionary Tale." *Negro Educational Review* 64, no. 1-4 (2013): 77-96.

Gordon, Rachel Singer. "Get Over the "Graying" Profession Hype." *Library Journal* 129, (January, 2004): 62.

Gulati, Anjali. "Diversity in Librarianship: The United States Perspective" *IFLA Journal* 36, no. 4 (December, 2010): 288-293. doi:10.1177/0340035210388244

Hodge, Megan and Nicole Spoor. "Congratulations! You've Landed an Interview." *New Library World* 113, no. 3 (2012): 139-161.

Holt, Rachel, and Adrienne L. Strock. 2005. "The Entry-Level Gap." *Library Journal* 130, no. 8: 36-38.

Honma, Todd. 2005. "Tripping Over the Color Line: The Invisibility of Race and Library and Information Studies." *InterActions: UCLA Journal of Education and Information Studies*. 1, no. 2 (2005):1- 26. http://escholarship.org/uc/item/4nj0w1mp.

Howland, Joan S. "Beyond Recruitment: Retention and Promotion Strategies to Ensure Diversity and Success." *Library Administration & Management* 13, no. 1 (1999): 4-14.

Hu, Sylvia S., and Demetria E. Patrick. "Our Experience as Minority Residents: Benefits, Drawbacks, and Suggestions." *College & Research Libraries News* 67, no. 5 (May 2006): 297-300.

Jayne, Randy. "Making Recruitment Part of Your Talent Management Process." In *The Talent Management Handbook: Creating a Sustainable Competitive Advantage by Selecting, Developing and Promoting the Best People*, 2nd ed., edited by Lance A. Berger Dorothy R. Berger, 471-478. New York: McGraw Hill, 2011.

Johnson, Peggy. "Retaining and Advancing Librarians of Color." *College & Research Libraries* 68, no. 5 (2007): 405-417.

Jones, Deetta. "The Definition of Diversity." *Journal of Library Administration* 27, no. 1-2 (1999): 5-15. doi:10.1300/J111v27n01_02.

Joyce, Leslie W. "Building the Talent Pipeline." In *Strategy-Driven Talent Management*, edited by Rob Silzer and Ben E. Dowell, 123-158. San Francisco: Jossey Bass, 2010.

Institute of Museum and Library Studies Grant Search page, accessed June 13, 2014. http://www.imls.gov/recipients/grant-search.aspx

Kayongo, Jessica, LeRoy LaFleur and Ira Revels. "Reaching High School Students: Sowing the Seeds of Librarianship." In *Achieving Diversity*, edited by Barbara Dewey and Loretta Parham, 102-113. New York: Neal-Schuman Publishers, 2006.

Kim, Kyung-Sun and Sei-Ching Joanna Sin. "Increasing Ethnic Diversity in LIS: Strategies Suggested by Librarians of Color." *Library Quarterly* 78, no. 2 (2006): 153-177.

Kelly, Erin and Frank Dobbin. "How Affirmative Action Became Diversity Management: Employee Response to Antidiscrimination Law, 1961 to 1996." *American Behavioral Scientist* 41, no. 7 (1998): 960-984. doi:10.1177/0002764298041007008.

Kelly, Michael. "The New Normal." *Library Journal*, 137, no. 1 (January, 2012): 37-40.

Klein, Frieda Kapor, Martha Mendoza, and Kimberly Allers. *Giving Notice: Why the Best and the Brightest Leave the Workplace and How You Can Help Them Stay.* San Francisco: Jossey Bass, 2008.

Knowledge River Institute, accessed June 19, 2014, http://sirls.arizona.edu/KR/about#kr1

Laroche, Lionel and Don Rutherford. *Recruiting, Retaining, and Promoting Culturally Different Employees.* Burlington, MA: Butterworth-Heinemann, 2007.

Mack, Thura, and Jill Keally. "Seeding the Vision: Designing a Minority Librarian Residency Program." *Southeastern Librarian* 52, no. 1: (2004) 4-8.

Maatta, Stephanie. "Closing the Gap." *Library Journal* 130, no. 17 (2005): 26-33.

———. "What's an MLS Worth?" *Library Journal* 132, no. 17 (2007): 30-38.

———. "The Emerging Databrarian." *Library Journal* 138, no. 17 (2013): 26.

Mack, Thura, and Jill Keally. "Seeding the Vision: Designing a Minority Librarian Residency Program – Part 2." *Southeastern Librarian* 52, no 13 (Spring 2004): 4-8.

Mahajan, Ritu. "The Naked Truth: Appearance Discrimination, Employment and the Law." *Asian American Law Journal* 14, no. 1/6 (2007): 165-203.

Martinez, Elizabeth. "Chicano Librarianship." *American Libraries* 41, no. 11/12 (2010): 40-43.

McCook, Kathleen de la Peña, and Paula Geist. 1993. "Diversity Deferred: Where are the Minority Librarians?" *Library Journal* 118, no. 18 (1993): 35-38.

Michaels, Ed, Helen Handfield-Jones, and Beth Axelrod. *The War for Talent*. Boston: Harvard University Press, 2001.

Minnesota Institute for Early Career Librarians, accessed June 29, 2014, https://www.lib.umn.edu/sed/institute.

Montiel-Overall, Patricia and Sandra Littletree. "Knowledge River: A Case Study of a Library Information Science Program Focusing on Latino and Native American Perspectives." *Library Trends* 59, nos. 1-2 (2010): 67-83.

Music Library Association. ARL/MLA Diversity & Inclusion Initiative, accessed June 29, 2014, http://www.musiclibraryassoc.org/?page=ARLMLADiversity.

Neely, Teresa Y. "Assessing Diversity Initiatives: The ARL Leadership and Career Development Program." *Journal of Library Administration* 49, no. 8 (2009): 811-835. doi:10.1080/01930820903396830.

Neely, Teresa Y., and Kuang-Hwei (Janet) Lee-Smeltzer, eds., *Diversity Now: People, Collections, and Services in Academic Libraries*. New York: Haworth Press, 2002.

Neely, Teresa Y., and Lorna Peterson. "Achieving Racial and Ethnic Diversity among Academic and Research librarians: The Recruitment, Retention, and Advancement of Librarians of Color—A White Paper." *College & Research Libraries News* 68, no. 9 (2007): 562-565.

New York Public Library. "Opportunities for Students and Interns." Accessed June 23, 2014, http://www.nypl.org/node/81769.

Reese, Gregory L., and Ernestine Hawkins. *Stop Talking Start Doing! Attracting People of Color to the Library Profession.* Chicago: American Library Association, 1999.

Ross, Janell. "For Black Kids in American, a Degree is No Guarantee." *Atlantic.* Last modified May 27, 2014. http://www. theatlantic.com/education/archive/2014/05/when-a-degree-is-no-guarantee/371613/.

Ross, Kevin. "Purposeful Mentoring in Academic Libraries." *Journal of Library Administration* 53, nos. 7-8 (2013): 412-428. doi: 10.1080/01930826.2013.882195.

St. Lifer, Evan, and Corinne O. Nelson. "Unequal Opportunities: Race Does Matter." *Library Journal* 122 (1997): 42-46.

Salo, Dorothea. "Can We Block the Pipeline Out?" *Library Journal* 139, no. 6 (April 2014): 16.

San Jose State University School of Library & Information Science. "About the Circle of Learning." Accessed June 24, 2014. http://slisweb.sjsu.edu/research/center-information-research-and-innovation-ciri/projects/featured-projects/circle-learnin-0.

Shakelford, William. "The New Face of Bias in the Workplace – 2011, Part 1 – The Subtlety of Bias," Workforce Diversity Network, http://www.workforcediversitynetwork.com/res_articles_newfaceofbias_Shackelford.aspx.

Steele, Joe. "Sharing the 'Unwritten Rules' Impacts Retention." *Cultural Diversity at Work* 9, no. 6 (July 1997): 6; quoted by Musser, Linda. "Effective Retention Strategies for Diverse Employees." In *Diversity Now: People, Collections, and Services in Academic Libraries*, edited by Teresa Y. Neely and Kuang-Hwei (Janet) Lee-Smeltzer, 63-72. New York: Haworth Press, 2002.

Sullivan, John. "A Low Turnover Rate Could Mean That You Have Ugly Employees." ERE.NET. Last modified August 8, 2011. http://www.ere.net/2011/08/08/a-low-turnover-rate-could-mean-that-you-have-ugly-employees/.

Tewell, Eamon C. "Employment Opportunities for New Academic Librarians: Assessing the Availability of Entry Level Jobs." *portal: Libraries and the Academy* 12, no. 4 (2012): 407-423.

Thomas Jr., R. Roosevelt. "The Daily Experience of Genuine Workplace Diversity." *Harvard Business Review* 68, no. 2 (1990): 115.

United States Census Bureau. "U.S. Census Bureau Projections Show a Slower Growing, Older, More Diverse Nation a Half Century from Now." Last modified December 12, 2012. https://www.census.gov/newsroom/releases/archives/population/cb12-243.html.

United States Department of Labor, Bureau of Labor Statistics. *Occupational Outlook Handbook, 2014.* http://www.bls.gov/ooh/education-training-and-library/librarians.htm.

Wallace, Danny P., ed. *Library and Information Science Educational Statistical Report 2012.* Association for Library and Information Science.

Winston, Mark. "Diversity and the Lack of Progress." *New Library World* 109, no.3/4 (2008): 130-149. doi:10.1108/03074800810857595.

Winston, Mark D. "The Role of Recruitment in Achieving Goals Related to Diversity." *College & Research Libraries* 59, no. 3 (1998): 240-247.

Winston, Mark D. "Recruitment Theory: Identification of Those Who are Likely to be Successful as Leaders." *Journal of Library Administration* 32, no. 3-4 (2001): 19-34.

Zhang, Xiaoyin. "Library Minority Managers: Ways to Survive and Succeed." *Journal of Educational Media & Library Sciences* 39, no. 3 (2002): 227-234.

SECTION TWO:

HOW DIVERSITY BENEFITS

THE PROFESSION

Chapter 6

CRITICAL RACE THEORY AND THE RECRUITMENT, RETENTION AND PROMOTION OF A LIBRARIAN OF COLOR: A COUNTERSTORY

Shaundra Walker

Introduction

Despite the proliferation of residency programs, institutes, and scholarships designed to increase the numbers of African American and other academic librarians of color, academic librarianship, in contrast to the American population, continues to lacks racial diversity. According to the American Library Association's most recent *Diversity Counts* report, credentialed academic librarians are 86.1% white. African Americans make up 12.6% of the American population, but only account for 5.4% of credentialed academic librarians.[1]

Origins of Current Diversity Efforts

The current fight for diversity in the library profession has its roots in the American Civil Rights Movement. In the late 1960s and early 1970s, despite the gains of the Civil Rights movement, and much like

---

1. Denise M. Davis and Tracie D. Hall, *Diversity Counts*, ([Arlington, VA]: American Library Association, 2007).

many members of their race as a whole, African American librarians were still experiencing racism in recruitment, retention, and promotion within the profession.[2]. Frustrated with this embedded, institutionalized racism, a group of African American librarians, led by E.J. Josey, banded together in 1970 to form the Black Caucus of the American Library Association (BCALA), the first of the ethnic library associations. Several other organizations for other librarians of color, including REFORMA, the Asian American Library Caucus, and the American Indian Library Association, were founded shortly thereafter.[3] Over the years, these organizations have played a central role in holding the library profession accountable not only for equity issues, but also for responding to a variety of social justice issues, such as access, in communities where African American librarians have been employed.[4]

Critical Race Theory (CRT)

Because the calls for diversifying the library profession grew out of the frustrations of the American Civil Rights Movement, Critical Race Theory (CRT), a theoretical framework that challenges many of the assumptions of this movement, provides an appropriate lens through which these efforts might be analyzed. CRT is distinguished from other critical theories because it uses race as central point of analysis in examining the intersection of issues related to law and power. The theory emerged in the 1970's from another critical theory, critical legal studies, which challenged the neutrality and objectivity of the law. In developing the framework, several scholars, most notably Derrick Bell, Kimberle Crenshaw, and Alan Freeman, expanded on critical legal studies, arguing

---

2. E.J. Josey, "Introduction," in *The Black Librarian in America*, ed. E.J. Josey (Metuchen, NJ: Scarecrow Press, 1970), vii.

3. Tami Echavarria and Andrew B. Wetheimer, "Surveying the Role of Ethnic-American Library Associations," *Library Trends* 46, no. 3 (1997): 374.

4. Maurice B. Wheeler, "Averting a Crisis: Developing African American Librarians as Leaders," in *The Handbook of Black Librarianship*, eds. E.J. Josey and Marva DeLoach (Lanham, MD: Scarecrow Press, 2000), 176.

that both politics and "social situations" influence jurisprudence in the United States. Since the 1970s, CRT's influence has expanded to other disciplines, including education, political science, and ethnic studies.[5]

Five major tenets form the basis of CRT that provide boundaries for the framework are: 1) the embedded and persistent nature of racism 2) a critique of liberalism, notions of color-blindness, meritocracy, neutrality, and objectivity 3) the value of the experiential knowledge of people of color 4) interest convergence, or the belief that the needs of the minority group are only accommodated when their interest intersect with those of the majority group, and 5) the breakdown of systemic racism. This essay will utilize several of these tenets to explore the problem.

Critical Theory, CRT, and LIS

A review of the literature suggests that critical theory is no stranger to library and information science, as different strains of the body of theory have been used to explore a variety of issues within the field, such as technology and information literacy, among other areas. However, it appears that CRT as a specific critical theory is lesser known and underutilized. For example, a recent study to investigate librarians' familiarity with critical theory and how it informs their professional practices found that while most librarians were familiar with critical theory in general, few were familiar with CRT and its associated theorists.[6]

Within the LIS literature, CRT as a specific critical theory has been used to examine areas such as representations in children's and young adult literature, archives and cataloging. However, the use of the theory to explore the profession's approach and success in diversifying its ranks is limited; only a few such works dealing with these issues within

---

5. Floyd D. Beachum, "Critical Race Theory and Educational Leadership," in *The Handbook of Educational Theories*, eds. Beverly J. Irby, Genevieve Brown, Rafael Lara-Alecio, and Shirley Jackson (Charlotte, NC: Information Age Publishing, 2013), 923.

6. Robert Schroeder and Christopher V. Hollister, "Librarians' Views of Critical Theories and Critical Practices," *Behavioral and Social Sciences Librarian* 33, no. 2 (2014): 16.

academic libraries, such as recent work by Demasco and Hodges[7] and Griffin,[8] appear in the literature. Much more popular in the LIS literature on this important topic are personal narratives,[9] descriptive narratives of diversity programs and their components,[10] and summaries of post-training evaluations. Critical approaches to examining diversity efforts, which have the potential to add value to the current narrative, are sorely lacking.

In the years since the founding of the ethnic caucuses, the profession has taken baby-steps toward addressing the lack of ethnic diversity among its ranks. Robert Wedgeworth, an African American, became ALA's first and only African American executive director in 1972. E.J. Josey was elected the first African American president of the American Library Association in 1984. Perhaps most notably, ALA established the Spectrum Scholarship Program in 1997. Other library organization and individual academic libraries have also developed diversity programs and residencies of their own. Yet despite these efforts, on the issue of racial diversity, it appears that only incremental improvements have been seen, resulting in a profession that remains overwhelmingly white. Librarians of color remain underrepresented in leadership positions; within the American Library Association, there have only been

---

7. Ione T. Damasco and Dracine Hodges, "Tenure and Promotion Experiences of Academic Librarians of Color," *College and Research Libraries* 73, no.3 (2012): 279-301.

8. Karin L. Griffin, "Pursuing Tenure and Promotion in the Academy: A Librarian's Cautionary Tale," *Negro Educational Review* 64, no. 1-4 (2013): 77-96.

9. For personal narratives of the Minnesota Early Career Institute and the Spectrum Scholarship Program, respectively, see Mark A. Puente, "Leadership Training Programs and Institutes: Models for Learning to Lead," pp. 121-138; and Tamika M. Barnes and Iyanna Sims, "Tilling Fresh Ground: Cultivating Minority Librarians for Library Leadership through Programs and Initiatives," pp. 139-158, both in *Staff Development Strategies that Work! Stories and Strategies from New Librarians,* eds. Georgie L. Donovan and Miguel A. Figueroa (New York: Neal-Schuman Publishers, 2009).

10. For background information and descriptions of the Association of Research Libraries' various diversity programs, see Barbara I. Dewey, "The Imperative for Diversity: ARL's Progress and Role." *portal: Libraries and the Academy* 9, no. 3 (2009): 355-361.

five African American presidents in the organizations 136 year history. Clearly, there appears to be a contradiction "between what people in the library profession say and what they do."[11] In addition to the persistent lack of librarians of color in the profession and in library leadership roles, African American and other librarians of color continue to report discriminatory practices that impede their retention and promotion.

Recruitment

Neely and Peterson state: "academic librarianship recruitment history cannot be divorced from the history of education and federal education policy in the United States."[12] With this in mind, CRT requires a consideration of the impact of legislation and federal policy on the recruitment, retention, and advancement of librarians of color. Although *de jure* segregation is no longer the law of the land, an understanding of years of legally segregated and unequal educational systems adds perspective to the current discussion. Successful recruitment into library education programs, the gateway to increased numbers of African American and other librarians of color in academic librarianship, has always required navigation through the American secondary and higher education systems, both of which remain racially constructed. Because an undergraduate degree is a requirement for admission to LIS master's programs, historical as well as current federal legislation and policy have the potential to impact the pool of African American undergraduates who are prepared to enter library education programs and eventually qualify for employment in academic libraries.

The low numbers of African American and other academic librarians of color is not a new phenomenon. For this reason, CRT is an appropriate framework, because it "extends beyond disciplinary boundaries

---

11. Wheeler, "Averting a Crisis," 170.

12. Teresa Neely and Lorna Peterson, *Achieving Racial and Ethnic Diversity among Academic and Research Librarians: The Recruitment, Retention, and Advancement of Librarians of Color* (Chicago: Association of College and Research Libraries, 2007), p. 8.

to analyze race and racism within both historical and contemporary contexts."[13] Historically, the underrepresentation of African American librarians has been attributed to various factors, most of which are related to race and racism. One early explanation was offered in 1935 by Florence Rising Curtis, the first and only leader of the segregated library school at Hampton Institute (now Hampton University). Curtis stated that "the economic and educational conditions of the institutions which might command their services" was a factor in the lack of African American library school students, a thinly veiled reference to the underdevelopment of historically black colleges and universities and segregated public libraries.[14] Similarly, when questioned on the performance of African American library school students in 1939, one Northern library school explained its lack of African American students this way:

> While we have every sympathy for the Negro woman student of course no prejudice, we discourage them for trying to enter the ____ School for Library Science or indeed any department of the University, because there is literally no satisfactory place for them to live in ____. We have had, therefore, no Negro graduates since 1936.[15]

Others have been more forthright, suggesting that African Americans' slow entry into the profession was affected by their inability to attend southern colleges and universities, relegation to inferior public 1890 land grant colleges and inadequate preparation for higher education in segregated elementary and high schools[16]

---

13. Tara J. Yosso, Laurence Parker, Daniel G. Solorzano, and Marvin Lynn, "From Jim Crow to Affirmative Action and Back Again: A Critical Race Discussion of Racialized Rationales and Access to Higher Education," *Review of Research in Higher Education* 28 (2004): 4.

14. Florence Rising Curtis, "Librarianship as a Field for Negroes," *Journal of Negro Education* 4, no. 1 (1935): 94.

15. Tommie Dora Barker, Evalene Jackson, and the American Library Association Board of Education for Librarianship, "Memorandum on the Need in the South for a Library School or Schools for Negroes" (Chicago: American Library Association, 1939), 41.

16. Rosemary Ruhig Dumont, "The Educating of Black Librarians: An Historical Perspective," Journal of Education for Library and Information Science 26, no. 4 (1986): 233.

African American Education, Law, and Legislation

The recruitment of African American librarians has been strongly influenced by the intersection of race, law, and federal policy and must be viewed within this larger context. Congressional acts, such as the Morrill Land Grant Acts of 1862 and 1890, in addition to being credited with establishing public universities throughout the United States, are also responsible for establishing a dual, two-tiered, and racially strati- fied system of public higher education which persists into the present. Many public historically black colleges and universities (HBCU) were not established in the interest of providing much-needed education to this population, but to secure federal funding for white-land grants, to relegate African American education to vocational training, and to prevent them from attending White land grant institutions.[17] As late as 1917, only one of the 16 black land grants in existence at the time offered college courses. Between Reconstruction and the Great Depression, the bulk of African American higher education was provided through a network of private, African American liberal arts colleges.[18] The Higher Education Act states that the federal government discriminated against HBCUs in the allocation of land, and in the distribution of financial resources, such as grants and contracts, and other federal resources.[19] Recent research from the Association of Public Land Grant Institutions reveals that the underfunding of these institutions is a contemporary issue, finding that from 2010-2012, 68% of HBCU land grant institu- tions did not receive their state matching funds, totaling a loss of nearly $57 million in funding.[20] The implications of federal legislation/policy

17. Julian B. Roebuck and Komanduri S. Murty, *Historically Black Colleges and Universities: Their Place in American Higher Education* (Westport, CT: Praeger, 1993), 27.

18. James D. Anderson, *The Education of Blacks in the South, 1860-1935* (Chapel Hill, NC: University of North Carolina Press, 1988), 235.

19. Higher Education Act of 1965, 20 U.S.C. 1060 § 321 (2013).

20. John Michael Lee, Jr., and Samaad Wes Keys, *Land-Grant but Unequal: State One-to-One Match Funding for 1890 Land-Grant Universities* (Washington, DC: Association of Public and Land-Grant Universities, 2013).

on HBCUs and the current issue of recruitment to the academic library profession is quite relevant when one considers that despite the fact they no longer monopolize African American education, HBCUs still contribute disproportionately the number of African Americans who earn undergraduate degrees. Whether enrolled at predominately white institutions or HBCUs, African American undergraduates' completion rates are influenced by other federal policy initiatives, such as changes in the PLUS Loan and Pell Grant programs. When policy changes negatively impact recruitment, retention, and progression at the under-graduate level, fewer African American and other students of color will be available for recruitment into library education programs and ultimately into work in academic libraries.

Library Education for African Americans and Interest Convergence

Library education has also been racially constructed. African American library education was first offered, not within the halls of the academy, but at the Louisville Free Public Library's Western Colored Branch, where Thomas Fountain Blue, a graduate of Hampton Institute, began training library workers for service in segregated Southern libraries.[21] Prior to 1926 when a segregated library school at Hampton Institute, a private HBCU, was established, fewer than 70 African Americans had obtained professional library training.[22] Historically, two private historically Black colleges/universities, Hampton Institute and Atlanta University (now Clark-Atlanta University), with the support of several private foundations, concerned individuals, and the American Library Association, bore the brunt of preparing African Americans for work in academic libraries. History reveals that library education for African Americans was only accommodated when its provision converged with

---

21. Lillian Taylor Wright, "Thomas Fountain Blue, Pioneer Librarian, 1866-1935" (master's thesis, Atlanta University, 1955), 34-35. http://digitalcommons.auctr.edu/dissertations/369.

22. Curtis, "Librarianship as a Field", 95.

the interests of its benefactors, which varied from expanding public library services in the South, to supporting the accreditation and maintenance of segregated secondary and higher education. For these reasons, education for librarianship for African Americans has been perilous, vulnerable, and uneven. Once the benefactors ceased support or interests shifted, library education for African American librarians became uncertain. When Florence Rising Curtis announced her retirement from Hampton, one of the primary funders of the library program gradually withdrew its financial support. Lack of this support and Hampton Institute's inability to operate the library school independently ultimately forced it to close in May 1939.[23] For two years, there was no formal library education for African Americans in the South, other than a librarian-teacher training program that operated on the campus of four HBCUs.[24] The library education program at Atlanta University, which opened in 1941 and was perhaps the most significant supplier of African American librarians, faced a fate similar to Hampton. When the Georgia Board of Regents announced that it would open a publicly-supported library education program at Valdosta State University, a predominately white institution (PWI), the school's administrators became concerned that a state grant partially funding the program would cease.[25] Much like the program at Hampton Institute, this real or perceived dependence on external funding is considered a primary reason for the closure of the CAU program in 2005.[26] The impact of the closure of the Clark

---

23. Arthur Clinton Gunn, "Early Training for Black Librarians in the U.S.: A History of the Hampton Institute Library School and the Establishment of the Atlanta University School of Library Service" (dissertation, University of Pittsburgh, 1986), 87.

24. Allison Sutton, "Bridging the Gap in Early Library Education History for African-Americans: The Negro Teacher-Librarian Training Program, (1936-1939)," *Journal of Negro Education* 74, no. 2 (2005): 138.

25. Paul Donsky, "Final Try to Save Library Program Too Late: Supporters Try, but Clark Atlanta Officials Say Decision Won't be Revisited," *Atlanta Journal-Constitution*, October 15, 2004.

26. Risa L. Mulligan, "The Closing of the Clark Atlanta University School of Library & Information Studies" (master's thesis, University of North Carolina at Chapel Hill, 2007), 15. https://cdr.lib.unc.edu/ indexablecontent/ uuid:800b5b93-3710-4c5e-9a19-4a6fd54f9f1e

Atlanta University library school remains unexplored, but considering its historical contribution, the fact that it no longer operates has certainly had an effect on the profession's diversity efforts.

Federal Policy and Support for African American Library Education

In addition to legislative influence, the recruitment of African American and other librarians of color has also been shaped by federal policy. In the 1970s, the Title-IIB program made a significant contribution to the education of African American librarians through the provision of fellowships for library school attendance and funding to support minority outreach programs at various library schools. DeLoach states that "only when the federal government mandated that Title II-B funds be utilized to equalize opportunities for minorities did library schools show a commitment to recruitment of minorities."[27] Between 1970 and 1989, that support dwindled from \$2,986,000 to just \$277,600. The numbers of African American library degree recipients followed a similar trajectory, declining significantly.[28]

Federal investment in library education for future librarians of color has also come through the Institute of Museum and Library Services (IMLS), which was established in 1996. IMLS was formed through a merger of the Institute of Museum Services and the Library Programs Office of the Department of Education.[29] Its signature recruitment

---

27. Marva DeLoach, "The Higher Education Act of 1965, Title II-B : the fellowships/ traineeships for training in library and information science program : its impact on minority recruitment in library and information science education" (dissertation, University of Pittsburgh, 1980), 5.

28. Mary F. Lenox, "Reflections of a Dean" in *The Black Librarian in America Revisited*, ed. E.J. Josey (Meutchen, NJ, Scarecrow Press, 1994), 23.

29. Linda Smith, "From Foundation to Federal Funding: The Impact of Grants on Education for Library and Information Science," in *Influence of Funding on Advances in Librarianship*, eds. Danuta A. Nitecki and Eileen G. Abels (Bingley, UK: Emerald Group Publishers, 2008), 153.

program is the Laura Bush 21st Century Grant Program, which provides financial support to projects that support the education of practicing librarians, LIS faculty and library leaders; the program also supports LIS research.[30] An analysis of the current and projected library workforce and the impact of federal funding concluded that while IMLS programs such as the Laura Bush 21st Century Grant Program had exceeded their projections for recruiting "diverse" and "non-traditional" students, the reliability of statistics on which this determination was based was unknown, because of inconsistencies in the way that diversity data was reported. Further complicating matters was the fact that the program used a very broad definition of diversity, which could include self-determined demographic characteristics, such as race and ethnicity, but could also include other aspects of diversity, such as underserved communities and special needs patrons, among others.[31]

Lorna Peterson, Associate Professor Library and Information Science at the State University at Buffalo, warns about the dangers of such broad definitions:

> If policy language makes no distinction among differences, the legacy of segregation, discrimination, and oppression can be denied. If "quirkiness" (a term heard in workshops), knitting skills, and being African American are all measures of diversity, social injustice becomes an individual, not institutional, matter. Institutions can more easily maintain the status quo, because the well-intended multiculturalists have diluted racism into a happy-faced discussion of difference.[32]

---

30. Institute of Museum and Library Services, "Laura Bush 21st Century Librarian Program," accessed June 23, 2014, http://www.imls.gov/applicants/detail.aspx?GrantId=9.

31. Carlos A Manjarrez, Joyce Ray, and Karmen Bisher, "A Demographic Overview of the Current and Projected Library Workforce and the Impact of Federal Funding," *Library Trends* 59 no. 1-2 (2010): 22.

32. Lorna Peterson, "Multiculturalism: Affirmative or Negative Action?" *Library Journal* 120, no. 12 (1995): 31.

Retention

In addition to the persistent lack of minorities in the profession, among those African American and other librarians of color who ultimately gain employment in academic libraries, reports of discriminatory practices abound. Current scholarship indicates that despite the passage of time and the existence of various diversity initiatives, these experiences and practices continue. One participant in a recent study of the tenure and promotion experiences of librarians of color expressed her frustration as follows:

> Mentoring programs and institutes targeted at librarians of color are not the answer. I believe they are making the situation in academic libraries worse. These programs imply that the problem is with the librarians of color, that librarians of color need to be taught to assimilate. The real problem is institutionalized racism in academic libraries. Instead of sending me to a program/institute, administrators...need to be sent to programs to raise their awareness about how their attitudes and behaviors are forms of discrimination and create barriers for librarians of color who are trying to obtain tenure and/or promotion.[33]

The promotion and tenure process is one area of academic librarianship where inequity can become institutionalized. The fact that this process is governed by institutional policy implies that it is color-blind, based on merit, and race-neutral; however the experiences of librarians of color suggest otherwise. The advancement of diversity initiatives and programs in academic libraries appears to be a double edged sword in some cases, as new librarians of color report feeling more likely than their White counterparts to be asked to serve on diversity committees and as liaisons to diversity-related campus groups.[34] New librarians of color also report being asked to serve on search committees for

---

33. Demasco and Hodges, "Tenure and Promotion Experiences," 295.

34. Kawanna Bright, Pambanisha King, and Deborah Lilton, "When Diversity is Too Much: New Librarians of Color and Expectations for Involvement in Library Diversity Initiatives" (paper presented at the National Diversity in Libraries Conference, Louisville, KY, October 3, 2008).

diversity-related positions and being asked to work on "special projects that related to diverse, ethnic, racial or cultural issues" is also reported.[35] This work, however valuable, has the potential to result in a "hidden workload," an unseen consequence of being a person of color. Such appointments raise particular concern when they impact the abilities of these librarians to focus on other areas of their tenure portfolios, such as research, which in some environments may have more value than committee work and service. Episodes such as these also have implications for annual performance evaluations in instances where performance expectations were not made clear, such as reported in the Damasco and Hodges study, or when librarians of color were asked to perform work for which they were assigned based on race instead of qualifications. One librarian reported being asked to serve as the library's Hispanic collection coordinator, although he/she had no subject background, interest, or language proficiency in that area.[36] When librarians of color are forced to work under such conditions, their ability to not only achieve tenure but to remain in the institution is likely compromised.

Promotion

One criticism of current library diversity efforts is their focus on recruiting new librarians instead of developing leaders. Indeed, positioning librarians of color in leadership roles has the potential to address retention issues, such as mentoring, valuing research that deals with diversity issues, and fairly applying promotion and tenure policies. Maurice Wheeler offers the following summary of the leadership diversity issue:

> Nothing short of a rebellion will cause librarians, associations, and individuals to step forward and act upon the affirmation action and diversity rhetoric notion that the cream always rises to the top. Often adjustments have to be made in systems and cultures that encourage and support growth and development. Libraries and associations must acknowledge

35. Ibid.
36. Ibid.

that they, too, have a responsibility in eradicating the underrepresentation of people of color in leadership roles.[37]

Experiential Knowledge of People of Color as Translated through Counterstories

With few exceptions, much of the literature on diversity and recruitment programs consists of program descriptions and anecdotal, mostly positive reflections from program participants. Aside from a small body of work that uses a critical lens, these reflections form a master narrative that virtually ignores the experiences of people of color who have not seen positive outcomes or reaped the benefits of the diversity initiatives. Monticenos warns of the dangers of such a narrative:

> The use of a master narrative to represent a group is bound to provide a very narrow depiction of what it means to be Mexican-American, African-American, White, and so on....A master narrative essentializes and wipes out the complexities and richness of a group's cultural life...[38]

With this in mind, the use of a CRT framework, with its focus on counterstories and experiential knowledge of people of color, provides an opportunity to add a new and much-needed perspective to the discourse. According to Solorzano and Yosso:

> [a] counter-story...is a method of telling the stories of those people who experiences are not often told (i.e., those on the margins of society). The counter-story is also a tool for exposing, analyzing, and challenging the majoritarian stories of racial privilege. Counter-stories can shatter complacency, challenge the dominant discourse on race and further the struggle for racial reform.[39]

---

37. Wheeler, "Averting a Crisis," 171.

38. Carmen Monticenos. "Culture as an Ongoing Dialogue: Implications for Multicultural Teacher Education," in *Multicultural Education, Critical Pedagogy, and the Politics of Difference* (Albany: State University of New York Press, 1995), 293.

39. Daniel G. Solorzano and Tara J. Yosso, "Critical Race Methodology: Counter-Storytelling as an Analytical Framework for Education Research," *Qualitative Inquiry* 8, no. 1 (2002): 32.

Using CRT as a framework, the following counterstory will provide an alternative perspective on the recruitment, retention, and promotion of librarians of color.

My Family and Educational Background

I was born in the decade following the Civil Rights movement. Though I never personally experienced the sting of legalized segregation, the days of Jim Crow's reign were not so much of distant memory for my parents, grandparents, and other elders in my community. As a child, my parents attempted to shelter me from the reality of racism and I wholeheartedly believed that such beliefs were relics of a bygone era. In my mind, racism wore a hood and sheet, rode around on a horse, and put burning crosses in black people's yards. Or, sometimes it wielded a fire hose and ferocious dogs. But I never saw those things in my community and so it was easy to for me to believe that racism did not exist.

My baby-boomer parents were approaching first grade the year *Brown v. Board of Education* (1954) was decided, but to my surprise, they never attended desegregated or integrated schools. Schools in our hometown did not desegregate until 1970, well after my mother had graduated from college and my father had been honorably discharged from the armed forces; the schools never truly integrated. Like my parents and grandparents before me, I attended segregated schools at the secondary level. Although this segregation was not legally enforced, the separation was almost as distinct as during the days of segregation. The numbers of non-African American children gradually decreased, beginning in elementary school, to the point that by the time I entered high school, there were only a handful of White students, mostly those who were unable to afford tuition at one of the private academies in town. A flurry of White private schools opened when the desegregation order was enforced, so there were many options available. If *Brown v. Board of Education* (1954) had as its goal to integrate the schools, it failed miserably, at least in my town. In addition to attending schools that mirrored the racial demographics of pre-Civil Rights movement era, I and other African American children in my hometown, with few exceptions, attended school in the same segregation-era buildings where our parents were educated. My middle school, which was my mother's high school and which was constructed in 1959, still stands today, ill-equipped to meet the needs of 21st century learning.

My post-secondary education was also largely segregated. Even though there were numerous public universities within my home state where I would qualify for state merit-based financial aid, my family felt it was in my best interest to attend a private HBCU. I had always attended schools where most of the students and faculty members looked like me and I sought a similar experience at the collegiate level. Following graduation, I toyed with the idea of attending law school, but happened upon a job advertisement for an academic librarian position and changed my mind. I soon learned that professional library positions required a Masters of Library and Information Science degree. Upon doing some research, I learned that the closest option for this degree was at Clark-Atlanta University, just across the street from my undergraduate alma mater. I also discovered several of the library diversity initiatives that arose during this time, such as the Spectrum Scholarship Initiative and the various academic library residency programs. I was confident that I had found the right profession and believed strongly that the profession was eager to bring in minorities, buying into what CRT refers to as the myth of meritocracy, colorblindness, neutrality, and objectivity.

To complement my library school education, I decided to pursue employment within the library field while attending graduate school. I had no prior experience in the library field and I noticed that even entry level professional positions often preferred some library experience. My initial attempts to find library employment were challenging. One of my first applications was at a large urban university. I shall never forget the interview; instead of telling me about the benefits of the position or asking position-specific questions, the interviewer presented me with a list of negative attributes about the job to gauge my interest. I was peppered with questions/statements, such as "Can you handle dust? It's very dusty around here." "Are you allergic to mold? We sometimes have problems with mold in the library." "Can you function in the cold? It gets very cold in our library." Puzzled, I answered affirmatively to the litany of questions/statements that I received. I left the interview and waited on a phone call that never came. After several additional attempts to find employment, I finally received a call back from a local public library system, where I had applied for a para-professional position. I wanted to gain experience in an academic library, but after so many letdowns, I accepted the position.

It was in this position that I began to notice some of the racial division within the library profession, an experience that directly contradicted my expectations. I noticed that most White librarians that I encountered had attended library school either at Emory or out of state; most African American librarians had attended Clark-Atlanta's program. I observed a similar division when I attended the statewide library association conference where there were usually very few African American librarians in attendance. Only later would I learn about how library education had been segregated and how E.J. Josey had forcibly integrated the Georgia Library Association.

My Experience Obtaining an Internship

I progressed through the coursework at Clark-Atlanta very smoothly. I ended up leaving the first para-professional library position that I obtained for a competitive paid summer internship program within an archive. My graduate program required an unpaid internship as a requirement to graduate. Through that experience, I learned a little more about the segregated history of library education, not only in Georgia, but throughout the southeast. In my experience, one of the residual effects of this dual, segregated system was a lack of interaction among librarians in the state. When it came time to find a site for my unpaid internship, my coordinator was at a loss for a site to place me. I needed an internship in my hometown, but when I discussed this with my internship coordinator, she told me that she did not know anyone professionally at any of the three colleges in my area. However, she did know the library director at Fort Valley State University, a public, land-grant HBCU in the area. The library director there had attended Atlanta University and was a colleague of hers, so arrangements were made for me to complete my internship there. Through this experience, I learned a valuable lesson about the value of "social capital" and the implications when one does not possess it. The term is used to describe "social relations that have productive benefits."[40] Social capital is very valuable, because it allows one to network and to gain access to resources that might not otherwise be available. These relationships are often built around common experiences, such as being alumni of the same institution, membership in social and civic organizations, or possessing common professional or personal associates. For academic librarians of color, social capital is often illusive.

After completing my internship at Fort Valley, which I believed would qualify me for an entry-level professional position in an academic library, I found the process of securing my first post-MLS position to be as or more challenging as my attempts to secure paraprofessional employment. My first application for a professional library position resulted in a telephone interview, which went very well, but did not result in the promised in-person interview. My second application for a professional position resulted in a face-to-face interview and a second, more informal interview, where I met with the Vice-President of Academic Affairs. In a very awkward exchange, he questioned me on the relevance of various databases to research needs. A short while later, I was offered the position, with conditions. Although the position was not tenure track, I told that my appointment would be a "visiting" position. I would receive a one-year contract, during which time I would be closely evaluated. If the library director found my performance to be satisfactory, I would then receive another one-year contract; after some time, if my evaluations were good enough, I might qualify for a three or five-year contract. Even though I was largely ignorant about the academic appointment

---

40. *Salem Press Encyclopedia*, s.v. "Social Capital," accessed October 27, 2014, http://www.ebscohost.com.

system, I knew enough to be offended. I met the qualifications for the position, both in terms of education and experience. I had even secured the endorsement of one of the few African American faculty members at the college, who knew the library director personally. Yet, the combination of my education, work experience, and enthusiasm was not enough to get me over this initial hurdle. The college could not legally come out and state that they did not want to hire me because I was African American, so the visiting professor assignment was proffered as a subtle way to convey the intended insult. Clearly, there was no need to put me on visiting status, because the only type of contract that I could earn, even if I had regular faculty status, was one-year contract.

During my employment at that library, I experienced what are called racial micro-aggressions, "brief and commonplace daily verbal, behavioral, or environmental indignities, whether intentional or unintentional, that communicate hostile, derogatory, or negative racial slights and insults toward people of color."[41] The final straw came when the library director, quite casually and matter-of-factly, informed me that the person they made the initial offer to turned them down, so that's how they had gotten me. Needless to say, I decided to pursue employment elsewhere.

My next library job was at a larger, better-funded public university. Unlike my first professional library position, my second professional position was a tenure-track position. By that time, I was familiar with tenure and knew that it was something that "teaching faculty" at my former employer enjoyed, but I knew little about the power, protection, and security that it provided. I liked my new job because the library was larger and more dynamic; even though I was the only librarian of color, there were more librarians and the environment was a bit more collegial. Still, I felt socially and culturally isolated. Just like at my first professional job, I made "black history" at my second professional job, too; as far as I was able to tell, I was the first professional librarian of color in the

---

41. Derald Wing Sue, Christina M. Capodilupo, Gina C. Torino, Jennifer M. Bucceri, Aisha Holder, Kevin L. Nadal, and Marta Esquilin. "Racial Micro-aggressions in Everyday Life: Implications for Clinical Practice," *American Psychologist* 62, no. 4 (2007): 273.

institution's history. Very often, when I went to non-library meetings, I was the only person of color in the room, "a fly in the buttermilk."[42] There was a network of African American faculty of color on campus, but even there, I felt awkward, because my work experiences and tenure and promotion expectations were very different.

The racial micro-aggressions continued at my second professional library job. Once, while attending a reception for a faculty member, I was approached by a White faculty member who assumed I was a domestic worker, and asked me where the coat check was. I informed her that I did not know where the coat check was located and that I was a faculty member, just like her. She stated, unapologetically, "Oh, I thought you worked here!" When I recounted my experience to another faculty member of color who was in attendance, she stated that the same faculty member had also approached her regarding the coat check. Another time, I encountered several White students at the reference desk, who refused to accept the information that I provided. They stated that they would return to the desk later, when the librarian was on duty or ask their professor for the information they needed. These experiences confirmed for me that even though I had received the necessary credentials, dressed the part, and assumed the position, my presence in the academy was still filtered through a colored lens.

In addition to my work in Predominantly White Institutions (PWIs), I have also worked at an HBCU, an experience that provided me with a framework to further explore and understand my prior work experiences. In the HBCU environment, I was able to leverage the social capital that I was sorely lacking when I worked in PWIs. Even though I was not well connected personally with colleagues across the campus, I was able to leverage other connections, such as my alumni network, participation in social and civic organizations, and even church affiliations. These

---

42. Mitzi Davis, Yvonne Dias-Bowie, Katherine Greenberg, Gary Klukken, Howard R. Pollio, Sandra P. Thomas, and Charles L. Thompson, "'A Fly in the Buttermilk': Descriptions of University Life by Successful Black Undergraduate Students at a Predominately White Southeastern University," *Journal of Higher Education* 75, no. 4 (2004): 420.

relationships allowed me access to critical information, resources, and other benefits. When I compared my experiences at the two types of institutions, I realized that the benefits that I enjoyed at the HBCU were probably already enjoyed by my White colleagues at other institutions. For the first time in my professional career, I was able to experience the equivalent of "white privilege" and it felt very comforting.

Quite often during my professional career, I have received comments from White colleagues that have not always felt complimentary. I have had individuals tell me that due to the fact that I am African American and female, I should have no problem advancing within the profession. These types of comments denigrate the well-rounded portfolio of education, experience, scholarship, and technical skill that I have developed during my career and suggest that my color and gender would give me a ticket wherever I wanted to go, no matter my accomplishments or ability. I have also been told on several occasions that I am very articulate and that I "speak well." My admirers seem not to understand that these statements have double meaning for persons of color and suggest that by speaking well, I exceed the low expectations for African Americans and am somehow different from other members of my race.

Despite these challenges, I remain committed to working within the library field. I enjoy helping people and I enjoy learning something new every day. However, I often wonder how many potential and actual librarians of color will become frustrated along the way. Achieving real diversity within our profession will require a coordinated effort to address inequitable practices that impede the recruitment, retention, and progression of librarians of color. Very often these behaviors have become so ingrained that they are difficult to identify and even harder to rectify.

Changing the demographics of the academic library workforce will require new approaches for assessing progress. Traditionally, we have focused nearly exclusively on quantitative measurements that evaluate progress over short periods of time. Tackling this problem necessitates the consideration of new approaches. CRT, with its focus on the experiential knowledge of people of color, interdisciplinary approaches, and the intersection of race, policy/law, and power, among other tenets, presents a lens through which many of our assumptions about the problem and how it might be solved could be further analyzed.

References

Barker, Tommie Dora, and Evalene Parsons Jackson. *Memorandum on the Need in the South for a Library School or Schools for Negroes.* Chicago: American Library Association, Board of Education for Librarianship, 1939.

Barnes, Tameka M., and Iyanna Sims. "Tilling Fresh Ground: Cultivating Minority Librarians for Library Leadership through Programs and Initiatives." In *Staff Development Strategies that Work! Stories and Strategies from New Librarians,* edited by Georgie L. Donovan and Miguel A. Figueroa, 139-157. New York: Neal-Schuman, 2009.

Beachum, Floyd D. "Critical Race Theory and Educational Leadership." In *The Handbook of Educational Theories,* edited by. Beverly J. Irby, Genevieve Brown, Rafael Lara-Alecio, and Shirley Jackson, 923-928. Charlotte, NC: Information Age Publishing, 2013

Bright, Kawanna, Pambanisha King, and Deborah Lilton. "When Diversity is Too Much: New Librarians of Color and Expectations for Involvement in Library Diversity Initiatives." Paper presented at the National Diversity in Libraries Conference, Louisville, KY, October 3, 2008.Top of Form

Curtis, Florence Rising. "Librarianship as a Field for Negroes." *Journal of Negro Education* 4, no. 1 (1935): 94-98.Bottom of Form

Damasco Ione T., and Dracine Hodges. "Tenure and Promotion Experiences of Academic Librarians of Color." *College and Research Libraries* 73, no. 3 (2012): 279-301.

Davis, Mitzi, Yvonne Dias-Bowie, Katherine Greenberg, Gary Klukken, Howard R. Pollio, Sandra P. Thomas, and Charles L. Thompson. "'A Fly in the Buttermilk': Descriptions of University Life by Successful Black Undergraduate Students at a Predominately White Southeastern University." *Journal of Higher Education* 75, no. 4 (2004): 420-445.

DeLoach, Marva LaVerne. "The Higher Education Act of 1965, Title II-B: The Fellowships/Traineeships for Training in Library and Information Science Program : Its Impact on Minority Recruitment in Library and Information Science Education." PhD diss., University of Pittsburgh, 1980.

Dewey, Barbara I. "The Imperative for Diversity: ARL's Progress and Role." *portal: Libraries and the Academy* 9, no. 3 (2009): 355-361.

Donsky, Paul. "Final Try to Save Library Program Too Late: Supporters Try, but Clark Atlanta Officials Say Decision Won't be Revisited." *Atlanta Journal-Constitution*, October 15, 2004.

Dumont, Rosemary Ruhig. "The Educating of Black Librarians: An Historical Perspective." *Journal of Education for Library and Information Science* 26, no. 4 (1986): 233-249.

Echavarria, Tami, and Andrew B. Wertheimer. "Surveying the Role of Ethnic-American Library Associations." *Library Trends* 46, no. 2 (1997): 373-91.

Griffin, Karin L. "Pursuing Tenure and Promotion in the Academy: A Librarian's Cautionary Tale." *Negro Educational Review* 64, no. 1-4 (2013): 77-96.

Gunn, Arthur Clinton. "Early Training for Black Librarians in the U.S.: A History of the Hampton Institute Library School and the Establishment of the Atlanta University School of Library Service." PhD diss., University of Pittsburgh, 1986.

Higher Education Act of 1965, 20 U.S.C. 1060 § 321 (2013).

ICF Incorporated. 2013. Laura Bush 21st Century Grant Program Evaluation. http://www.imls.gov/assets/1/AssetManager/LB21%20Evaluation%20Report.pdf

Institute of Museum and Library Services. "Laura Bush 21st Century Librarian Program." Accessed June 23, 2014, http://www.imls.gov/applicants/detail.aspx?GrantId=9.

Josey, E.J. "Introduction." In *The Black Librarian in America*, edited by E.J. Josey, vii-xvi. Metuchen, NJ: Scarecrow Press, 1970.

Kumasi, Kafi. "Roses in the Concrete: A Critical Race Perspective on Urban Youth and School Libraries," *Knowledge Quest* 40, no. 5 (2012): 32-37.

Lee, John Michael, Jr., and Samaad Wes Keys. *Land-Grant but Unequal: State One-to-One Match Funding for 1890 Land-Grant Universities*, Washington, DC: Association of Public and Land-Grant Universities, 2013.

Lenox, Mary F. "Reflections of a Dean." In *The Black Librarian in America Revisited*, edited by E.J. Josey, 19-29. Meutchen, NJ: Scarecrow Press, 1994.

Manjarrez Carlos A., Joyce Ray, and Karmen Bisher. "A Demographic Overview of the Current and Projected Library Workforce and the Impact of Federal Funding." *Library Trends* 59, no. 1-2 (2010): 6-29.

Monticenos, Carmen. "Culture as an Ongoing Dialogue: Implications for Multicultural Teacher Education." In *Multicultural Education, Critical Pedagogy, and the Politics of Difference*, edited by Christine E. Sleeter and Peter McLaren, 291-305. Albany: State University of New York Press, 1995.

Mulligan, Risa. L. "The Closing of the Clark Atlanta University School of Library & Information Studies" Master's thesis, University of North Carolina at Chapel Hill, 2007. https://cdr.lib.unc.edu/ indexablecontent/uuid:800b5b93-3710-4c5e-9a19-4a6fd54f9f1e

Neely, Teresa and Lorna Peterson. *Achieving Racial and Ethnic Diversity among Academic and Research Librarians: The Recruitment, Retention, and Advancement of Librarians of Color*. Chicago: Association of College and Research Libraries, 2007.

Peterson, Lorna. "Multiculturalism: Affirmative or Negative Action?" *Library Journal* 120, no. 12 (1995): 30-33.

Puente, Mark A. "Leadership Training Programs and Institutes: Models for Learning to Lead." In *Staff Development Strategies that Work! Stories and Strategies from New Librarians,* edited by Georgie L. Donovan and Miguel A. Figueroa, 121-138. New York: Neal-Schuman, 2009.

Roebuck, Julian B., and Komanduri S. Murty. *Historically Black Colleges and Universities: Their Place in American Higher Education.* Westport, CT: Praeger, 1993.

Schroeder Robert, and Christopher V. Hollister. "Librarians' Views on Critical Theories and Critical Practices." *Behavioral and Social Sciences Librarian* 33, no. 2 (2014): 91-119.

Smith, Linda. "From Foundation to Federal Funding: The Impact of Grants on Education for Library and Information Science." In *Influence of Funding on Advances in Librarianship,* edited by Danuta A. Nitecki and Eileen G. Abels, 141-165. Bingley, UK: Emerald Group, 2008.

Solorzano, Daniel G., and Tara J. Yosso. "A Critical Race Counterstory of Race, Racism, and Affirmative Action." *Equity & Excellence in Education* 35, no. 2 (2002): 155-68.

Sue, Derald Wing, Christina M. Capodilupo, Gina C. Torino, Jennifer M. Bucceri, Aisha Holder, Kevin L. Nadal, and Marta Esquilin. "Racial Microaggressions in Everyday Life: Implications for Clinical Practice." *American Psychologist* 62, no. 4 (2007): 271-286.

Sutton, Allison M. "Bridging the Gap in Early Library Education History for African Americans: The Negro Teacher-Librarian Training Program (1936-1939)." *Journal of Negro Education* 74, no. 2 (2005): 138-150.

Wright, Lillian Taylor. "Thomas Fountain Blue, Pioneer Librarian, 1866-1935." Master's thesis, Clark Atlanta University, 1955. http://digitalcommons.auctr.edu/dissertations/369.

Yosso, Tara J., Laurence Parker, Daniel G. Solorzano and Marvin Lynn. "From Jim Crow to Affirmative Action and Back Again: A Critical Race Discussion of Racialized Rationales and Access to Higher Education." *Review of Research in Education* 28 (2005): 1-26.

Chapter 7

SERVING WITH A SENSE OF PURPOSE: A BLACK WOMAN LIBRARIAN IN RURAL NEW MEXICO

Akilah Shukura Nosakhere

Introduction

In rural communities where there are few Black women in professional and leadership positions, gender and racial bias is problematic.
Gender bias and racial prejudice can block development on both the
personal and institutional levels. Such are the challenges I face in Carlsbad, New Mexico where I serve as the director of a small community
college library.

Carlsbad is a small town of 27, 653 residents with hopes of becoming
a city of 50,000 by 2035. It is located on the Pecos River and serves as
the county seat of Eddy County and is situated along the northern edge
of the Chihuahuan Desert.[1] The town's population is majority White at
77% mirroring the percentage of Whites in the United States.[2] Carlsbad
is a community of families with strong ties to the ranching, mining,
and oil and gas, and nuclear industries. Some White families trace their
legacy to the territorial period of great cattle drives and ranching prior

---

1. "Long Term Planning Committee," *City of Carlsbad, New Mexico*, accessed
December 21, 2014, http://www.cityofcarlsbadnm.com/longtermplan.cfm.

2. "United States: USA Quick Facts," *U.S. Census Bureau*, accessed December 14, 2014, http://quickfacts.census.gov/qfd/states/00000.html.

to the arrival of working class families from the coal mining regions of West Virginia, Ohio, and Kentucky.

The Hispanic or Latino population is a significant portion of Carlsbad and Eddy County in southeastern New Mexico, making up some 43% of Carlsbad and 48% of the county population, respectively. The U.S. Census reported that Hispanics own 16.2% of all businesses, and over 30% of Hispanic households in Carlsbad and Eddy County speak Spanish in the home.[3] A vital part of the region's workforce, Hispanics are employed in potash mining, oil and gas extraction, and nuclear industries in Eddy County. The local community college, New Mexico State University Carlsbad, is a Title V Hispanic Serving Institution (HSI) and certifies Hispanic students in nursing and other healthcare fields.

The percentage of Blacks in Carlsbad is less than 2% (fewer than 1,000 persons) according to the latest census data.[4] Black residents of Carlsbad belong to various social and economic classes, similar to all populations. Descendants of agricultural workers, who arrived in the area from Texas and the South during the 1930s and 1940s, are the backbone of the local African American community on the south end of the city. Carlsbad is also home to a small community of African nationals employed mainly in the medical and mining industries. There is also a high profile transient community of Black medical professionals from the United States and elsewhere who keep to themselves. This population is believed to be recent medical school graduates who serve poor rural communities for a short time in exchange for reduction or cancelation of medical school debt. Few members of this affluent group establish civic relationships or interact with the community college during their stay. Once their obligation is fulfilled they move on to establish their careers elsewhere.

Interaction between the African and African American communities in Carlsbad is service based. Unless there is an occupational or

3. "New Mexico: State and County Quick Facts," U.S. *Census Bureau*, accessed July 10, 2015, http://quickfacts.census.gov/qfd/states/35/35015.html.

4. "New Mexico: USA Quick Facts," U.S. *Census Bureau*, accessed December 14, 2014, http://www.census.gov/quickfacts/table/PST045214/00.

service relationship there is little communication between the two groups. African nationals have not attended African American cultural events organized for the general community by the local NAACP or the Martin Luther King Scholarship Foundation. Research indicates that African and African American transplants who fail or desire not to gain access to the local Black community often form their own support network along occupational or class lines.[5] The existence of separate support networks is the case among the African and African American communities of Carlsbad; cultural differences make for a complicated relationship between the two groups as well.

African and African American youth are noticeably absent from community college classrooms in Carlsbad. Through my participation in the Eddy County NAACP, I have learned that college-age children of many African American residents attend post-secondary institutions outside of the region. Like young people in other racial and cultural groups, Black youth leave the town upon graduation from high school to attend New Mexico State University (NMSU) – Las Cruces or other universities in New Mexico or Texas. In general, young people leave Carlsbad to build successful careers elsewhere then return to raise their children or to retire.

African and African Americans engage in civic activities in Carlsbad and Eddy County, but none are counted among the stakeholders of NMSU – Carlsbad. I met two West African students during my first year who were commuters from Hobbs, NM and have since graduated from the NMSU – Carlsbad nursing program. I have not have the opportunity to see or interact with more than seven Black students since 2010.

Racial separation was the norm in Carlsbad until the spring of 1951 when the local school system voted to accept the solitary Black high school senior, Jimmy Thomas, into the all-White Carlsbad High School 1951 graduating class.[6] The local school board decided that it was more

---

5. Carol Parker Terhune, "Coping in Isolation: The Experience of Black Women in White Communities," *Journal of Black Studies* 38, no. 4 (March 2008): 555.

6. Don Eskins, "CHS and Integration," *Carlsbad Our Town: Carlsbad Current Argus* (2011): 14.

economical to include the Black student than provide a separate ceremony as required at that time under the separate but equal law. By the fall, the Carlsbad school system had moved to include the small community of African American students into the city schools—three years before the 1954 Brown Supreme Court decision.[7] Carlsbad restaurants and motels gradually followed suit and accommodated African American tourists and local residents.[8]

Arriving from Atlanta where African Americans are the majority, my husband and I experienced a bit of culture shock to the point that we acknowledged every Black person we saw in Carlsbad while shopping or driving around the city. The two African American churches, Pilgrim's Rest and Mt. Olive Baptist, serve primary Black congregants and have strong historical roots to certain African American families in the community. They are maintained through extended family connections. The Eddy County NAACP has a membership of about 75 adult and youth members, with one active White member. An active committee of about ten faithfully organizes Black History Month and Juneteenth events that are open to the entire town. The local NAACP also participates in annual fundraising dinners of the Carlsbad Foundation and the Martin Luther King, Jr. Scholarship Foundation. Since my arrival in Carlsbad, I have served as the link between the NAACP and the NMSU – Carlsbad campus. During these past five years, the relationships between the two has grown; however, there is yet to be any formal representation from the NAACP or other Black organization serving on community-focused college committees or advisory councils.

Land of Enchantment

Black New Mexicans (African American, Caribbean, and African) make up less than 3% of the state's population.[9] However, The African

---

7. Ibid.

8. Ibid.

9. "New Mexico: USA Quick Facts," *U.S. Census Bureau,* accessed December 4, 2014, http://quickfacts.census.gov/qfd/states/35000.html.

presence in New Mexico is well documented, dating from the period of Spanish exploration to early statehood. Black soldiers, known as "buffalo soldiers," were stationed throughout southern and western New Mexico to protect western White settlements and to battle Native Americans, in order to expand the western border of the country.[10] Throughout New Mexico, Black laborers worked in agriculture, ranching, and on the railroads. Black migrants making their way West after the Civil War. Vado and Blackdom were towns established by Blacks in the late 19th century[11] The Black populations of these towns have since migrated to nearby cities of Las Cruces in southern New Mexico and Roswell in the southeastern region. Only Vado and Dora remain today, leaving a legacy of independence and self determination of early Black New Mexicans.[12]

I fell in love with New Mexico in 1998 while attending a North American Serials Interest Group (NASIG) conference in Albuquerque. During the early years of NASIG, attendees booked dorm rooms instead of hotel rooms. My room in Hokona Hall on the campus of the University of New Mexico had a Mayan image painted on the wall. I copied it on the back of a conference flyer, along with the accompanying Spanish phrase and tucked it in my book. That evening I skipped dinner, deciding to stay in the room to read and to listen to the radio. As the evening progressed, the music became intoxicating I put down the book and I danced all over that room! Weeks later, I finally looked up the translation of the Spanish phrase on my makeshift bookmark and learned that "vivir a bailar!" in English means "live to dance!" The following morning, a group of us were scheduled to hike in the Sandia Mountains. On the tram ride up to Sandia Peak, the sudden appearance of hang gliders launching from steep ledges was breath-taking. Perhaps my most enchanting experience was witnessing circus elephants being

---

10. Frank N. Schubert, *Black Valor: Buffalo Soldiers and the Medal of Honor, 1870 - 1898* (New York: Rowman & Littlefield, 2009), 41-42.

11. Bruce A. Glasrud, *African American History in New Mexico: Portraits from Five Hundred Years* (Albuquerque: University of New Mexico Press, 2013), 112, 116-19.

12. Ibid., 11.

led through the streets of Albuquerque, making their way from the railroad depot to the fairgrounds amidst cheers of excitement.

In 2003, I returned to New Mexico for professional development. This time I spent a week at Bishop's Lodge in Santa Fe as a participant in the fourth class of the Association of Research Libraries (ARL) Leadership and Career Development Program (LCDP).[13] While we spent most of our time in tightly scheduled sessions, we used our free time to explore the Lodge's extensive grounds and the city of Santa Fe, a short cab ride down the mountain. New Mexico soon became my favorite vacation destination. My husband and I traveled to the state to visit historical sites and the museums of Santa Fe and Albuquerque. So when I read the 2009 job announcement for a library director at NMSU – Carlsbad, I applied and began to think about making New Mexico my next home base. My husband and I visited northern New Mexico several times and we enjoyed the openness and loved the beautiful terrain. After a bit of research we learned that the southeastern region was not as developed as Albuquerque or Santa Fe, but we were still as interested in making the move to a rural and less hectic place. We understood that an offer meant moving far away from family, sacrificing easy access to the arts and fine vegetarian dining, and getting used to the ranching and cowboy culture of southeastern New Mexico. The offer came and I accepted without hesitation. Soon we were on our way to Carlsbad, New Mexico to pursue new opportunities for professional and personal growth.

Public art prospects are important for my husband Charles, who makes his living as a muralist. I encouraged him to join the Carlsbad Chamber of Commerce and was delighted when he was asked by the Chamber to address the weekly 'Friday Focus' breakfast meeting. We prepared a presentation highlighting his 35 years of public art in the cities of Los Angeles and Atlanta and were pleased with the warm welcome

---

13. "Past LCDP Fellows & Career Coaches," *Association of Research Libraries*, accessed November 22, 2014, http://www.arl.org/leadership-recruitment/diversity-recruitment/leadership-career-development-program/2531-past-fellows-a-career-coaches#.VKCWG14AKA.

extended by the community leaders. Charles even received several inquiries about providing artwork for local businesses. Off to a good start, we were hopeful about business prospects until I noticed that Charles was listed on the Chamber's website as a "handyman," even though he had been formally introduced as a professional public artist. His many years of full-time experience in the 'mural capital city' of Los Angeles, California was totally ignore . My husband, being the kind-hearted soul that he is, just shrugged his shoulders and smiled. Me? I was furious!

Fortunately, Charles encountered a group of kindred spirits and together they established the Carlsbad Mural Project that has been a mutual blessing for him and the city of Carlsbad. He stays busy beautifying the "town of desert hues" with colorful murals of native landscapes and outdoor activities. On the homefront, we no longer hunger for our favorite vegetarian restaurants over 1200 miles away in Atlanta. Thanks to our new friends, we learned to grow a few vegetables in the desert to prepare tasty Mexican-inspired vegetarian cuisine at home.

New Mexico State University – Carlsbad: Getting to Know You

The New Mexico State University system is designated as a 'Hispanic serving' institution with 51% of the student body being of Hispanic descent.[14] The Carlsbad campus is one of the four community colleges within the NMSU system; the campus also serves a high percentage of Hispanic students. Unlike the main campus in Las Cruces, NMSU – Carlsbad does not have senior administrators who are Hispanic. Top administrators at NMSU – Carlsbad reflect the 'White male' majority of the southeastern region; three of the four administrators are White males. The women and racial and cultural minorities on staff serve as directors or department chairpersons with limited presence and responsibilities on campus governance committees. In 2010, the Carlsbad campus

---

14. "Top Colleges," *Forbes.com*, accessed November 23, 2014, http://www.forbes.com/colleges/new-mexico-state-university-main-campus/.

was awarded a five-year grant from the U.S. Department of Education (USDE). The Title V grant was awarded to provide career opportunities in nursing and health care for low income Hispanic/Latino students in southeastern New Mexico.[15] As noted, Hispanics make up 42.5% of Carlsbad's total population and the community college as a designated HSI actively recruits low-income Hispanics to improve their educational skills and career options. Hispanic students are well represented in the dual credit program that enables eligible high school students from Carlsbad and Loving High Schools to take college courses. Credits gained through this program count toward the attainment of both the high school diploma and an associate degree.[16]

The NMSU – Carlsbad strategic plan speaks eloquently of a commitment to "diversity at all levels."[17] Recent hires in adminstration demostrate a sincere effort to fulfill the institution's diversity goals. After all, humanity is naturally diverse and human diversity is exhibited through multiple group identities as official enumerators are beginning to recognize. The intersection of group identities reveals the natural intricacy of human life. NMSU – Carlsbad, like most American higher education systems, wrestles with the increasing complexity of diversity with the goal of expanding diversity within the organization and eradicating a legacy of racial and gender bias.[18]

---

15. "Title V Program Office," *NMSU Carlsbad,* accessed November 30, 2014, http://carlsbad.nmsu.edu/departments/title-v/.

16. "Dual Credit Program," *NMSU Carlsbad,* accessed November 30, 2014, http://carlsbad.nmsu.edu/departments/academics/dual-credit-program/.

17. "NMSU Carlsbad Strategic Plan: Building the Vision," *NMSU Carlsbad,* accessed November 30, 2014, http://carlsbad.nmsu.edu/files/2014/07/plan1.pdf.

18. Susan Sturm, Tim Eatman, John Saltmarsh, and Adam Bush, *Full Participation: Building the Architecture for Diversity and Public Engagement in Higher Education,* accessed May 18, 2014, http://inclusion.uwex.uwc.edu/sites/inclusion.uwex.uwc.edu/files/Full%20Participation%20-Civic%20Engagement%20and%20Inclusion_0.PDF.

That Black Woman in the Library

It is not surprising that most people found it difficult to comprehend that I made a conscious and informed decision to come to rural Carlsbad, New Mexico. I sized up the campus library during my interview and wanted to manage the transformation of that facility. I was thrilled with the prospect of planning and creating a functional learning facility that could serve as a comfortable and inspiring center of student activity. I gave little thought to my life outside of the campus library. Outside of hiking and reading, there was very little else I was interested in doing in my off time. So, I devoted 50 to 60 hours a week for 14 months planning for the renovation. The library support staff of three employees shared my enthusiasm for the library's transformation.

My new library colleagues in Carlsbad and around the state were endlessly curious to know why a Black woman would leave Atlanta, the "Black Mecca," to settle in the rustic White working-class town of Carlsbad. A Black man, a state employee I met at Library Legislative Day in Santa Fe did not hold his tongue once he learned that I had recently moved to Carlsbad from Atlanta. He expressed his disbelief stating: "You must be out of your mind to leave *black* Atlanta for *redneck* Carlsbad!" I just smiled at him and slowly moved away. My motives are rooted in community service and adventure. Another incident occurred at a roadside store near Cloudcroft, New Mexico where we stopped to purchase cherry cider. An elderly White man, curious about this Black couple in a shiny red pickup, asked us where we were from. "Carlsbad," we replied. Astonished, he screwed up his face and snorted, "What the heck are you doing in that redneck town?" Again, I just smiled, knowing that my presence in a white rural community was not unusual for me or any other Black professional person pursuing career opportunities. Most recently, I was thought to be the community college library director who had relocated as the result of Hurricane Katrina. But it was the director of another NMSU community college, and she is White.

Blacks rarely have the option of living in towns where there are no other racial groups. Many Blacks reside in multicultural environments and have learned to cope with all types of people, biases, and attitudes. The same is probably true of White professors who join the faculty of historically Black colleges and universities (HBCUs). People are naturally curious and sometimes suspicious of your motives. They find it hard to believe that you made a conscience decision to become a part of an institution where there are few, if any, others like you.

Since occupying a tenure-track faculty position as library director in the community college, I have been subjected to marginalization because of intersecting group identities related to my race, gender, and occupation. Aparicio (1999) concluded that the "very presence of the Black woman simultaneously disrupts the status quo and challenges traditional boundaries"[19] in American institutions of higher education. My status is further discounted and my accomplishments trivialized because I am a librarian by profession. Librarianship is perceived as a low status occupation that is not recognized, valued, or rewarded by American higher education.[20] In light of negative perceptions in the workplace, it is important that I demonstrate that I am fully capable of performing the job I was hired to do. Black women in higher education have learned to work with and around those who doubt their personal and professional worth. Bell (1990) revealed that Black women working in all-White environments are guarded emotionally; some reportedly "don't feel safe when interacting with whites, there is a sense of distrust."[21] In her powerful narrative, Karin L. Griffin writes about feeling pressure from departmental peers who refuse to allocate time for her

---

19. Frances R. Aparicio, "Through My Lens: A Video Project about Women of Color Faculty at the University of Michigan," *Feminist Studies* 25, no. 1 (Spring 1999): 119. http://libezp.nmsu.edu:2185/stable/3216674.

20. Prins Hans and Wilco de Gier, *The Image of the Library and Information Profession: How We See Ourselves an Investigation: A Report of an Empirical Study Undertaken on Behalf of IFLA's Round Table for the Management of Library Associations,* (Munchen: International Federation of Library Associations, 1995), 21-22.

21. Ella Louise Bell, "The Bicultural Life Experience of Career-Oriented Black Women," *Journal of Organizational Behavior* 11, no. 6 (1990): 474. DOI:10.1002/job.4030110607.

information literacy sessions and who frequently ask if library faculty "conduct research and are required to publish."[22] Griffin reminds us of how campus administrators may also exhibit professional indifference to librarians when new curricula is proposed (and approved) without inquiring of library staff what level of support they would be able to offer."[23]

As a Black academic librarian in a tenure track position, Griffin confesses that she struggles with stress from the assumption that she is "expected to work twice as hard to be treated as equal."[24] Research and personal observation indicate that "value placed on the contributions of faculty of color may carry unequal weight in comparison to contributions of white counterparts."[25] Having to prove one's worth traps women professionals into roles where they are performing like superwomen[26] who are "always competent and ready to perform."[27] Such behavior is a defense and coping mechanism that is unsustainable; yet many Black professional women succumb to the pressure of having to prove to doubtful colleagues that they are "capable of achieving."[28] The ability to manage such stressful situations is found in a coping mechanism defined as "racial socialization messages."[29] Terhune (2008) argues that coping mechanisms are instilled by one's parents and community during childhood. They serve as "reinforcement of a secure racial identity

---

22. Karin L. Griffin, "Pursuing Tenure and Promotion in the Academy: A Librarian's Cautionary Tale," *Negro Educational Review* 64, no.1-4 (2013): 85.

23. Ibid.

24. Quoted in Karin L. Griffin, "Pursuing Tenure and Promotion in the Academy: A Librarian's Cautionary Tale," 85.

25. Nicole Pagowsky and Miriam Rigby, *The Librarian Stereotype: Deconstructing Perceptions & Presentations of Information Work*, (Chicago, IL: Association of College and Research Libraries, 2014), 159.

26. Bell, "The Bicultural Life Experience of Career-Oriented Black Women," 473.

27. Ibid.

28. Ibid.

29. Terhune, "Coping in Isolation: The Experience of Black Women in White Communities," 558.

grounded in history, heritage, and culture, buffering overt and covert racist and negative stereotypes."[30] In other words, coping mechanisms are grounded in a group identity that protects the psyche through the neutralization of negativity and enables tolerance of an action or comment in the interest of self- preservation.

For example, one afternoon I was called to the service desk to help identify a plant found along the nature trail near the campus. The patron appeared startled to see me and when I was introduced as the library director, she stiffened. Being familiar with several works on Chihuahuan Desert plants, I promptly found a color illustration of the plant in question and presented it to the patron. She looked at me and said, "Good girl." I did not perceive the remark to be a compliment or innocent comment. I thought it was an inappropriate comment to make to the director of the library or to a woman you are meeting for the first time. I did not smile when she said it, and she instantly looked away. I am sure it was meant to be an insult, but my coping mechanism kicked in and I let it go.

Information Literacy Instruction: The Ultimate Strategic Goal

The campus president sent an invitation soliciting ideas from faculty and staff for the latest edition of the Carlsbad campus strategic plan. I was at ALA midwinter in Seattle when I received the email, but I took the time to email some suggestions related to the inclusion of information literacy as a strategic goal for the campus. I received the standard, "Thanks, Akilah" email, but little else. There were no comments, questions for clarification, or reasons stating why it would not be considered. When the revised strategic plan was unveiled there was no mention of information literacy anywhere in it. Without feedback from the president I was left to speculate as to why the suggestion was rejected and why I did not merit a response. Perhaps it was because I

---

30. Ibid.

had no relationship with this new president and I soon realized that he had very little experience with Blacks, let alone Blacks in positions of authority. To him, I am just the "library director," or perhaps just the "Black woman library director"? Undeterred, I remain hopeful that I will have other opportunities to advocate for information literacy in a more formal manner.

Since my arrival at NMSU – Carlsbad, it has been my goal to promote library services among the students and faculty while positioning the library as an equal partner in the educational process. After a year of observation and planning for renovation, the provost encouraged me to create a task force to revise the library strategic plan. Following a survey of library facilities and services, a series of focus groups with campus and community users, and eight months of analysis and writing, the task force produced a five-year library strategic plan based on three broad goals: 1. Improve the User Experience; 2. Enhance the Library Space; and 3. Boost Community Outreach. The transformation of library services and facilities continued through achievement of key performance indicators (KPI) based on the three objectives. Adherence to these objectives in campus programming also helped students and faculty understand the multi-faceted role of an academic library.

As a teacher-librarian, I piloted a two-credit course in collaboration with the Department of Developmental Studies to increase information skills in first year students by providing instruction in information literacy during the 2012 summer term. The course, *Twenty-First Century Information Access*, proved helpful to the four students and the science instructor who completed the course. Convincing students to sign up for the information literacy course was challenging. By the fall semester, I drafted the full-time library staff and offered the 8-week course as professional development. It turned out to be a productive and valuable opportunity to library improve service. Their registration also saved the course from being cut by the new provost who was not too interested in offering courses with three students or less.

The following spring semester the information literacy course was cut due to low enrollment. The loss of the course sent me back to the drawing board. Within weeks, I began collaborating with the chair of the Department of College Studies to include information literacy instruction as a unit within the college studies curriculum. I shared data to illustrate the value of an information literacy course on our campus, and as a result, the suggestion was fully embraced by the department chair. We began promoting library visits and a one-shot library orientation sessions among the College 101 instructors teaching face-to-face courses. At faculty orientations for adjunct and full-time faculty, I invited instructors to work with me by bringing their students to the library or inviting me to their classroom for a short introduction to library services. My efforts increased foot traffic into the physical library, where students used the library computer lab and resources, and boosted the number of users of online resources from the library website.

NMSU – Carlsbad was scheduled for a reaccreditation visit from the Academic Quality Improvement Program (AQIP) during the 2012-13 academic year. AQIP is one of several pathways leading to reaffirmation of accreditation with the Higher Learning Commission.[31] I prepared a review of the library program for use in the campus AQIP report. The library review served as the basis for my report to the provost, and later, the stakeholders committee. Again, I requested inclusion of information literacy instruction goals in the campus strategic plan. The report included feedback from students and graphs illustrating increases in the use of library-based online resources. Additionally, the report emphasized the role of the librarian in the education of NMSU – Carlsbad students and the opportunity for collaboration with faculty to boost the library and information skills of first-year students. The timing was perfect for formal acknowledgement of the library as a partner in the education of our students. My outreach to faculty represented the best way to introduce the information literacy program, and I was making progress toward my goal.

---

31. *"Higher Learning Commission: A Commission of the North Central Association, The AQIP Pathway,"* accessed November 23, 2014, https://www.ncahlc.org/Pathways/aqip-home.html.

In my presentation to the stakeholders committee, I shared the 2008 American Association of Community Colleges (AACC) 2008 position statement noting the importance of information literacy as a component of the curriculum design. The statement further noted that an "effective curricula offer both current and classic content across disciplines within a design that engages students, meets their learning needs, aids in student success in courses and retention in academic programs."[32] The AACC position statement also emphasized the importance of faculty/librarian collaboration in producing student academic success, stating that "classroom faculty should partner with library and learning resource center staff to form instructional teams to encourage information literacy outcomes in credit and noncredit instruction."[33]

At the conclusion of my presentation there was total silence. I looked at my colleagues around the table and noted a couple of smiles and a few nods of agreement but little else. By the time my eyes met the chair he was chanting "fine job" and started an applause that everyone nervously copied before quickly moving on to the next agenda item. There was no discussion or questions. It was a complete dismissal and disregard of my professional work as director of library services. I felt humiliated and devalued.

When new committee assignments were announced at the end of the spring semester, I had been replaced as faculty representative to the stakeholders committee and assigned to the diversity committee. Transferred along with me was the "Taste of Culture," a cultural food tasting event I inherited when I served as interim chair of the stakeholders group. I served on the diversity committee for one year and chaired the "Taste of Culture" event for the second time. When committee assignments were released the following year, I asked to be removed from the diversity committee and reassigned to a committee where my professional skills and education could be used.

---

32. *"AACC Position Statement on Information Literacy,"* accessed November 4, 2014 http://www.aacc.nche.edu/About/Positions/Pages/ps05052008.aspx.
33. Ibid.

Event planning is great skill to have, and I give thanks to the Indiana church women who trained me in the niceties of party planning, but I do not aspire to be the Martha Stewart of the campus! I agree wholeheartedly with Theresa Byrd's observation that minority librarians are subject to be restricted to service on the diversity committee. Such assignments isolate minority librarians from the mainstream of the organization and limit opportunities for advancement.[34] As a permanent fixture on the diversity committee, you could find yourself planning and executing cultural programs and parties for all eternity! In my case, I found it best to provide the chair with an event timeline of required tasks, and promise to be avaliable to answer any questions. In my first year as a member of the developmental studies committee, I participated in instructional initiatives such as "Writing Across the Curriculum" and training tutors to use key resources to help students academically. Service on this committee best fit my educational and professional background, and I look forward to increased collaboration with developmental studies faculty and staff to support first year students. At NMSU – Carlsbad, chances are slim that a librarian or a woman of color would be named committee chair—a position apparently reserved for male faculty with doctorate degrees.

Academic Librarian: Clerk or Educator?

The low status of librarianship in American higher education is due to many factors. The most prevalent reason is a lack of awareness of what academic librarians do. Most of the professional work is performed out of the sight of library users. Common clerical tasks that have dominated our profession during the last two centuries have been replaced with high-level management responsibilities thanks to integrated technologies

---

34. Theresa S. Byrd, "Managing the Academic Library: The Role of the Black Librarian Leader in Three Different Institutional Environments," in Andrew P. Jackson, Julius C. Jr. Jefferson, and Akilah S. Nosakhere, eds., *21st-Century Black Librarian in America: Issues and Challenges* (Lanham, MD: Scarecrow Press, 2012), 108.

that aid in analyses and assessment of library services. Routinely, academic librarians analyze and develop budgets, negotiate and manage service contracts, evaluate learning products, study the curriculum, and assess and select materials, keeping in minds the varying needs of various user groups. All of this is performed and managed long before the need becomes apparent.

Most faculty, administrators, and stakeholders would be envious of the savvy technology skills possessed by today's academic librarian. Many plan and manage library websites and social media sites, and describe, digitize and launch digital collections and repositories that are accessed by academic scholars and students near and far. Few library users know that there are schools of library and information studies specializing in management of libraries of all types and that an accredited library degree is earned at the master's level. For the majority of librarians the MLS degree is sufficient for career advancement, particularly if one is conscientious about keeping up with professional reading and participating in continuing education. However, for academic librarians in senior library positions, the MLS is not enough to convince faculty and administration of the academic librarian's knowledge of subject content. It is becoming apparent that an additional credential is required.[35]

Increasingly, academic librarians teach information literacy courses and seek increased collaboration with faculty to incorporate information literacy into course content at the design level. This practice is not new yet it continues to be controversial as academic librarians advocate for strategic initiatives on information literacy and request to team teaching with faculty. Some faculty and administrators believe that academic librarians are over-stepping their service role when it comes to promotion of the teacher-librarian model. Research maintains that librarians differ from teaching faculty because as knowledge workers they enable the creation of knowledge through the dissemination of information;

---

35. T.D. Webb, *Divided Libraries: Remodeling Management to Unify Institutions,* (Jefferson, NC: McFarland, 2012), 114.

faculty create new knowledge through research.[36] Badke (2005) argues that librarians and faculty and librarians have a "different culture and different priorities" when it comes to teaching. While collaboration with librarians for instruction has experienced limited success over the years, it is still widely resisted by faculty, with the perceived lack of credentials and differences in research approach being among the major reasons.[37]

This credibility issue faced by academic librarians in higher education is heating up once more as information literacy is aggressively promoted among first year college students. Individual librarians and library administrators in higher education are finding it worthwhile and necessary to seek additional credentials to gain respect in academia. Retired university librarian and researcher T. D. Webb advises that earning a Ph.D. is "critical for librarians who expect to be taken seriously by university and college faculty."[38] Mayer and Terrill found in their survey of 686 academic librarians that 56.55% of them agree with the statement that "academic librarians should have an advanced subject degree."[39] Armed with doctorate degrees, will academic librarians of color be accepted and treated as equal to teaching faculty and campus administrators?

The Triple Negative: Black Female Librarian

Graubard and Leclerc reveal that librarianship is devalued in higher education because it is considered service, and because service is perceived as a feminine quality of low in status in our society, librarianship

---

36. Stephen Richards Graubard and Paul Omer Leclerc, *Books, Bricks and Bytes: Libraries in the 21st Century* (New Brunswick, NJ: Transaction Publishers, 1995), 87.

37. William B. Badke, "Can't Get No Respect: Helping Faculty to Understand the Educational Power of Information Literacy," *Reference Librarian* 43, no. 89-90 (2005): 64. https://acts.twu.ca/Library/Respect.pdf.

38. T.D. Webb, *Divided Libraries: Remodeling Management to Unify Institutions,* (Jefferson, NC: McFarland, 2012), 113.

39. Jennifer, Mayer and Lori J. Terrill, "Academic Librarians' Attitudes about Advanced Subject Degrees" *College & Research Libraries* 66, no. 1 (2005), 62.

is low in status and lacks prestige within the academic arena.[40] This low status and lack of prestige that librarianship has within the academic arena results in librarians not being taken seriously in higher education. Additionally, Graubard and Leclerc argue that librarianship was never scholarly even when the profession was dominated by men in the mid-nineteeth century.[41] In light of these findings, and when combined with racial bias, it is clear that societal stereotyping of women and librarianship can certainly compound the negative perception of Black women library directors in academic institutions.

Given the complex issues of race, gender, and occupation bias within American higher education it is no wonder that Black women with academic library careers find themselves isolated and devalued, and their professional work discounted. It is detrimental to all parties when racial, gender, and cultural diversity are perceived as threatening and offensive when these qualities add rich perspectives and are beneficial to the educational mission of any institution. The stereotyping and devaluation of my person and profession restricts my effectiveness within the institution. Racial and occupational bias denies me opportunities to excel as a knowledge worker and educator. Fortunately, my strong sense of identity nurtured with regular doses of Black cultural reading and prayer strengthens my coping abilities and keeps me from internalizing mean-spirited comments.

Epstein (1973) reported in her ground-breaking study of Black women professionals that multiple group identities can enhance career opportunities of Black women professionals.[42] Those professionals exhibiting strong intellectual skills and equally stout self-confidence could find success in their chosen careers in spite of societal stereotypes and long-held perceptions of incompetence and inferiority.[43] While these

---

40. Graubard and Leclerc, *Books, Bricks and Bytes*, 82.

41. Ibid., 82-83.

42. Cynthia Fuchs Epstein "Positive Effects of the Multiple Negative: Explaining the Success of Black Professional Women," *American Journal of Sociology* 78, no. 4, (January 1973), 920.

43. Ibid., 921-922.

findings have some merit, it is important to note that Black women tend to be successful in these racially isolated situations because we choose to ignore the racially demeaning comments and work twice as hard to be professionally successful wherever we are. Microaggressions[44] thinly disguised as compliments, and assumptions about our abilities and why we were hired in the first place are all physically and psychologically exhausting, yet "we rise."

"Do Your Best Work" - Dr. John Henrik Clarke

My five years as library director and tenure-track faculty at NMSU – Carlsbad has offered many challenges and a few setbacks, yet I continue to advocate for information literacy instruction. I have encountered situations where my professional accomplishments have been quietly ignored, my faculty rank has been questioned, and my authority dismissed, yet I continue to teach, write, and promote information literacy skill development as a vehicle for social and intellectual growth for students. My goal as a library professional is to create environments that foster learning and positive change in the lives NMSU – Carlsbad students. I am committed to this goal in spite of the racist and sexist stereotypes I have faced knowingly and unknowingly throughout my career. Microaggressive racial behaviors rooted in historical racial stereotypes heaved upon Black librarians occur not only in small rural towns and institutions but also in urban America as well.[45]

Rejection and dismissal of the professional expertise of an individual because of identity group membership is prevalent in higher education and in all aspects of the national life. Careful dissection and sincere discussion on the individual and community levels are required to combat

44. Roxanne A. Donovan, David J. Galban, Ryan K. Grace, Jacqueline K. Bennett, and Shaina Z. Felicié, "Impact of Racial Marco- and Microaggressions in Black Women's Lives: A Preliminary Analysis." *Journal of Black Psychology* 39, no. 2 (2012): 186. DOI: 10.1177/0095798412443259.

45. Andrew P. Jackson, Julius C. Jr. Jefferson, and Akilah S. Nosakhere, eds., *The 21st Century Black Librarian in America: Issues and Challenges,* (Lanham, MD: Scarecrow Press, 2012), 203.

the negative effects of racism, gender bias, and professional stereotyping. Unfortunately, these challenges are faced by each generation in the United States and beyond. Racial and cultural minorities and women professionals pursuing careers outside of their comfort zones have to develop tough skins to tolerate ignorant and hateful comments in the workplace. As we build our careers, remember that we have the power to neutralize the effects of race, gender, and occupational bias through intellectual and emotional nurturing of ourselves. Only then can we provide our professional best in service to the institutions of our choice.

References

American Association of Community Colleges. *AACC Position Statement on Information Literacy.* Accessed November 3, 2014. http://www.aacc.nche.edu/About/Positions/Pages/ps05052008.aspx.

Aparicio, Frances R. "Through My Lens: A Video Project about Women of Color Faculty at the University of Michigan." *Feminist Studies* 25, no.1 (Spring 1999):119-130. http://libezp.nmsu.edu:2185/stable/3216674.

Association of Research Libraries. *Past LCDP Fellows & Career Coaches.* 2014. Accessed November 22, 2014. http://www.arl.org/leadership-recruitment/diversity-recruitment/leadership-career-development-program/2531-past-fellows-a-career-coaches#.VKCWG14AKA.

Badke, William B. "Can't Get No Respect: Helping Faculty to Understand the Educational Power of Information Literacy." *Reference Librarian* 43, no. 89-90 (2005): 63-80. https://acts.twu.ca/Library/Respect.pdf.

Baker, Neal, and Aletha D. Stahl. "What I Want in a Librarian." *Reference and User Services Quarterly* 37, no. 2 (1997): 133-135.

Bell, Ella Louise. "The Bicultural Life Experience of Career-Oriented Black Women." *Journal of Organizational Behavior* 11, no. 6 (1990): 459-477. DOI: 10.1002/job.4030110607.

Bowden, Russell, and Donald E. Vijasuriya. "The Status, Reputation and Image of the Library and Information Profession." *Proceeding of the IFLA Pre-Session Seminar.* Delhi, India: International Federation of Library Association, 1992.

Byrd, Theresa S. "Managing the Academic Library: The Role of the Black Librarian Leader in Three Different Institutional Environments." In *The 21st-Century Black Librarian in America,* edited by Julius C. Jefferson, Akilah S. Nosakhere, and Andrew P. Jackson, 105-109. Lanham, MD: Scarecrow Press, 2012.

City of Carlsbad, New Mexico. *City of Carlsbad, New Mexico Long Term Planning Committee.* Accessed November 21, 2014. http://www.cityofcarlsbadnm.com/longtermplan.cfm.

Donovan, Roxanne A., David J. Galban, Ryan K. Grace, Jacqueline K. Bennett, and Shaina Z. Felicié. "Impact of Racial Macro- and Microaggressions in Black Women's Lives: A Preliminary Analysis." *Journal of Black Psychology* 39, no. 2 (2013): 185-196. DOI: 10.1177/0095798412443259.

Epstein, Cynthia Fuchs. "Positive Effects of the Multiple Negative: Explaining the Success of Black Professional Women." *American Journal of Sociology* 78, no.4 (January 1973): 912-935. http://libezp.nmsu.edu:2185/stable/2776611.

Eskins, Don. "CHS and Integration." *Carlsbad Our Town: Carlsbad Current Argus,* 2011.

Forbes.com. *Top Colleges.* Accessed November 23, 2014. http://www.forbes.com/colleges/new-mexico-state-university-main-campus/.

Glasrud, Bruce A. *African American History in New Mexico: Portraits from Five Hundred Years.* Albuquerque: Univesity of New Mexico Press, 2013.

Graubard, Stephen Richards, and Paul Omer Leclerc. *Books, Bricks and Bytes: Libraries in the 21st Century.* New Burnswick, NJ: Transaction Publishers, 1995.

Griffin, Karin L. "Pursuing Tenure and Promotion in the Academy: A Librarian's Cautionary Tale." *Negro Educational Review* 64, no.1-4 (2013): 77-96. http:// ebscohost.com/c/articles/91870115/

Hans, Prins, and Wilco de Gier. "The Image of the Library and Information Profession: How We See Ourselves an Investigation." In *A Report of an Empirical Study Undertaken on Behalf of IFLA's Round Table for the Management of Library Associations, 21-22.* Munchen: International Federation of Library Associations, 1995.

Higher Learning Commission: A Commission of the North Central Association. *The AQIP Pathway.* Accessed November 25, 2014. https://www.ncahlc.org/Pathways/aqip-home.html.

Jackson, Andrew P., Julius C. Jr. Jefferson, and Akilah S. Nosakhere, eds. *The 21st Century Black Librarian in America: Issues and Challenges.* Lanham, MD: Scarecrow Press, 2012.

Manuel, Kate, Susan E. Beck, and Molly Molloy. "An Ethnographic Study of Attitudes Influencing Faculty Collaboration in Library Instruction." *Reference Librarian* 43, no. 89-90 (2005): 139-161.

Mayer, Jennifer, and Lori J. Terrill. "Academic Librarians' Attitudes about Advanced Subject Degrees." *College & Research Libraries* 66, no. 1 (2005): 59-73.

Muhs, Gabriella Gutierrez y, Yolanda Flores Niemann, Carman G. Gonzalez, and Angela P. Harris. *Presumed Incompetent: The Intersections of Race and Class for Women in Academica.* Boulder, CO: Utah State University Press, 2012.

New Mexico State University – Carlsbad. *Building the Vision NMSU Carlsbad Strategic Plan.* Accessed May 10, 2014. http://carlsbad.nmsu.edu/files/2014/07/plan1.pdf.

New Mexico State University – Carlsbad. *Dual Credit Program.* Accessed November 30, 2014. http://carlsbad.nmsu.edu/departments/academics/dual-credit-program/

New Mexico State University – Carlsbad. *Title V Program Office.* Accessed November 30, 2014. http://carlsbad.nmsu.edu/departments/title-v/.

Pagowsky, Nicole, and Miriam Rigby. *The Librarian Stereotype: Deconstructing Perceptions and Presentations of Information Work.* Chicago: Association of College and Research Libraries, 2014.

Passet, Joanne. Culture Crusaders: *Women Librarians in the American West, 1900-1917.* Alburquerque: University of New Mexico, 1994.

Schubert, Frank N. *Black Valor: Buffalo Soldiers and the Medal of Honor, 1870 - 1898.* New York:Rowman & Littlefield, 2009.

Sturm, Susan, Tim Eatman, John Saltmarsh, and Adam Bush. *Full Participation: Building the Architecture in Higher Education* (White paper). Columbia University Law School: Center for Institutional and Social Change, 2011. http://inclusion.uwex.uwc.edu/sites/inclusion.uwex.uwc.edu/files/Full%20Participation%20-Civic%20Engagement%20and%20Inclusion_0.PDF

Terhune, Carol Parker. "Coping in Isolation: The Experience of Black Women in White Communities." *Journal of Black Studies* 38, no.4 (March 2008): 547-564. http://www.jstor.org/stable/40034421.

U.S. Census Bureau. *New Mexico: USA Quick Facts.* Accessed December 14, 2014. http://quickfacts.census.gov/qfd/states/35000.html.

U.S. Department of Labor. *Occupational Outlook Handbook, 2014-2015, Librarians.* Accessed May 13, 2014. http://www.bls.gov/ooh/education-training-and-library/librarians.htm.

Webb, T.D. *Divided Libraries: Remodeling Management to Unify Institutions.* Jefferson, NC: McFarland, 2012.

Wellington, Darryl Lorenzo. "Black in Santa Fe." *Santa Fe Reporter.* Accessed July 7, 2014. http://www.sfreporter.com/santafe/article-7838-black-in-santa-fe.html.

Chapter 8

LIKE A FISH OUT OF WATER, BUT FORGING MY OWN PATH

Vince Lee

Introduction

From day one I knew I was different. Ever since the first day of class in library school, I knew that I was the only one who looked as I did. Looking at my classmates, I saw Caucasians and some African Americans; what I didn't see were Asian Americans. I was the only one there. Unfortunately, studies on racial diversity in academic and research libraries have confirmed that not much has changed in over a 30-year period. Chang states that from 1981-2011, "overall minority representation has only increased from 10 percent to 14.2 percent. The percentage of library professionals who are black has only increased from 3.10 percent to 4.4 percent, Hispanic has increased from 1.39 to 2.6 percent, Asian/Pacific Islander has increased from 5.4 to 6.8 percent and American Indian/Alaskan Native increased from 0.09 percent to 0.30 percent."[1] While other Asians pursued more lucrative professions,

---

1. Hui-Feng Chang, "Ethnic and Racial Diversity in Academic and Research Libraries: Past, Present, and Future" (paper presented at the annual Association of College & Research Libraries Conference, Indianapolis, Indiana, April 10-13, 2013), 183.

such as being a physician, lawyer, or even an engineer, I chose to become a librarian and archivist.

It wasn't just that there was a lack of Asians in library school, but also that I did not see many Asians in the profession when I began my academic career. I feel I have been granted two unique opportunities in my in my professional academic library career—the first was when I was hired as an archivist for a newly created African American Library and the second is in my current position as archivist for the Carey C. Shuart Women's Archive and Research Collection. In both situations I felt that I was breaking the color line as the first Asian to occupy these positions. I felt I did not fit neatly into public preconceived notions of what an archivist should be. In the first, I was a Chinese American serving an African American repository. In the second, I am a male Chinese American serving a repository that represents the history of women in Houston and Texas. Thus the title of this essay: I felt I was like a fish out of water in both instances.

Being in these situations has given me an opportunity to reflect not only on preconceived ideas and stereotypes of who archivists in academic libraries should be, but there are self-imposed biases in regard to how we see ourselves and how we fit into the profession. I believe these factors fed into the insecurities I felt that constantly fed the need to constantly prove myself, and in my opinion, work twice as hard to show that I was worthy of the opportunities that had been given to me. These feelings also influenced me in terms of donor relations and cultivating donors. I continually felt cautious about how I was perceived within the community and how I represented the institutions that entrusted me to acquire archival materials. Internally it is a fine-line, balancing relationships with donors while being careful not to offend them, especially individuals who were not expecting an Asian male archivist. Yet, I was usually able to keep donors at ease and convince them that I was qualified and could do the job as archivist.

All of these competing and conflicting emotions, both internally and externally, can feel overwhelming and suffocating at times, especially when the facade one tries to project is one of calm, control, and amiability, while trying to fit in. This perception is what is known in the Asian community as being the model citizen; the model minority myth has been perpetuated by those in hegemonic power who want to categorize or explain an ethnic group's performance in comparison to others. However, this myth isn't unique to the Asian American experience. In every ethnic minority group, there are examples of successful individuals to be found, whether they identify as being Black, Hispanic, or Native American, to name but a few groups in addition to the Asian community. There are other complex factors that contribute to academic and occupational success besides something that is inherent in one racial minority group over another, not to mention the individual talents and aptitudes of the individuals within that group.

There are social and psychological costs to the model minority label. Some studies have revealed that Asian Americans' psychological well-being has suffered as a result of the image and the pressures that go along with trying to live up to the image. These include studying longer hours and enduring feelings of loneliness and isolation.[2] Because I have been given an opportunity within the profession, I feel must be twice as good as the next candidate to justify my hire. That means producing excellent work, being self-motivated, not making mistakes, and getting along well with everyone. In short there is no room for error, no down time, and all eyes are on you. You are not only representing yourself, which in my case is a first generation Chinese American, but you are representative of an entire community of people who look and act like you—a tall order indeed.

Also, within the African American community there is a "tension" as to how Asian Americans are perceived, especially when that group has stereotypically been depicted as outsiders or foreigners even though the individuals within that group are born within the United States.[3] One

---

2. Paul Wong, et. al., "Asian Americans as a Model Minority: Self-Perceptions and Perceptions by Other Racial Groups," *Sociological Perspectives* 41, no. 1 (1998), 98.

3. Ibid., 99. Based on author's synthesis and summation of the article along with personal experience.

of the few studies that have been done on this topic, Michael Thornton and Robert Taylor's 1988 study entitled "Intergroup Attitudes: Black American Perceptions of Asian Americans," concluded that based on familiarity as a determining factor of one group's perception of another, African Americans did not feel close to Asian Americans. If one group doesn't identify or share commonalities of experience with another, it is often easier to devise "shorthand" stereotypes for the group, even though they may be wrong, than to take the time and try to understand the individuals within the group.[4]

Gregory School, Houston's First African American Public Elementary School

I applied to the African American Library at the Gregory School because I wanted the opportunity to be hired as an archivist for its newly created special collections library. There aren't many opportunities in an archivist's life where you come into a position at the ground floor and shape the direction of that institution. I found this to be a compelling reason and an exciting opportunity to build something special within the African American community. It would take me to a new place away from Michigan, which would involve relocating with my wife and six-month-old son. I also applied for the position because I believed my experience gained as a volunteer and practicum student in processing the African World Festival Collections and the Papers of Mayor Coleman Young would serve me well as a candidate who had worked on collections documenting the African American community. I also thought that my experience working at one of the premier African American institutions in the Detroit area would translate well as an incoming candidate for a new archive. I felt fortunate that I had worked at the Charles H. Wright Museum of African American History. I ended up doing my practicum at the Charles Wright not so much as a choice, but because it was one of the few options that were available.

---

4. Wong, et al, "Asian Americans as a Model Minority," 98.

Had there been other positions available and closer to my home, I am not so sure that I would have taken the position.

I was surprised to be hired as the lead archivist for The African American Library at the Gregory School. I remember it well. I was going through a phone interview for the position and it was February of 2009. They were interviewing me for the position and the only experience I had had was as a practicum student at the Charles H. Wright Museum of African American History in downtown Detroit. I thought that they would be in pursuit of a more seasoned candidate with much more experience in establishing and running an archive. I was someone who was newly minted and fresh out of school. After my practicum had ended I decided to stay on as a volunteer and continue processing collections to gain additional experience until I landed a full time job as an archivist. To be honest, I didn't think I had much of a chance to land the position as I thought they would want to hire an African American candidate. I tried though because at that point I was desperate to land a full time job—any job for that matter—that would allow me to finally become an archivist. Surprisingly, the phone interview went very well. I was interviewed by three individuals—the hiring manager for the Gregory School, the assistant manager for the Houston Metropolitan Research Center, and the Chief of Central Services for Houston Public Library. After the phone interview concluded, there was a follow-up call with some additional questions that I was able to answer and elaborate on. That phone interview would be my one and only interview prior to them offering me the position, which I thought unusual at the time. I thought that at least there would be another round of face-to-face interviews.

When the offer was made and I accepted the job, I thought to myself, surely they made a mistake. Don't they know that they are hiring an Asian American to be the lead archivist for the newly designed and soon to be opened African American Library at the Gregory School?

I realized that employers and HR cannot discriminate or take into consideration hiring based on a person's race, creed, religion, or orientation, but still I was expecting the offer to be retracted at some point, once they realized the mistake they made in the hire. Looking back though,

I believe I was hired because I had shown initiative and persistence in continuing on at the Charles Wright, even though my practicum had ended. Perhaps that persistence I had shown as a volunteer demonstrated to the hiring manager my professionalism and a passion for what I was doing even though I wasn't being compensated as a volunteer. I also think that being a new graduate with limited experience may have worked in my favor because I was energetic and eager to prove myself. I was coming into a new situation with an open mind and without the baggage or predispositions that a more experienced candidate might bring.

In short, the newly created special collections and I would have an opportunity to grow together as we went along and I would have the opportunity of putting my imprint on it. With that being said, I still felt ill equipped for the job at hand and had my doubts. Apart from my experience at Charles H. Wright Museum of African American History, I did not have a lot of experience for the position, besides being able to convince the prospective employer that I was the right person for the job. I felt like I had gotten away with something and it would only be a matter of time before I was found out and this whole charade would come crashing down all around me.

I didn't know if they knew what they were getting themselves, but I made the trek down to Houston from Michigan, taking my family with me when I relocated. The first day I reported into work, my supervisor and colleagues welcomed me with open arms and expressed their gratitude that I had taken the job and tried to make me feel comfortable. However, I couldn't shake off the feelings of inadequacy and feeling like somewhat of a fraud. Actually, I felt that I did not know enough about the Fourth Ward or Freedmen's Town; and I wasn't sure how the community would react to an Asian coming into their community and soliciting their materials for the African American Library at the Gregory School. What I did know was that I was a trained archivist who was knowledgeable about how to process, assess, appraise, and arrange collections I came across, and could make them usable and available to researchers. In times of uncertainty or trouble, I would always go back to what I knew and take it from there. The rest of the work, I would have to learn day-by-day, week-by-week, month-to-month, one step at a time, until I gained experience and credibility.

I wondered if the community could trust me? How could I gain their trust? How would I win them over? Those questions weighed heavily on me when I began my position, because I was not African American. How would someone like me do well in the Third Ward, Fourth Ward, and Fifth Ward, Independence Heights, Acres Homes, and Sunnyside, as well as in the high schools in the area such as Phillis Wheatley, Jack Yates, and Booker T. Washington? These were historically black neighborhoods and schools going back generations, in which African Americans who were freed after Emancipation decided to settle and build their lives in these communities. Without their trust how would I acquire their materials? How would I get them to donate and entrust the materials to the African American Library at the Gregory School to build the archive from the ground up? Without that I might be dead in water from day one.

These communities are tight knit. They are mistrustful of others who are not like them and outside of their community, however well-intentioned they might be. These communities have been burned too many times, both historically and by what they consider betrayal by the "white man," because they had materials that were taken in the name of archives or preservation and later they found out that their materials did not end up in the agreed upon place or may have been sold or auctioned off for profit. Historically, this concept has been referred to in literature within the black community as "racial mistrust."[5] These feelings of mistrust developed within the African American community through a process of being exposed directly and/or indirectly, to prejudicial practices on the part of the dominant white society.[6] Materials from these communities—photos, documents, ephemera—are some of the most rare and precious things within their family possessions

5. F.A. Biafora, Jr., et al., "Cultural Mistrust and Racial Awareness among Ethnically Diverse Black Adolescent Boys," *Journal of Black Psychology* 19, no. 3 (1993), 98-99.

6. Ibid., 269.

that links their history and legacy. It is difficult for people who have no experience working with archives and archivists to give up and turn over control of their items, especially if they don't understand what an archives is or what an archivist does, not to mention having dealt with unscrupulous individuals in the past who have stolen items from them.

Fortunately for me, the process had already started and the groundwork had been laid before I arrived, by a local community historian named Patricia Prather. Ms. Prather was and is the local neighborhood historian who knows many of the longtime residents in the Third, Fourth, and Fifth Wards. She was born and raised in Fifth Ward, and her father Clifford F. Smith was the first African American electrician in Houston in 1943 and his business C.F. Smith Electric Company serviced many African American homes and businesses in the area. So as a young girl she knew many of the residents and businesses through her father's business connections.

Ms. Prather introduced me and gave me entry into the African American community that I would not have had access to on my own. She brought me along on donor visits and into residents' homes. Through her goodwill and relationships within the African American community I was entrusted to handle and secure their materials for the archives. Donor visits with Pat were an educational opportunities in themselves. I would visit donors within the community, many times in their homes, talking about their family, their legacy and history, and how they settled into the area. On the drive over to the donors, Ms. Prather would also explain buildings, landmarks, and cemeteries, and their significance to African American history and the community. Also, I think that in meeting African American donors face-to-face I allayed many of their apprehensions once they discovered I was a person of color and started to get a sense of who I was. The single most important thing I have learned in my dealings with the African American community and donors is to be genuine—just be yourself. Don't try to be or portray something you're not; they will see right through that. They know when they are being conned and when someone is representing themselves falsely. I also think that my experience in having grown up and worked in my father's Chinese restaurant business served me well in donor relations. It taught me not only customer service skills, but how to treat people with respect, how to be transparent, and how to put people at ease by answering any questions they had about the process. The key is to treat them like you want to be treated if the tables were turned. In donor relations and archival theory this is known as "public trust."[7] There are forces at work every day that endanger the trust archivists have been allotted and worked so hard to build up over time, whether through misdeeds such as theft, misappropriation, and obfuscating and misrepresenting facts within the archives.[8] Just as working in my father's restaurant had taught me, once you lose a customer it's awfully hard to win them back once that trust has been broken.

This is not to say that there weren't incidents where not everything went smoothly. I have had encounters where visitors looked at me funny and some even had the temerity to say to me to my face that they expected an African American archivist to be present to process the collections, not an Asian American. Some even questioned me in sarcastic tones, about what I knew about their community and what my exact qualifications were to process their materials and collections. At other times, working with donors to secure their collections could be like pulling teeth, the back and forth of yes, they were going to donate, and then the next week, no, they weren't, or they had a change of heart; other times, it would be asking how much we would give them (in monetary terms) for their materials. In educating and managing donor expectations, I explained that there are organizations that could purchase collections through their collection development policy or a specific endowment, but that as a public library we did not possess an endowment, especially in the tight economic times we faced in 2009. Others asked about the possibility of donating a surrogate copy of the materials to the archives while retaining the originals. Although

---

7. Jason G. Speck, "Protecting Public Trust: An Archival Wake-Up Call," *Journal of Archival Organization* 8, no. 1 (2010), 33.

8. Ibid., 38.

unique arrangements for partnerships do exist between independent community archives who retain custody and ownership of the original materials, while at the same time benefitting from the expertise and security that a mainstream archive can provide, this would be a highly irregular for individual donors to enter into, especially for those who lacked the expertise, experience, and responsibilities such an arrangement would entail for all parties involved.[9] I had to deal with all of these scenarios, questions, and expectations as well as explain processes to donors during our meetings.

As I continued doing my work, I grew into my job, and I found the process to be educational, but at times it was slow, taxing, and required patience. I needed to educate African American donors from the community about what an archives is and what an archivist does, managing expectations and explaining that no, your item is not guaranteed to be displayed in the permanent exhibit, and that we preserved documents, photographs, and ephemera. At times, I also needed to show donors how materials would be processed, housed, and stored before they would be used by researchers. I had to explain what a finding aid was, how it was used to locate information, and also what an oral history was and how the sessions would be conducted and recorded. Through each donor meeting and meeting within the community, I was trying to slowly but gradually win the hearts and minds of the individuals within the community. As I was doing this, I was also trying to be less self-conscious about being an Asian American archivist at an African American Library, dealing with my self-doubts and fears, trying to do my job perfectly, and being all things to all people while trying to please everyone. If I did that or attempted to do that I would go crazy, because that just wasn't possible and I would lose sight of who I was and what I was trying to do in my job, which was to acquire collections, process them, and make them available. If I did my job to the best of my ability, in such a way that the community could be proud of it, while also educating donors,

9. Flinn Andrew, Mary Stevens, and Elizabeth Shepherd, "Whose Memories, Whose Archives? Independent Community Archives, Autonomy and the Mainstream," *Archival Science* 9 (2009), 80.

making them feel respected and comfortable through the process, all the while being transparent, then I have done my job. That is all I could ask and hope for. Any of the other biases, insecurities, and fears about whether I belonged would eventually fall by the wayside, because frankly they weren't important—that was just baggage added onto the equation to complicate things or justify things in our minds about how things should be, instead of how they could be if we step away from ourselves.

Carey Shuart Women's Archives (Special Collections, University of Houston Libraries)

I did well over the next several years at the African American Library at the Gregory School. I started bringing in increasing numbers of African American collections from the surrounding community. I was establishing great relationships with donors. I even had a hand in doing oral histories. In effect, I had made my mark and built the archival collection from the community at the Gregory School from the ground up. The irony is that as things were progressing well, I knew it was time to leave. Since the beginning, I knew in my heart that I wanted to return to academia and academic libraries. That's when I saw an opportunity at the University of Michigan, where I began my career. If a job opportunity presented had itself, I would have jumped at it and taken it. Knowing how I felt, one of my colleagues at Houston Public Library suggested I apply for a position at the University of Houston Libraries, Special Collections. The only catch was that the position was for Archivist of the Carey C. Shuart Women's Archive and Research Collection, and involved papers and materials from the Department of Women's, Gender and Sexuality Studies. Despite this fact, I applied for the position because I felt that my skills and the experience I had acquired while working at the Gregory School for nearly three years were transferable, including my donor relations experience. I had also supervised and delegated responsibilities as assistant manager to library staff and was ready to supervise others under my charge. As a seasoned archivist, I was ready to take on the next challenge that an academic library would provide.

Despite my qualifications and experience, I was still my own worst critic. I felt as though I was taking on a position that I was ill equipped to handle and unqualified for. My own biases and predilections for what the position entailed started to kick in once again. I felt like there were a lot of strikes working against me. First, I wasn't a woman. I was a man applying for a position that would represent the Shuart Women's Archive to campus, faculty, and the public that utilized the archives. Second, I was a Chinese American man who was applying for the position. Traditional stereotypes (negative and positive) abound for Asian Americans. Concepts such as "foreigners," "smart or technologically savvy," "academically successful or intelligent," "hard-working or diligent," "obedient or submissive," "docile," and "accommodating" to name but a few are often used.[10] Based on these stereotypes Asian American men have often times been emasculated and deemed more feminine or less of a man by western society and culture. With these stereotypes in place, how much further afield could I get by applying for the position? Third, I did not possess any sort of undergraduate or graduate degree in Women's Studies or Sexuality Studies. So my credibility in the eyes of donors who were women or organizations founded by women weighed heavily on my mind. As an archivist for the Shuart Women's Archive, I would be expected to work closely with a group called the Friends of Women's Studies. They were responsible for starting the Women's Archives, the Department of Women's, Gender and Sexuality Studies and I would be working with them to identify and add to the collections. The benefactor, Carey Shuart, had been heavily involved with this group, and I wondered how I would be received by them as a man—would I be viewed suspiciously, as an outsider?

Another challenge that I faced was that the position required outreach at events such as Table Talk, an annual fundraising event that raises money to support the Friends of Women's Studies and the Shuart Women's Archive. I also faced the challenge of working towards keeping

10. Yueh-Ting Lee, et al., "How Are Asian Americans Seen and Evaluated? Examining Ethnic Stereotypes and Their Cultural Complexity," *Cross-Cultural Communication* 10, no. 2 (2014), 99.

a continuing appointment position. What that means is that even though we are not technically considered teaching faculty, we are still expected to perform and meet the requirements necessary to be promoted from Assistant Librarian to Associate Librarian within six years' time and then ultimately, with substantial experience, to full Librarian status. This is akin to tenure in the faculty ranks. Also, each librarian is expected to demonstrate a record of library service and scholarship through committee work, publications, presentations, awards, professional development, and outreach to the campus and surrounding community.

I went through the interview process at the University of Houston, which was an all-day interview with dinner the night before and breakfast the following morning with a group of librarians. Following breakfast, there would be an open forum presentation, then interviews with the Dean and Assistant Deans, then lunch with the librarians, followed by more interviews with the Special Collection Department, and then concluding with an interview by the search committee. It was a very thorough vetting process that tests your mental abilities, as well as one that challenges stamina. My main thought and goal was to stay consistent and on point and that this was a marathon, not a sprint. I will say that the recruiting and interview process was consistent; after a day spent in interviews, you come away with the impression that the questions posed are the same throughout to see if there are inconsistencies in your response and to gauge whether you would be the right candidate and fit for the existing culture.

To my great surprise and relief, I was hired for the position. I really did not think I had much of a chance based on my background and work experience at the African American Library at the Gregory School. Although I did well in the interview process, at the time I thought my interview may have been granted as more of a formality than it was as an opportunity to be considered for the position. I also knew going into the interview process that I would be the only person of color within the department, as well as the only male to hold a librarian's rank. As an archivist and librarian of color, I felt like I had a big disadvantage compared to some of my colleagues who had been publishing, working on the committees, and doing professional development. I felt as though my CV and resume were light and inadequate in many areas. I didn't think that many of the things I had done at the Gregory School would be counted toward any of requirements for promotion, and that I would be in effect starting from scratch in building my academic career. Feelings of inadequacy and distress are not uncommon among Asian Americans in any profession.[11] These emotions are often tied into strong feelings of guilt, shame, and trying to live up to a perceived standard, as well as seeking approval. Asian Americans are more willing to present problems related to academics and career to counseling because they can be easily addressed and fixed. However, discussing feelings of inadequacy could bring shame or stigma, and present a sense of weakness to others perceive them, so these emotions are repressed and brushed aside.[12]

I had insecurities and still do, but it is a different kind of insecurity from what I experienced at the Gregory School, where I had to contend with acceptance by the African American community and donors. I felt isolated, by myself, and on my own in my new job. I also felt the need to perform twice or three times as hard because of who I was. I felt the need to prove myself and justify my hire, feeling as though I would be looked at under the microscope. I had no role models or anyone like myself within Special Collections or within my particular environment who could show me the way or advise me on how to manage my career within the academic library setting. I know it is cliché to say, but I felt as though I was a pioneer or trailblazer of sorts, that I was forging my own path for the first time and figuring things out for myself as I went along. Apparently I am not alone in feeling this way, according to studies of job satisfaction among teaching faculty of color. Recurrent themes encountered are: feelings of isolation and tokenism; lack of access to social networks; lack of mentors; perceptions that their research was undervalued; challenges in terms of negotiating identity; hidden

---

11. David Cheng, Frederick T.L. Leong, and Robert Geist, "Cultural Differences in Psychological Distress Between Asian and American College Students," *Journal of Multicultural Counseling & Development* 21(3) (1993), 183.

12. Ibid.

workloads; lack of support; differing expectations; and organizational climate issues.[13] Although I did not experience all these themes, a few stood out, particularly isolation and hidden workloads which did give me pause. With that amount of pressure, it sometimes feels like the loneliest place in the world, not knowing who to turn to or where to go, while trying to keep it all inside and perform well at the same time. My work/life balance could not be characterized as good in this situation. I would say it is skewed more toward work, at the expense of life and family at this point.

It's been over two years since I was hired on at the University of Houston Libraries Special Collections. Within that time I have cultivated the collections and brought in additional papers and collections for the Shuart Women's Archive, worked with donors, and built relationships with the Director of Women's, Gender and Sexuality Studies and with members of the Friends of Women's Studies. Through their networking and referrals I have been in touch with prominent women in the area who have been involved with or started organizations that have been instrumental in shaping history within Houston and the State of Texas. I have also been invited to serve on and chair committees, such as the Library Strategic Directions and the Micro-grant Committee. I have performed library service to external constituents such as the University Commission on Women, whose mission is promoting and addressing issues important to women faculty, staff, and students all across campus. I have also represented the library as a member of Houston Area Rainbow Collective History (ARCH), sharing my expertise on archival best practices and procedures for individuals and organizations interested in preserving gay history. I have developed an exhibit for the Women's Archive, promoted collections at the annual Table Talk event, given a presentation, conducted tours, and submitted articles for publication. In short, it has been a very eventful and productive two years.

---

13. Ione T. Damasco and Dracine Hodges, "Tenure and Promotion Experiences of Academic Librarians of Color," *College & Research Libraries* 73 (2012), 282.

Despite my own insecurities and reservations about how this would all play out as a Chinese American man in the position of the Shuart Women's Archivist, I have found that my colleagues within the library and also the members of the Friends of the Women's Studies genuinely like working with me and have welcomed me with open arms. I attribute this to my "can do" attitude, my professionalism, and the way that I treat others as I would like to be treated. I believe that other people sense that I am a genuine person who is willing to collaborate with them and make things work for the sake of the team or the department. There is also a sense of trust because in the years that I have worked with the library and the department, I have cultivated good will and demonstrated my competence in dealing with donors, processing collections, and honoring my commitments in a timely manner. Above all, I think that my collegiality and my ability to show that I care have endeared me to others and served me well both at the African American Library and in my current position. It seems that other Asian Americans within the field who have progressed into upper management also attribute their success to these qualities. Kenneth Yamashita, former president of the Asian/Pacific American Library Association, stated in a 2013 article that "inclusiveness and consensus-based decision making are very important to me. These qualities might be characterized as my Asian American (emphasis on "American") leadership style."[14]

There is a price to be paid for being well received and being the model citizen. Damasco and Hodges caution that "new library faculty are advised to be organized, to seek out peer mentors, to develop a balanced and regularly updated portfolio, to set realistic expectations, to avoid too many service commitments, and to recognize job stressors in order to seek help when needed."[15] This sounds logical and reasonable

---

14. Melissa I. Cardenas-Dow, "APA Library Leader Interview: Kenneth A. Yamashita, Stockton, California," accessed June 28, 2014, http://www.apalaweb. org/apa-library-leader-interview-kenneth-a-yamashita-stockton-california/.

15. Ione T. Damasco and Dracine Hodges, "Tenure and Promotion Experiences of Academic Librarians of Color," *College & Research Libraries* 73 (2012), 281.

in the theoretical sense, but in my experience it has been anything but that. When you are thrust into a new situation and you have to prove yourself, oftentimes you do take on more than you can chew to show that you can do it. Sometimes you don't know what has hit you until it is too late. There is also the factor of pride, which prevents asking for help and knowing when to seek it. I suspect some librarians of color such as myself may not ask for help both out of a sense of pride and for fear of showing weakness and failure. As a result, more and more individuals have sought me out for serving in various capacities or for partnering in papers and projects. Difficult as it may be, I have had to learn to scale back and say "no" to many individuals' requests as I must guard my time and really focus on the events and projects that have a greater impact on my promotion. Speaking of promotion, I am currently in the process of compiling my CV, documentation, and portfolio for my third year review by the Library Promotion Committee. All the materials need to be submitted by mid-September of this year for consideration. Fortunately I have had a librarian promotion mentor who has coached me through the process. We would meet bi-monthly to discuss goals, accomplishments, and work I have done that could be included in my portfolio. She has also been instrumental in answering any additional questions I have had in regards to the promotion criteria and selection of references. Having undergone the same process herself, she has helped to demystify what is involved in the process and is making sure that I have all my ducks in a row before submitting my materials. In her article, "Retaining and Advancing Librarians of Color," Johnson emphasizes that "mentoring can enhance an individual's capacity to make progress and develop skills that will satisfy performance and promotion criteria."[16]

This is not to say I am still not worried, but my mentor has made it more manageable. She provides me with what Johnson would call "career enhancing and psychosocial"[17] functions through mentorship.

---

16. Peggy Johnson, "Retaining and Advancing Librarians of Color," *College & Research Libraries* 68 (2007), 405.

17. Ibid.

My worries are mostly about what is unknown, and the sense of losing control and turning my life's work over to others to decide the outcome. I also wonder if I have done enough to date with my accomplishments and professional activities, and will they be fully reflected in the portfolio that I am about to present? This is where my insecurities and sometimes self-doubt rear their ugly heads; in addition to the feeling that I am not good enough. I am also afraid that I will be discovered or considered a fraud or worse among my peers. Rather than reach out to a support group or resource such as the Archivists and Archives of Color Roundtable, I chose to try to deal with it myself, or suppress my feelings externally. I have felt that my feelings of shame, inadequacy, and guilt have caused me to avoid confronting the emotional turmoil. Yet by doing so, I have perpetuated what Cheng, Leong, and Geist (1993) have identified as honoring the family name by not admitting there is an emotional problem in order to save face and avoid shame.[18]

As hard as it is to say, I really do care what others think of me, especially among a panel of peers and colleagues. I have always been one who worked to please my superiors, donors, and colleagues, sometimes at the expense of my own time and self-worth. At other times have overextended myself. I can be my own worst personal critic. This is one of the cross-roads I face as an aspiring Assistant Librarian who hopes to make it onto the continuing appointment track as Associate Librarian by my sixth year. I wish I could tell you a happy story and say that I will make it. The truth of the matter is I am not sure at this point. I truly hope to have an opportunity to provide an update or retrospective into my tenure process, providing insight for other librarians and archivists regarding what I went through and ultimately hopefully accomplished in receiving a continuing appointment in my profession. I suppose that if things turn out to be less than favorable, then what I will have to say

---

18. David Cheng, Frederick T.L. Leong, and Robert Geist, "Cultural Differences in Psychological Distress Between Asian and American College Students," *Journal of Multicultural Counseling & Development* 21, no. 3 (1993), 183-184.

will also prove to be instructive on what not to do and guide others in areas where I came up short.

Conclusion

What I have learned in the final analysis is that communities and institutions care more about the work that you do and the amount that you care than the color of one's skin. It is my personal opinion that the measure is more of your work and not your racial category. Sure, there are those who will continue to judge, fairly or not, about who they would like to see as their ideal, but that is their problem. We shouldn't and needn't take them to heart and let it interfere with our worth as professionals. As archivists and librarians of color we need to get out of our own head and out of our own way. As professionals of color, we have a unique and valuable skill set that is transferable to positions outside of our own communities and comfort levels. If anything, this skill set is the great equalizer—the position at hand usually doesn't care what color you are. They only care that you get the job done, are accountable, and produce a good product. If anything, I think that library schools that prepare future librarians and archivists should embrace a new paradigm shift and offer courses and practicums that push graduates outside of their comfort levels. This sentiment was echoed in a 2008 paper delivered at the National Diversity Libraries Conference: "As new librarians of color we should be aware of how institutions think of us and benefit from us and we must carefully consider the implications for our careers."[19] Bright, King, and Lilton add, "some might enjoy and thrive in this environment but other new librarians of color might be more interested in the functional side of librarianship and might want

---

19. Kawanna Bright, Pambanisha King, and Deborah Lilton, "When Diversity is Too Much: New Librarians of Color and Expectations for Involvement in Library Diversity Initiatives" (paper presented at the annual National Diversity in Libraries Conference, Louisville, Kentucky, October 1-4, 2008: 1-45), 41.

to think of strategies to develop their careers accordingly."[20] Professionals may end up working with constituents and communities that don't look like they do or are not what they initially envisioned for their linear career path, just as I certainly didn't. But I still managed to not only survive but to thrive, even though at times I felt like a fish out of water, gasping for its last breath. I am still managing to forge my own path.

References

Biafora, F.A., Jr., D. L. Taylor, G. J. Warheit, R.S. Zimmerman, and W. Vega. "Cultural Mistrust and Racial Awareness among Ethnically Diverse Black Adolescent Boys." *Journal of Black Psychology* 19, no. 3 (1993): 266-281

Bright, Kawanna, Pambanisha King, and Deborah Lilton. "When Diversity is Too Much: New Librarians of Color and Expectations for Involvement in Library Diversity Initiatives." Paper presented at the annual National Diversity in Libraries Conference, Louisville, KY, October 1-4, 2008.

Cardenas-Dow, Melissa I. "APA Library Leader Interview: Kenneth A. Yamashita, Stockton, California." Accessed June 28, 2014. http://www.apalaweb.org/apa-library-leader-interview-kenneth-a-yamashita-stockton-california/.

Chang, Hui-Feng. "Ethnic and Racial Diversity in Academic and Research Libraries: Past, Present, and Future." Paper presented at the annual Association of College & Research Libraries Conference, Indianapolis, IN, April 10-13, 2013.

Cheng, David, Frederick T.L. Leong, and Robert Geist. "Cultural Differences in Psychological Distress Between Asian and American College Students." *Journal of Multicultural Counseling & Development* 21, no. 3 (1993): 182-189.

---

20. Ibid.

Damasco, Ione T. and Dracine Hodges. "Tenure and Promotion Experiences of Academic Librarians of Color." *College & Research Libraries* 73 (2012): 279-301.

Flinn, Andrew, Mary Stevens, and Elizabeth Shepherd. "Whose Memories, Whose Archives? Independent Community Archives, Autonomy and the Mainstream." *Archival Science* 9 (2009): 71-86.

Johnson, Peggy. "Retaining and Advancing Librarians of Color." *College & Research Libraries* 68 (2007): 405-417.

Lee, Yueh-Ting, Victor C. Ottai, Canchu Lin, and Sydney Xinni Chan. "How Are Asian Americans Seen and Evaluated? Examining Ethnic Stereotypes and Their Cultural Complexity." *Cross-Cultural Communication* 10, no. 2 (2014): 98-111.

Speck, Jason G. "Protecting Public Trust: An Archival Wake-Up Call." *Journal of Archival Organization* 8, no. 1 (2010): 31-53.

Wong, Paul, Chiengpin Faith Lai, Richard Nagasawa, and Tieming Lin. "Asian Americans as a Model Minority: Self-Perceptions and Perceptions by Other Racial Groups." *Sociological Perspectives* 41, no. 1 (1998): 95-118.

Chapter 9

RACIAL REALISM OR FOOLISH OPTIMISM: AN AFRICAN AMERICAN MUSLIM WOMAN IN THE FIELD

Rebecca Hankins

Defining the Problem

Since starting this essay the public outrage at the epidemic killings of black males by white police officers throughout this country has made me rethink my words. As a mother of four black males and grandmother to three black males, I understand the vulnerability and anguish of Black communities. These are not new dangers suffered by people of color, or black males specifically. These are part of a larger problem that makes the discussion of issues concerning the lack of people of color in librarianship and archives seem insignificant. I am angry and my essay reflects that anger, but I ask you to think critically about how the lack of representation, even in libraries and archives, is symptomatic of the society as a whole. If there's one thing we can be assured of, as evidenced by some of the pronouncements of our Supreme Court's new female judges, the lack of representation of people of color has a significant impact on one's understanding of injustice; i.e. shared experiences and mutual empathy have consequences that can mean the difference between valued inclusion vs. "alienated agency." Alienated agency means that not only are people alienated from what is considered normal society or what Dr. Joe Feagin terms "the white racial frame," but they no longer have agency, status, or a sense that they belong to that society.

Understanding the *white racial frame* helps to comprehend the structural and systemic racism within American society and why adopting Bell's notion of *racial realism* is part of the title of this essay. The *white racial frame* theory, as outlined by Feagin, is defined as "an overarching worldview, one that encompasses important racial ideas, terms, images, emotions, and interpretations. For centuries now, it has been a basic and foundational frame from which a substantial majority of white Americans-as well as others seeking to conform to white norms-view our highly racialized society"[1]. This theory is useful in understanding race relations amongst those who wish to adopt whiteness as a means of mobility in the U.S. and how that affects their interactions with African Americans. Feagin argues that "[t]erms like 'American dream' and 'American culture' are typically used to refer primarily to the values, ideals, or preferences of whites"[2] which if looked at from an economic perspective requires some form of assimilation to white norms in order to acquire economic mobility. In a 1948 interview, Albert Einstein is quoted saying, "Race prejudice has unfortunately become an American tradition which is uncritically handed down from one generation to the next."[3] More surprising, however, is Einstein's statement in the same interview: "The only remedies [to racism] are enlightenment and education. This is a slow and painstaking process in which all right-thinking people should take part."[4] These statements are salient reminders of the enduring nature of racism.

In his article, "Racial Realism," the late Harvard Law Professor Derrick Bell wrote that many of our more conservative Supreme Court

---

1. Joe R. Feagin, *The White Racial Frame: Centuries of Racial Framing and Counter-Framing* (New York: Routledge, 2010), 3.

2. Ibid., 7.

3. Albert Einstein, "Interview with the *Cheyney Record*, October, 1948," quoted in Fred Jerome and Rodger Taylor, *Einstein on Race and Racism* (Rutgers, NJ: Rutgers University Press, 2006), 148.

4. Ibid.

Justices, similar to earlier pronouncements, "settled cases not by deductive reasoning, but rather by reliance on value-laden, personal beliefs... determined by one's particular environment."[5] He further notes that in the notorious UC Berkeley v. Bakke decision, "the Court effectively made a choice to ignore historical patterns, to ignore contemporary statistics, and to ignore flexible reasoning. Following a Realist approach, the Court would have observed the social landscape and noticed the skewed representation of minority medical school students."[6] This is the same thinking we face in hiring decisions, promotion, and retention of people of color. Bell's words, written in 1991, offer an amazing foresight into what has become our present, and I dare say, our future. "Today, blacks experiencing rejection for a job, a home, a promotion, anguish over whether race or individual failing prompted their exclusion. Either conclusion breeds frustration and eventually despair. We call ourselves African Americans, but despite centuries of struggle, none of us—no matter our prestige or position-is more than a few steps away from a racially motivated exclusion, restriction or affront."[7]

Racial Realism

The combination of racism and white racial framing are systemic, facts that all people of color generally and African Americans specifically, must understand and recognize in order to adopt a mindset that deals with these realities, hence Bell's racial realism.[8] For Bell, who eventually had to leave Harvard due to the reality that Harvard was not interested in hiring Black female law professors, racism is not only an impediment to Black mobility, but it was so systemic that to rid itself of racism, the society would have to be fundamentally changed and

---

5. Derrick Bell, "Racial Realism," *Connecticut Law Review*, 24, no. 2 (1992), 365. Accessed October 5, 2014, http://liberalarts.iupui.edu/mpsg/Essays/Bell%20-%20Racial%20Realism.pdf

6. Ibid, 369.

7. Ibid., 374.

8. Ibid., 365.

that was never going to happen. Bell's notion of racial realism is meant for African Americans to stop looking for some remedies from a racist system that can only lead to despair. We, as people of color, need to start thinking of ways to protect and advance our own interests rather than thinking society will remedy inequality and injustice. As Bell notes "The Racial Realism that we must seek is simply a hard-eyed view of racism as it is and our subordinate role in it. We must realize, as our slave forebears, that the struggle for freedom is, at bottom, a manifestation of our humanity that survives and grows stronger through resistance to oppression, even if that oppression is never overcome."[9] These are the ideas that continue to drive my career and what I personally face as an African American Muslim woman trying to find a job, earn tenure, and advance within the library science and archival fields.

Terrell Jermaine Starr's article on Alternet.org titled "Dear White People: Here Are 5 Reasons Why You Can't Really Feel Black Pain"[10] has sage advice, but Reason #3 is particularly relevant to the subject of my essay: "The employment market is incredibly racist." Starr's article is about representation, the lack thereof for black people and how it is allowed to define who we are, and more importantly, how it impacts our existence in America. Representation through a diverse workforce, in all areas but especially in the library/archival professions, has a significant and strategic impact on our daily lives. Providing a population access to information and history that is inclusive, broad, and diverse gives a sense of agency to all citizens. Starr succinctly touches on many of the issues people of color face in trying to find jobs and/or to reach some economic security. Understanding racism and its impact on my job prospects and work can be daunting and defeating, but necessary to maintaining my resolve.

---

9. Ibid., 378.

10. Terrell Jermaine Starr, "Dear White People: Here Are 5 Reasons Why You Can't Really Feel Black Pain," Alternet. org, last modified December 4, 2014, http://www.alternet.org/dear-white-people-here-are-5-reasons-why-you-cant-really-feel-black-pain.

The Archives

The essays in this monograph have touched on a number of significant and important areas in the field of librarianship, but its sister profession, archives, is only represented by one other the essay, by Vince Lee. My essay will discuss how the archival field has approached these issues of inclusion, representation, and diversity from the perspective of a tenured, African American, Muslim woman at a predominantly white institution. My experience is sufficiently unique in that, as the literature notes, there are very few African American librarians of color, but for African American Muslim archivists the numbers are so small, we all know each other! A few years ago a few of us attempted to start a group of Muslim Librarians and Archivists, but it failed because there are so few of us. The notion of finding mentors or modeling leadership behaviors of predecessors is also non-existent for me within the archival profession. I don't know of any African American Muslims archivists or African American females that are directors or who lead archives within an academic environment in this country. A search of the Archivists and Archives of Color Roundtable's Directory of Members[11] attests that most of its members who are directors work in museums, programs, or archival environments that are not on academic campuses. There are a few African American women who lead academic libraries, but the archival world has traditionally been the domain of white male leadership, and there appears to be very little done to interrupt that paradigm. The few Muslim archivists I have met were either in government documents work or are primarily working in librarianship. I know of only one other African American Muslim woman who is an archivist working in academia, and we often commiserate!

In 2004 the Society of American Archivists, the largest professional archival organization in the world, conducted an extensive survey of the

---

11. Archivists and Archives of Color Roundtable, 2012 Directory of Membership, retrieved October 12, 2014, http://www2.archivists.org/sites/all/files/2012%20AAC%20Directory.pdf.

archival field titled A*CENSUS.[12] One of its four major challenges was "Ensuring that recruitment efforts focus on attracting archivists who more closely reflect the diversity of society at large." It is interesting that none of the solutions offered included providing leadership or mentoring opportunities for those minorities already in the field. As Agnes K. Bradshaw, writing in this volume, has noted, there appears to be a real lack of awareness or concern regarding what should be done with those already in the pipeline. Most of the initiatives target the recruitment, education, and skill development of younger archivists, with almost no mention of retention for older archivists. When older archivists are mentioned, their value is in relation to "transferring knowledge"[13] to younger members and stepping aside so that younger archivists can develop leadership skills. Putting aside all of these demographic issues in the archival field, the profession historically has been fraught with controversy.

The archival profession has had a troubling history of racial engagement as recounted in Alex H. Poole's recent article in the *American Archivist* titled "The Strange Career of Jim Crow Archives: Race, Space, and History in the Mid-Twentieth-Century American South"; he states that "the archive is never a neutral space"[14] —that someone's biases, preferences, and conceptions of what is important have long-term consequences for what we deem historical or whose history we value. Poole's article highlights the struggle to provide equal access to archival collections for African American historians and how, too often, it was those archivists charged with providing access who were the obstacles to that access. Poole's discussion of the University of North Carolina's troubling statements and practices related to segregation and access

---

12. A*CENSUS: Archival Census and Education Needs Survey in the United States, *American Archivist* 69, no. 2 (2006): 291-618. Retrieved November 20, 2014, http://www2.archivists.org/sites/all/files/ACENSUS-Final.pdf.

13. Ibid, 320.

14. Alex H. Poole, "The Strange Career of Jim Crow Archives: Race, Space, and History in the Mid-Twentieth-Century American South," *American Archivist* 77, no. 1 (2014), 23.

points out that such actions were not unique, especially in the South. Similarly, access to leadership roles that can often mitigate these kinds of behaviors has been significantly more difficult for African Americans specifically, and people of color generally, in the archival arena, especially within academic environments.

Foolish Optimism?

With all of these previously noted issues in the field of archives, lack of representation, marginalization, and outright discrimination, how does one remain optimistic and engaged? I have forged ahead in the archival profession with some successes. I have always been a minority within a minority, a living example of the double consciousness that W. B. Du Bois talks about. I am also a victim of double marginality, as an African American Muslim in a society that privileges African American Christians. I bring a unique perspective to archives and librarianship just by being who I am, representing those populations that we never consider. I am passionate about my career as an archivist and take every opportunity to inform others about this wonderful profession and the work we perform as archivists. I embody and take very seriously the definition of archivists used by Mark Greene in his SAA presidential address: "archivists are professionals with the power of defining and making accessible the primary sources of history, primary sources that protect rights, educate students, inform the public, and support a primal human desire to understand our past."[15] As a seasoned archivist I have also inculcated the ideas that are central to the Society of American Archivists' *Archival Values*, including "Recognizing that use is the fundamental reason for keeping archives, archivists actively promote open and equitable access to the records in their care within the context of their institutions' missions and their intended user groups. They

---

15. Mark A. Greene, "The Power of Archives: Archivists' Values and Value in the Post-Modern Age," *American Archivist* 72, no. 1 (2009), 40.

minimize restrictions and maximize ease of access."[16] To facilitate access, I have presented at conferences, served on committees, and published articles in library, archival, and other peer-reviewed journals on subjects that range from Black feminist writers and Black and Hispanic art in special collections, to Islamic science fiction, fantasy, and comic book literature. My professional work, service to the profession, and scholarly publishing have resulted in my recent successful tenure bid at Texas A&M University. As noted in the letter sent to me from the President of Texas A&M University, "Tenure is an earned recognition of capability, and promotion is an acknowledgment of performance. This measure of your achievement is also an indicator of the high esteem in which you are held by your peers."

I have done everything and attended all of the programs that were supposed to prime one for leadership in the profession, including attending the Minnesota Institute for Early Career Librarians, being selected for the Archival Leadership Institute, chairing both roundtables and sections in ALA, being elected to SAA Council, receiving a prestigious Archival Fellowship, and mentoring countless young people (some of whom have gone on to leadership positions) and other colleagues. I've developed workshops and classes, trained interns, provided leadership and service outside of the library, developed strong donor relations, written grants, developed world-renowned collections (Afro-centric, LGBTQ, Africana, and Women & Gender), published research that has received considerable notice (in that I've been invited to present nationally, regionally, and internationally), but yet I've never been given an opportunity to lead or work administratively in my library, except on a rotating basis for one committee. The numerous times I have applied for leadership opportunities in the archives or library, they have all been rejected with the note that I don't fit the qualifications; inadequate leadership or administrative experience are the most common reasons for rejection.

---

16. Society of American Archivists, "SAA Core Values Statement and Code of Ethics," 2011, http://www2.archivists.org/statements/saa-core-values-statement-and-code-of-ethics.

Conclusions

In my career I have attempted to embrace Kenji Yoshino's concept of "covering,"[17] trying to fit in and smile my way through a hostile environment. I've read about and tried to incorporate Melissa Harris-Perry's "dissemblance,"[18] concealing one's true self, which is similar to Yoshino's concept. I have also tried hard not to be Devon Carbade's "fifth Black woman,"[19] the one outlier to the four successful Black women, but my presentation as a hijab-wearing, African American Muslim woman always marks me as different. I have been the victim of micro-agressions and cultural biases on many levels. This occurs not only from the majority population; because my presentation distinguishes me as a religious minority, I experience double marginality and discrimination. Even so, the courts in the Carbade case rejected her claims of discrimination based on identity performance because they viewed it as a mutable trait. So according to the courts, I should change the way I look in order to fit in; but that is basically asking me to give up my practice of my religion and how I interpret it.

My adoption of Bell's racial realism has been extremely important to my ability to maintain a balance and remain productive. I am doing my part to diversify the historical record, focusing on alternative movements and activism by people of color. In numerous ways I have used the archival and library fields as a means of resistance, concentrating on collecting in areas of the invisible and voiceless. That means I have focused on Black and Brown participation in the communist/socialist parties, revolutionary and radical movements, radical journalists, the labor industry, and those who had a substantial impact on people of color in the late 1800s and early 1900s. Much of this material is

---

17. Kenji Yoshino, *Covering: The Hidden Assault on Our Civil Rights*, New York: Random House, 2006.

18. Melissa Harris-Perry, *Sister Citizen*, New Haven, CT: Yale University Press, 2011.

19. Devon Carbade and Mitu Gulate, "The Fifth Black Woman." *Contemporary Legal Issues* 11 (2001): 701-729.

concentrated in a few national archives, but these documents are not as widely held as the resources on the mainstream Modern Civil Rights movement material, or the non-violent or social activism movements of the late 1950s-1970s. I'm also focusing on other religious groups and their impact and the activities these groups chose to involve themselves in to realize the "American Dream." In the years to come there will be archives dedicated to Muslims, Hindus, Sikhs, Buddhists, South and Central Americans, Arab Americans, Pakistani, Iraqis, Syrians, and others immigrants who have been in this country for over a hundred years, but whose lives and activities have not been documented in a systematic or organized fashion.

My embracing of racial realism understands that this is a challenge for us all, to make our repositories more diverse in our collections and collecting policies, and to reduce the feelings of invisibility and marginalization of these overlooked populations. As Bell notes, resistance can take many forms; for me in the archival world, that means documenting the humanity of all of America's citizens. In his final anecdote about Mrs. MacDonald's work for equality, she sums up my determination in the face of racism and powerlessness, when she answers his question about why she continues by saying: "... I lives to harass white folks."[20] I love that note of defiance, but I prefer my defiance to be have a more positive spin, "I live to ensure that people of color have a voice and are not silenced in the archival record, the library, and the informational world."

References

Archivists and Archives of Color Roundtable. *2012 Directory of Membership.* http://www2.archivists.org/sites/all/files/2012%20 AAC%20Directory.pdf

"A*CENSUS: Archival Census and Education Needs Survey in the United States." *American Archivist* 69, no. 2 (2006): 291-618. Retrieved November 20, 2014. http://www2.archivists.org/ sites/all/files/ACENSUS-Final.pdf

20. Bell, "Racial Realism," 378.

Bell, Derrick. "Racial Realism." *Connecticut Law Review* 24, no. 2 (1992): 363-379.

Carbade, Devon W., and Mitu Gulate. "The Fifth Black Woman." *Contemporary Legal Issues* 11 (2001): 701-729.

Feagin, Joe R. *The White Racial Frame: Centuries of Racial Framing and Counter-Framing*. New York: Routledge, 2010.

Greene, Mark A. "The Power of Archives: Archivists' Values and Value in the Post-Modern Age." *American Archivist* 72, no. 1 (2009): 17-41.

Jerome, Fred, and Rodger Taylor. *Einstein on Race and Racism*. Rutgers, NJ: Rutgers University Press, 2006.

Perry, Melissa Harris. *Sister Citizen: Shame, Stereotypes, and Black Women in America*. New Haven, CT: Yale University Press, 2011.

Poole, Alex H. "The Strange Career of Jim Crow Archives: Race, Space, and History in the Mid-Twentieth-Century American South." *American Archivist* 77, no. 1 (2014): 23-63.

Society of American Archivists. "SAA Core Values Statement and Code of Ethics." 2011. http://www2.archivists.org/statements/saa-core-values-statement-and-code-of-ethics.

Starr, Terrell Jermaine. "Dear White People: Here Are 5 Reasons Why You Can't Really Feel Black Pain." Alternet.org. Last modified December 4, 2014. http://www.alternet.org/dear-white-people-here-are-5-reasons-why-you-cant-really-feel-black-pain

Yoshino, Kenji. Covering: *The Hidden Assault on Our Civil Rights*. NY: Random House, 2006.

SECTION THREE:

PERSONAL DIVERSITY STORIES

Chapter 10

THE VETERAN AND THE ROOKIE: OUR STORY, OUR EXPERIENCE

Rhonda E. Fowler and Karen Rogers-Collins

The Veteran

When I began my career in librarianship, it was at the end of an era that included the card catalog. The online catalog was slowly replacing physical cards and databases were replacing indices. Fast forward to 2014 and technology is one of the few things that has changed dramatically in the library where I am employed. Although technology has changed considerably, librarians in the institution have stayed the same. The gender representation of librarians has changed, but the ethnicity of librarians has remained the same. In the 1990s-2012, we managed to attract more men into the profession to achieve gender diversity, but we weren't as successful in recruiting people of color into the field and into the institution. Over the last 25 years, the library has hired three female librarians of color, seven white male librarians, and ten white females. According to the American Library Association (ALA) in their document "Diversity Counts 2009-2010," the total number of librarians is 118,666. Demographic totals include 104,392 Whites, 6,160 African Americans, 3,661 Latinos, 185 Native Americans including Alaskan, and 1,008 listed as two or more races.[1] The demographic information offered includes additional background on the racial make-up of librarians nation-wide.

Career and Evaluation Process

My path into academic librarianship might differ from other people in academic librarianship. After five years of working in the public library system as a library aide, I began working my current institution as a library assistant in the cataloging department. I took a leave from that position to pursue a library science degree at another institution, concentrating in reference and public service. I decided to concentrate on academic librarianship simply because I enjoyed working in an academic environment and hoped that there would be a vacancy by the time I received my Master's degree. Although there were no guarantees that there would be a position available when I graduated, I chose to pursue this area of librarianship. When I was offered a position in my library, I was concerned about accepting it (even though I wanted to work there), because librarians at my institution are required to attain faculty status. Some of the librarians I spoke with informed me that in order to be awarded tenure one had to publish just like regular teaching faculty. I asked myself, do I really wanted to spend time writing articles or engaging in presentations? I spoke with many of the librarians and was assured that I would receive mentoring and guidance throughout the tenure process if I was hired.

I was concerned about the "scholarship" aspects of the tenure process. I was intimidated by having to engage in scholarship that would be a requirement for tenure. I asked tenured librarians about the expectations for scholarship and was told that it was an unwritten policy that in order to fulfill the scholarship requirements, one needed to complete written articles by the time tenure was applied for. Scholarship could

---

1. American Library Association. Office of Diversity. *Diversity Counts, 2009-2010*, http://www.ala.org/aboutala/sites/ala.org.aboutala/files/content/ governance/officers/eb_documents/2012_2013ebdocuments/ebd12_10_ diversity_counts.pdf.

encompass an article in any journal on any subject you were interested in, a presentation at a conference, a book chapter, or a poster session.

In retrospect, in regards to the tenure process, I received considerable guidance and support, but at the time I questioned what possible scholarship I could produce that would be acceptable to the evaluation committee? I felt that even though I was offered a position that increased the diversity of the librarians, it didn't mean that I would be successful in the demanding tenure process. Damasco and Hodges, who have written about retention issues for librarians of color, have stated: "increased recruitment of faculty of color does not guarantee increased retention rates."[2] I became worried about being reappointed yearly, as well as the possibility of being denied tenure in my sixth year. However, my process towards tenure was easier than I had originally imagined. I didn't feel like I was put under any more scrutiny than any other librarian seeking tenure. So my career continued and I was promoted.

Although professionally I received guidance toward tenure and advancement there were other topics that didn't get discussed. The first twenty years of my career I felt isolated when it came to discussing topics such as race and discrimination. I felt that most of my colleagues wanted a pleasant working environment, and really didn't understand what I was talking about because it had not happened to them. According to Johnson, libraries do hire diverse librarians but they want you to conform to the dominant culture.[3] If you don't conform to the culture, then you might have experiences that they don't understand. Sometimes, when I tried to explain a negative encounter or micro-aggression with a patron who treated me differently because of the color of my skin, I felt my colleagues dismissed my experiences. This type of micro-aggression might be labeled as micro-invalidation, which is characterized by communications that exclude, negate, or nullify the psychological thoughts,

2. Ione T. Damasco and Dracine Hodges, "Tenure and Promotion Experiences of Academic Librarians of Color," *College and Research Libraries* 73, no. 3 (2012), 279.

3. Peggy Johnson, "Retaining and Advancing Librarians of Color," *College and Research Libraries* 68, no. 5 (2007), 408.

feelings, or experiential reality of a person of color.[4] My question is: how do librarians gauge experiences of micro-aggression? For example, a patron came to the reference desk and said she was looking for information on poverty and welfare. I asked what her focus of research was, and she informed me that she equated Blacks with poverty and welfare, which I was disagreed with. I thought it would be in the best interests of both of us if someone else assisted her, so I referred her to another librarian. As this example illustrates, it has been a constant battle for me as one of only two African American librarians in the library for numerous years. I was the only African American librarian until my colleague, another African American librarian, was hired four years ago. Could it be that my colleagues suffered from aversion to racism, which is when many white Americans believe that they are non-prejudiced?[5] Their inability to empathize and sometimes acknowledge my feelings has made me wonder.

Many of the librarians tend to be isolated according to the work they do in the library. In the previous library we had shared offices, so during the day we were able to talk with each other as well as confer and share ideas with each other. Being surrounded by colleagues, informal mentoring took place. Back then mentoring was more natural and one didn't have to seek someone out like you do now. At the time at that office there were three or four librarians that you could talk, brainstorm, and collaborate with. Most problems were taken care of quickly because you could have an informal meeting and discuss, and would get feedback about whatever the issue was that needed to be solved. Prior to when the new librarian of color was hired, I was isolated on the second floor because the government documents are located on that floor and I felt I needed to be near the collection. Now I just have to step out of my office into the office next door for a quick conversation about work or other topics.

---

4. Dearald Wing Sue, "Racial Microaggressions in Everyday Life: Implications for Clinical Practice" *American Psychologist* 62, no. 4 (2007), 275.

5. Samuel L. Gaertner and John F. Dovidio, *Reducing Intergroup Bias: The Common Ingroup Identity Model* (Philadelphia: Psychology Press, 2000), 13.

Another part of the environment is not related to colleagues but rather others who will often let you know that they could do your job and that you should be doing what they would do in your position. Eventually, this behavior weighs you down and you ask yourself if you really want to spend the next ten years listening to opinions from other librarians who are not in your position and don't have your responsibilities, but they think they can do your job better than you. At some point, it wears you down.

As I reflect on my professional career, I have been in the same work place for over twenty-five years. I have seen many things change over the years, from our profession to the political climate we live in. However, even with these changes and the respect that I feel my colleagues give me, I have to wonder why most of them are not more open to collaborating on scholarship with me. In the twenty-five plus years that I have been here I have only had one non-librarian of color ask me to work on scholarship with her. Could it be that my colleagues are guilty of aversive racism as referred to above? Could it be that they don't know how to approach me? Or could it be that they think we cannot find topics we can collaborate on? I don't know why other colleagues haven't asked me to collaborate with them on scholarship. It bothers me because I watch other librarians collaborate on projects and often think that I would have been interested in working on that topic. The flip side of the argument is that I could approach my colleagues about working on scholarship, but I often ask myself why I should have to be the one to seek them out?

I came to the profession having to transition from being a paraprofessional and after receiving my MLS, to becoming a new librarian, a role that was a process. I listened to those who mentored me and assisted me to establish my job duties and expectations. In a study on new academic librarians, it was found that the study participants "made sense of job boundaries, duties, and expectations" during their first year or two as librarians.[6] Although this study did not talk about issues the participants

---

6. Laura Sare, Stephen Bale and Bruce Neville, "New Academic Librarians and Their Perceptions of the Profession," *portal: Libraries and the Academy* 12, no. 2 (2012), 193.

had with social problems such as racism, for me this making sense of job duties and boundaries was possible because of the group mentoring I received. In an article written by Peggy Johnson, group mentoring is defined "as a function of professional associations in which the career development of members of that professional group is influenced by the group's exertion of social norms and roles."[7] In her article Johnson studied group mentoring and created learning communities on retention at the University of Minnesota (UM).

At UM they held a biennially training institute geared toward early career librarians of color.[8] Johnson states: "mentoring is particularly critical in the retention of minority librarians."[9] Although the mentoring I received was not geared toward any one group, some of the ideas were similar. For example, I was encouraged to work on professional development and continuing education by attending conferences and pursuing a second master's degree. These are examples of how retention is fostered.[10]

Presently my main area of responsibility is the Government Documents Collection. As the Federal Depository Coordinator, I am responsible for maintaining the collection that is housed in the library. Even though I have not been asked to collaborate on scholarship, when it comes to professional work someone is always there to collaborate and help out. For example, for over thirty years there had always been a full time library clerical assistant in the government documents area. A few years ago the position was cut, which would have left me without clerical assistance and having to do the work of two people. The technical services librarians stepped in and together we developed a plan of action to distribute the workload to other library assistants in

---

7. Johnson, "Retaining and Advancing Librarians of Color," 406.

8. Ibid., 405.

9. Ibid., 407.

10. Ibid., 408.

the Periodicals/Governments Department, as well as the Cataloging Department.

As I approach the last 8-10 years of my career, I look back on it and think about how we have progressed from the card catalog to almost all our work being done on the computer. In spite of the fact that the racial makeup of librarians hasn't changed much and the missed opportunity for scholarship collaboration, the mentoring that I have received towards tenure, as well as the camaraderie over the years, have helped my experience in academic libraries serve as a great and rich experience.

The Rookie

Career

I came to academia in a less traditional way than most of my colleagues. I call myself the "rookie," but that's only as it relates to my time in academic libraries. Before accepting a tenure-track position at a university with 23,000 students pursuing undergraduate, graduate, specialist, doctoral and certificate degrees, I worked for 17 years in special libraries (law, medical, pharmaceutical/corporate).

When I arrived for my interview at the university library in 2010, I was pleasantly surprised to see another African American librarian on the search committee. The university's total workforce is 54% women, 20% minorities, and 12% African American (as reported in the school's annual diversity report). I grew up in the geographical area of the university and acquired my undergraduate degree from it, so I was familiar with the geographical, racial, and ethnic make-up of the area. While working for a global research facility in the past, I had worked with library colleagues nationally and internationally, but I had never worked anywhere that had so many librarians all in one building. There were 23 total faculty librarians – but only one librarian of color. I was somewhat disappointed in, but not surprised by this number.

Tenure Track and Evaluative Process

As a seasoned librarian coming from a special libraries background, riding the faculty tenure-track train has been challenging, particularly in the areas of scholarly and creative activities. With no formal training in developing presentations, conducting original research, and writing for publication, these activities were outside of my comfort zone. I was a practitioner, not a scholar. My previous opinion of life in academia was not positive. The horror stories about what professors endured to make tenure, the tale of publish or perish, was initially a turnoff for me. I knew not all librarians in academia are tenure track faculty, but at our institution they are. A tenure track librarian hired as an instructor spends 6 years in the "evaluation" or probationary stage, and at the beginning of year 6 applies for tenure. I am beginning year 5 of the tenure process, so I have been through a full review at my third year. It has been a stressful and demanding process. The idea of an evaluation committee (of my peers) judging my work and making recommendations on whether or not the university should offer tenure was odd to me. Not being familiar with this type of process, in the back of my mind I wondered and worried if my work would be judged fairly, objectively, and without bias. Generally, the make-up of the evaluation team needs to reflect an understanding of the range of duties and activities of the faculty as a whole, but certainly, that is not always the case. The only criteria for serving on the library evaluation committee are that the faculty members be tenured. The idea is that one is not practicing their profession at a higher level than their tenured colleagues, or that they have an exceptional track record of service and scholarship. I was used to a more simplified performance review process being conducted by a direct supervisor, along with a self-review. Evaluations would be based on written job responsibilities and duties, and merit increases were based on whether one had consistently met and/or exceeded objectives.

I learned from my full review in my third year that it's not just about the work (projects) you complete, and listing achievements and accomplishments, but how you "sell" it. I've been in the workforce long enough to understand the importance of documenting accomplishments, but mastering the art of self-promotion is an ongoing challenge for me; I am learning it.[11]

Most members of an evaluation committee take their roles very seriously and serve honorably on the committee. Members are supposed to deliberate the strengths and weaknesses of each case in good faith and with objectivity, but what about those few librarians who "unknowingly" bring their own biases to the table? Is it easier to positively judge someone who is similar to you in background, culture, work style, or work duties? I don't know the answer to that question. I believe that the relationship one has with one's colleagues on the evaluation committee plays a crucial role in determining the success of the outcome of the process. The evaluation is supposed to be collegial and fair. In a paragraph relating to ratings and how they're determined, the Departmental Evaluation Document (DED) covers the need for candidates to be able to demonstrate the ability to work effectively within a faculty environment—this includes working cooperatively with other faculty members as well as staff. Having a mutually respectful or even a friendly relationship with one's fellow faculty members, the department head, and the Dean of Libraries also helps. If candidates do not establish a collegial relationship with the evaluation committee, they may still do well in the evaluation process if they have an intimidating personality; the evaluation committee may overlook certain weaknesses in one or more of the elements of the evaluation criteria to avoid a confrontation.

The library's DED also outlines the criteria required to achieve tenure: Professional Performance; Scholarly and/or Creative Activity; and Service. Professional Performance is the most important criterion. The library does not utilize any type of points or scoring system, so without a tool to quantify activities, there is room for a great deal of subjectivity in the evaluation process. On the one hand, this is a good thing, as it allows for more discretion on the part of the evaluation committee

---

11. Kerry Ann Rockquemore and Tracey Laszloffy, "Building a Supportive Network," in *The Black Academic's Guide to Winning Tenure—Without Losing Your Soul* (Boulder, CO: Lynne Rienner Publishers, 2008), 175-187.

and administration when rating and evaluating library faculty. On the other hand, the vagueness of the document leave candidates open to uncertainty about whether what they have accomplished is enough.

Each department at our university evaluates tenure-track faculty using criteria set forth in the individual department's Department Evaluation Document (DED) and the contract agreement negotiated by the university's chapter of the American Association of University Professors (AAUP). Our library DED states that the criteria for faculty evaluations must be applied in varying disciplines. Therefore each document is unique. This statement gave me some comfort, but I still wondered if the perspective of the evaluator, who may have unconscious biases or may be unfamiliar or ill-informed about what other faculty members do, would be reflected in the feedback? How does an evaluation team member judge the effectiveness of the tenure candidate in their professional duties and activities if they really don't know or understand or participate in those activities as part of their own day-to-day responsibilities?

As librarians, fitting into the standard criteria for tenure as applied to the teaching faculty is tough, especially for non-public service librarians. Librarians are considered non-teaching faculty so the criteria and techniques used for evaluation are slightly different from those outlined in the AAUP contract. For non-library faculty, teaching/scholarship/service is used for tenure evaluation. The activities and responsibilities of the library faculty are very diverse. It's easier for public service librarians to fit into the teaching faculty model than it is for the technical services librarians. As a technical services librarian, it's harder for me to show my work's impact on student success, even though more and more users are relying heavily on technology, including electronic and digital resources. Our library spends a large percentage of its budget on electronic resources. I lead the team that ensures reliable and optimal access to these information resources.

But how do you explain or prove this or quantify successes in student improvement? Where's the specific evidence? There is some evidence of librarians' impact on student learning outcomes, especially concerning how we contribute to student information literacy, but this is usually from a public service/instruction librarian perspective. Literature on assessment in libraries often looks at usage data and how it relates to collection development and cost per use. I know that's how we have more often used this data, as technical service librarians. Linking student success to how often or not a student uses library resources, particularly the electronic journal and database resources, is more difficult.[12]

Disciplinary faculty sometimes don't understand the technical aspects of what we do as librarians; they only understand the instruction and reference pieces of traditional librarianship. Many librarians in technical services are functional supervisors. This is not as common among public service librarians. The responsibility of overseeing the work of clerical and technical staff brings an extra dimension and challenge to our day-to-day workload. Even though our library evaluation document explains that the ability to organize and supervise staff is part of the professional responsibilities of some library faculty, it sometimes seems to be minimized by some library faculty colleagues. We hear statements like, "that's not faculty work."

It's library faculty work if a librarian was hired to do it. As librarians we work in an environment where not all administrators and disciplinary faculty within the broader campus community are convinced librarians should be faculty anyway. Library faculty colleagues, along with our administration, shouldn't undervalue the professional duties, service areas, and research activities of our own. We get that enough from those outside the profession. As Meredith Farkas researched whether academic librarians are seen as faculty or support staff by the disciplinary faculty, and noted that librarians have image problems regardless of whether they are in public or technical services, and tenure-track or not.[13]

---

12. Brian Cox and Margie Jantti, "Discovering the Impact of Library Use and Student Performance," *EDUCAUSE Review* (18 July 2012), accessed 6 October 2014, http://www.educause.edu/ero/article/discovering-impact-library-use-and-student-performance.

13. Meredith Farkas, "Librarians in Academia: Faculty or Support Staff?" in *Information Wants to Be Free*, last modified October 8, 2005, http://meredith.wolfwater.com/wordpress/2005/10/08/librarians-in-academia-faculty-or-support-staff/.

The university has no particular programs in place to specifically assist any new library faculty, let alone librarians of color, but they do offer a program through the Faculty Development Center, "Planning Your Scholarly Agenda," to help identify long- and short-term goals and objectives for creative and scholarly activity, which is available to all new faculty. This workshop focuses on how to develop a plan for scholarship, but it doesn't offer an overall strategy on how to navigate the path to tenure. Even though I had been a practicing librarian for over 15 years, I still would have benefited from a program that formally paired senior library faculty with new library faculty to provide research advice and opportunities for collaboration, along with mentoring, networking, and socialization into an academic work setting. I think because I have been a librarian for many years, colleagues thought that I didn't need as much help in navigating the academic library waters, and maybe I thought the same thing. I was wrong.

Surviving the tenure process is hard on anyone who has to go through it. Many of the obstacles mentioned are not unique to librarians of color. They cross all segments. I feel extremely fortunate to have a seasoned African-American academic librarian to turn to for guidance. She definitely has schooled me in the unwritten rules of the overall institution. I've also had strong support from non-librarians of color, male and female, but particularly male. I count some of them as my most trusted advisors. I learned early on in my professional career that having strong allies makes the difference in your success or failure in the workplace. If you don't build a safety net around you, when you stumble, the fall can be career ending. Sometimes people don't get tenure; it does happen.[14]

It's reassuring to have folks that have your back, are looking out for you, and guiding you along this process. In recent years the need for strong mentorship and support has become a cornerstone for success in many professions, not just academic librarianship. The ALA's series

---

14. Kimberly Flint-Hamilton, et al., "Surviving Tenure: The Plight of Black Faculty," (panel discussion presented at the Annual Meeting for the Black Catholic Theological Symposium, Boston, MA, 2006).

on mentoring discusses the benefits of providing new hires with both formal and informal mentoring. Cultivating "relational networks," as described in Rockquemore and Laszloffy's guide to winning tenure, relates to this idea of building a community of supporters to help face the challenges of the tenure process.[15]

Life in Academia

Most of our academic institutions claim that they are looking for and appreciate diversity, including diversity of thought and action. Successful organizations need diversity of thought, experiences, and skills. As John Linkner wrote in his *Detroit Free Press* column on April 6, 2014, too often organizations are built with self-lookalikes, because it's comfortable, but homogenous teams bring little innovation or inspiration. Great sports teams don't take the field with 11 quarterbacks, or 9 pitchers, as organizations cannot achieve their potential with only one viewpoint. They need different ages, genders, races, skill sets, experience, educational backgrounds, personalities, and cultures.[16]

Historically, librarianship has been very homogenous (female, Caucasian). Most librarians who are not of color have never been the only one, the "other." Gaertner and Dovidio discuss what they call "pro-ingroup bias."[17] This idea may be why there are so few librarians of color. It's not overt racism or prejudice, but favoritism towards one's own group. Unfortunately, if this theory is true, the consequences are the same. We don't look like them or they do not know people like us, so we're not present.

One study reported that women who don't identify ethnically or racially with their colleagues in the workplace are more likely to lower their career aspirations than women who are racially similar to their

---

15. Rockquemore and Laszloffy, "Building a Supportive Network," 175-187.

16. John Linkner. "A Mix of Ideas and Skills is the Key to Success." *Free Press*, April 6, 2014.

17. Gaertner and Dovidio, "Aversive Racism and Intergroup Bias," 17-20.

co-workers.[18] I don't necessarily agree with this idea, or see it to be true in librarianship; I can see how it could happen, though. Advancing in one's career is difficult. Similar to corporate America, in librarianship we lack the support of mentors and/or sponsors at the decision-making, influential levels. We could use someone to mention our name when new projects and opportunities arise, and to speak highly of us every chance they get. I've been fortunate to have mentors, what Rockquemore and Laszloffy refer to as sponsors, in my career.[19] I've yet to identify a sponsor at the university, and success often depends on our career aspirations. Shall it be a goal to be a director, dean, and administrator, a decision maker? How do we measure successful progress towards those goals? When I worked in corporate America the phrase, "lead from any chair" was commonplace. Over the years I've seen many library leaders with little influence over their staff. I believe the activity of leadership has more to do with one's ability to engage others in working towards a common goal, and less to do with a job title.

Why do librarians of color all sit together in the faculty lounge or faculty meeting? We do it for support and camaraderie. Often there is a reluctance to reveal too much personal negativity or weakness within ourselves or about our families, because it might confirm stereotypes that the media perpetuates about people of color.[20] Often, we are constantly on guard. Why do we as people of color care what others think about us? Do we only care about what those in power think of us? Maybe we need to get over the reluctance just to be ourselves, warts and all. Perhaps this way can we begin to reduce stereotyping and be as free as the next person to share or not share, and feel safe in bringing our whole selves. Various life experiences, insights, and values need to be recognized in the workplace, so our contributions to our organizations and institutions can be acknowledged.

---

18. Jennifer Thorpe-Moscon and Alixandra Pollack. *Feeling Different: Being the "Other" in US Workplaces,* Catalyst Report, January 16, 2014, 7.

19. Rockquemore and Laszloffy, "Building a Supportive Network," 175-187.

20. Thorpe-Moscon and Pollack, *Feeling Different,* 1.

Conclusion

You may ask, "Where are all the librarians of color in academia?" That question can also be asked for all libraries. It's not particularly true just for academic libraries. Being the only one or one of two African American librarians is nothing new, whether it's an academic, public, or special library. We often stand by ourselves or there are few of us in these institutions. Librarians of color often feel isolated. We often go out of our way to be inclusive because we don't want others to feel that way. We are sensitive to the person or group that is being marginalized. As people and not just as librarians of color, we have often felt we have not had a voice.

A word of advice to anyone feeling isolated—attend conferences and seek out librarians of color, exchange contact information, and communicate regularly. Join the Black Caucus of ALA and the African American Studies Librarians Section (AFAS) of ACRL. The camaraderie is beneficial and will help you to be comfortable in any work environment. Being active also helps professionals to stay in contact with what other librarians of color are working on and is a means for sharing information and ideas. Many campuses have associations for minority faculty and staff. Seek them out and get involved with campus and community issues.

References

American Library Association. APA. *Library Worklife: HR E-News for Today's Leaders.* Series on Mentoring, 1984. http://ala-apa.org/newsletter/.

American Library Association. Office of Diversity. *Diversity Counts, 2009-2010,* http://www.ala.org/aboutala/sites/ala.org.aboutala/files/content/governance/officers/eb_documents/2012_2013ebdocuments/ebd12_10_diversity_counts.pdf.

American Library Association, Office for Research and Statistics. *ALA Demographics Studies July 2013*. Accessed June 9, 2014. www.ala.org/research/sites/ala.org.research/files/ content/July13report.pdf.

Cox, Brian, and Margie Jantti. "Discovering the Impact of Library Use and Student Performance." *EDUCAUSE Review Online* (18 July 2012). http://www.educause.edu/ero/article/discovering-impact-library-use-and-student-performance.

Damasco, Ione T., and Dracine Hodges, "Tenure and Promotion Experiences of Academic Librarians of Color." *College & Research Libraries* 73 (2012): 279-301.

Dovidio, John F., and Samuel L. Gaertner. "Aversive Racism." *Advances in Experimental Social Psychology* 36 (2004): 1-52.

Dovidio, John F., and Samuel L. Gaertner. "Aversive Racism and Selection Decisions: 1989 and 1999." *Psychological Science* 11 (2000): 319-323.

Eastern Michigan University. Affirmative Action Audit (2010-2011) and Affirmative Action Plan (2011-2012): Executive Summary." Accessed May 30, 2014. www.emich.edu/hr/diversity/documents/executive_summary.pdf.

Farkas, Meredith. "Librarians in Academia: Faculty or Support Staff?" In *Information Wants to Be Free*. Last modified October 6, 2005. http://meredith.wolfwater.com/wordpress/ 2005/10/08/librarians-in-academia-faculty-or-support-staff/.

Flint-Hamilton, Kimberly, Diane Batts Morrow, John Morrow, Jr. and Jamie T. Phelps. "Surviving Tenure: The Plight of Black Faculty." Panel discussion presented at the Annual meeting for the Black Catholic Theological Symposium, Boston, MA, 2006.

Gaertner, Samuel L., and John F. Dovidio. "Aversive Racism and Intergroup Bias." In *Reducing Intergroup Bias: The Common Ingroup Identity Model*, 13-31. Philadelphia: Psychology Press, 2000.

Gilchrist, Debra, and Megan Oakleaf. "An Essential Partner: The Librarian's Role in Student Learning Assessment." National Institute for Learning Outcome Assessment. Occasional Paper #14, (April 2012).

Johnson, Peggy. "Retaining and Advancing Librarians of Color," *College and Research Libraries* 68, no. 5 (2007), 408.

Linkner, John. "A Mix of Ideas and Skills is the Key to Success." *Free Press,* April 6, 2014.

Miller, Jeannie P., and Candace R. Benefiel. "Academic Librarians and the Pursuit of Tenure: The Support Group As a Strategy for Success. *College & Research Libraries* 59, no. 3 (1998): 260-265.

Rockquemore, Kerry Ann, and Tracey Laszloffy. " Building a Supportive Network. In *The Black Academic's Guide to Winning Tenure-Without Losing Your Soul,* 175-187. Boulder, CO: Lynne Rienner Publishers, 2008.

Sare, Laura, Stephen Bale, and Bruce Neville, "New Academic Librarians and Their Perceptions of the Profession." *portal: Libraries and the Academy* 12, 2 (2012) 193.

Sue, Dearald Wing. "Racial MicroAaggressions in Everyday Life: Implications for Clinical Practice." *American Psychologist* 62, 4 (2007), 275.

Thornton, Joyce K. "African American Female Librarians." *Journal of Library Administration* 33, no. 1-2 (2008): 141-164. doi: 10.1300/J111v33n01_10.

Thorpe-Moscon, Jennifer, and Alixandra Pollack. *Feeling Different: Being the "Other" in US Workplaces.* Catalyst Report, January 16, 2014. http://www.catalyst.org/knowledge/feeling-different-being-other-us-workplaces.

Yamada, David. "What is Academic Tenure?" Minding the Workplace: The New Workplace Institute Blog, August 22, 2011. http://newworkplace.wordpress.com/2011/08/22/what-is-academic-tenure/.

Chapter 11

DiVeRsItY at Miami University Libraries: Four Unique and Similar Experiences

Stacy Brinkman, Jacqueline Johnson, Kwabena Sekyere, and Elías Tzoc

Introduction

Miami University is a coeducational public research university in Oxford, Ohio, located in the southwestern region of the state, approximately 30 miles from both Cincinnati and Dayton. Founded in 1809, Miami University is the 10th oldest public university in the United States and the second oldest university in Ohio. It has an estimated 16,000 undergraduate students, 1,500 graduate students, and 2,000 faculty and staff. It is best known for its focus on undergraduate teaching and research, and is considered one of the original eight "Public Ivy" institutions.

While the student and local population is predominantly white, Miami University and the Western College for Women (which is adjacent to, and merged with, Miami University in 1974) have historically been active in promoting diversity. Most notably, in 1964 over 1000 volunteers gathered at the Western College for Women to participate in Freedom

Summer, a campaign to register black voters in Mississippi.[1] The Miami University Libraries began actively hiring students and staff from Korea, Vietnam, and Taiwan in the late 1950s and 1960s, as the population of Asians at the university also began to grow. In 1969, Dr. Charles D. Churchwell became the first African-American director of the Miami University Libraries.[2]

In 1989, Miami University Libraries established a Minority Residency program in order to increase diversity among its staff and to encourage librarians of color to enter the profession. Since its inception, over twenty librarians have participated in the residency program. This chapter presents the experiences of five librarians, all of whom entered the profession through this residency program. Subsequently, they have moved into permanent positions within the library and have received promotion and tenure, and one has moved into the position of Dean and University Librarian. We share a common beginning and common institution, but our experiences have been diverse, reflecting the diversity in our backgrounds and in our positions: we are African-American, Asian American, Latino, and International (Ghanaian and Guatemalan), and each of us has very different professional responsibilities within the library. In this chapter, we will explore specific challenges and opportunities we have encountered in three areas: the recruitment process, retention and career development vis-á-vis the promotion and tenure process, and retention via diversity initiatives.

The five voices presented in this chapter are as follow:

- ELIAS is the digital initiatives librarian. Originally from Guatemala, he joined Miami in 2007 as an Academic Resident Librarian.

---

1. For additional information about Freedom Summer, consider the following: Kathy Emery, Linda Reid Gold, and Sylvia Braselmann, *Lessons from Freedom Summer Ordinary People Building Extraordinary Movement* (Monroe, ME: Common Courage Press, 2008); Tracey Sugarman, *We Had Sneakers, They Had Guns: The Kids Who Fought for Civil Rights in Mississippi* (New York: Hill and Wang, 1966); Tracy Sugarman. Stranger at the Gates (New York: Hill and Wang, 1966); and Bruce Watson, *Freedom Summer: The Savage Season that Made Mississippi Burn and Made America a Democracy* (New York: Viking Press, 2010).

2. Elizabeth H. Baer, *The History of the Miami University Libraries* (Oxford, OH: Friends of the Miami University Libraries), 251-252; 273.

- KWABENA is the electronic information services librarian. Originally from Ghana, he joined Miami in 2005 as a Minority/ Academic Resident Librarian.
- JACQUELINE is the Archivist of the Western College Memorial Archives. An African-American from South Carolina, she joined Miami in 1991 as a Minority Resident Librarian.
- STACY is the Art & Architecture librarian. A Japanese-American from Seattle, she joined Miami in 2005 as an Academic Resident Librarian.
- JEROME is the Dean and University librarian. An African-American from Indiana, he joined Miami in 1992 as a Minority Resident Librarian.

Recruitment: The Residency Program

Minority Residency programs were established in some academic libraries in the mid-1980s as a means to help increase the number of minorities within the profession of librarianship. Usually designed to offer entry-level librarians the opportunity for employment in professional library positions, residency programs have seen numerous individual examples of success. Still, the programs do not go unchallenged. Some critics are leery of these programs because they question the need to hire inexperienced librarians, while supporters see them as an opportunity to attract new librarians into the profession.[3] Others have commented that residency programs can make minorities and residents feel like "special children."[4]

---

3. Detrice Bankhead, "The University of California, Santa Barbara Fellowship: A Program in Transition," in *Diversity in Libraries: Academic Residency Programs*, eds. Raquel V. Cogell and Cindy A. Gruwell (Westport, CT: Greenwood Press, 2001), 3; Julie Brewer, "Reflections of an Academic Library Residency Program Coordinator," in *Diversity in Libraries: Academic Residency Programs*, eds. Raquel V. Cogell and Cindy A. Gruwell (Westport, CT: Greenwood Press, 2001), 13.

4. Toby A. Lyles, Charmaine Henriques, and Lamara Williams-Hackett, "The Three-Year Experience: The Minority Research Residency Program at the University of Iowa Libraries," in *Diversity in Libraries: Academic Residency Programs*, eds. Raquel V. Cogell and Cindy A. Gruwell (Westport, CT: Greenwood Press, 2001), 87.

The Miami University Libraries Minority Resident Program was established by Dean and University Librarian Judith Sessions 25 years ago as one component of the Libraries' overall Affirmative Action plan. It was intended to increase the representation of minority librarians at Miami and to further the growth and development of minority librarians within the profession. Designed to assist a recent library school graduate in making a successful transition to academic librarianship, the resident program traditionally recruited candidates from a national pool. The one- to two-year program was contingent upon availability of funds and performance, and residents were assigned positions and given areas of responsibility based on their individual interests as well as the needs of the Libraries, often after an orientation period during which the resident trained in multiple departments.

> JACQUELINE: I began as a Minority Resident Librarian at 1991. I remained in that position for two years. During my time as a resident I worked as a Cataloging Librarian in Technical Services and was transferred to Special Collection in 1999. While there I worked as a Special Collections Cataloger. In 2005, I began work as the Archivist of the Western College Memorial Archives and remain in that position.

> JEROME: I have thought about what has made experience at Miami Libraries so rich and wonderful, and the most important thing I think is having individuals at the top of the organization who are committed to ensuring that they have a body that is reflective of the society that we are a part of. And I totally commend Judith [Sessions] and the university's initiative to start a residency program. So when I read the ad that there was this place called Miami University in rural southwest Ohio that was committed to diversifying its librarian ranks, I thought, that's a place that I might want to be part of.

The majority of librarians who have participated in the Miami University Libraries' Resident Program remain for only the one or two years—the length of the program itself. Most librarians who have participated in the program have had very positive experiences. Several librarians have remained at Miami University Libraries when a permanent position opened up that fit their qualifications and areas of expertise. Others went on to positions at other academic libraries. However, some librarians who have participated in the program have had mixed experiences with the resident program. In the earlier years of the resident program, there was some confusion among existing staff as to what a "resident" means versus an "intern."

> JACQUELINE: There have been a few bumps in the road during my profession. One of the challenges that I experienced upon arrival in Oxford is that most of the librarians and staff members were not aware that I had already graduated from library school with my Master of Library Science. The majority of the staff thought that despite the fact that my title was Minority Resident Librarian, I was serving as an intern. I was proactive and met with my supervisor and asked him to inform the staff about my credentials. There were some employees in the cataloging staff who did not want to give me access to certain portions of the catalog because they thought that I was still in the learning process.

In 2006, Sylvia Hu and Demetria Patrick published an article in *C&RL News* on their experience with the program. While they describe their overall experience as positive and valuable, one frustration they identified was that they felt that residents were not seen as "real" librarians in the same way as non-resident new librarians.[5]

At the same time, it is important to clarify that residents, like "visiting assistant professors" or "instructors" among faculty, are in many ways different from tenure-track faculty, even if these positions are all full-time and professional.[6] Although some resident librarians have seen their experiences translate into full-time, tenure-track positions, this is not always possible, as tenure-track lines require further university approvals. Even though resident positions are not tenure-track, residents have the freedom to pursue professional development, and are included in

---

5. Sylvia S. Hu and Demetria E. Patrick, "Our Experience as Minority Residents: Benefits, Drawbacks, and Suggestions," *College & Research Libraries News* 67, no. 5 (2006): 297-300.

6. Miami University Libraries implemented a new promotion and tenure system in 2003. Around the time of the implementation of this new tenure system, resident librarians were given the added title "Visiting Assistant Librarian."

the pool of travel funds available to attend conferences, professional organization meetings, seminars, and training sessions.

Over the years, the structure, implementation, and even the name of the program have changed due to various factors, including legal challenges. In its early years, residents were called "Minority Residents," and the Libraries actively recruited minority candidates, and were particularly successful in bringing many African Americans into the workforce. However, beginning in the mid-1990s, pressure to disassociate race as a criteria for selection or recruitment began mounting after other states began banning Affirmative Action policies in higher education. While Ohio does not currently have a law that bans race as a criteria for selection, the Miami University legal counsel advised that the Libraries retract the word "Minority" from the residence program. In the early 2000s, the residence program was re-named the "Academic Resident Librarian" program.[7]

> KWABENA: I applied for a position at Miami University Libraries in 2005 in response to an advertisement for a "Minority Resident Librarian." However, when I began, my title was "Academic Resident Librarian."

Although the program encouraged librarians of color to apply, recruitment could no longer specify minority status as a preferred or a required criteria. Significantly, since 2005, of the 13 "Academic Resident Librarians" hired by the Miami University Libraries, only three have been persons of color.

---

7. Interview transcript of Judith Sessions by Elias Tzoc and Jacqueline Johnson. Oral History Interview: Diversity and Miami University Digital Collections (June 2012). Interestingly, Sylvia Hu and Demetria Patrick, the authors of the previously published article on their experiences in the Miami University Minority Resident Librarian program, were among the last librarians hired with this title. Miami University is not the only institution that has experienced change due to politics surrounding affirmative action: The University of California, Santa Barbara residence program also underwent a change in name due to political reasons. See Patrick Dawson and Neerea A. Llamas, "From Innovative to Controversial: The UCSB Library Fellowship," in *Diversity in Libraries: Academic Residency Programs,* eds. Raquel V. Cogell and Cindy A. Gruwell (Westport, CT: Greenwood Press, 2001), 143-153.

Along with the change in name, hiring practices and the structure of the resident program have changed. While Miami Libraries has conducted some searches for Academic Resident Librarians since 2005, a number of residents since that year were hired without a national search. Rather, they were hired directly by the Dean of Libraries to meet a need within the system, similar to the manner in which Visiting Assistant Professors are hired in academic departments. Therefore, some Academic Residents were hired into a particular position, and did not train in multiple departments.

> KWABENA: Overall, I had a very positive experience with Miami residency program. I had opportunity to learn a lot about computer applications and languages. It gave me the opportunity to attend my first professional library conference. Because of this experience I was able to start networking with other professionals with similar research interest as mine. The program was created to allow residents to work in different departments and finally select an area of librarianship of his/her interest but that wasn't the case for me. Fortunately, I was able to work as an Electronic Information Services Librarian and explore my interest in technology. I was disappointed that I wasn't given the opportunity to explore other department as advertised. Other than that it was a great experience.

> ELIAS: Although I was initially hired as a resident librarian, I only had this title for six months and in March 2008, I became the Digital Initiatives Librarian. I have always worked with the same departmental team—formerly Digital Initiatives and now the Center for Digital Scholarship. In my short time as a resident, I was invited to assist with an internal evaluation of the Digital Collections program, which allowed me to start working on some web development for CONTENTdm. I was also invited to join the Diversity Cluster and co-developed the first website for this group. One of the best early experiences I had at Miami was the opportunity to work on a digitization project of Música Colonial originally from Guatemala.

In some instances, a staff vacancy resulted in an Academic Resident starting their professional career as the head of a unit or program:

STACY: I began my Academic Resident Librarian position as the Art/ Architecture librarian—the head of a branch library. This was certainly daunting for a new professional. I embraced the challenge, but did at times feel a bit isolated, especially in the first few months. I found myself wishing I had a mentor or at least a colleague with an office in the same building, and I know that I made some mistakes along the way as I was learning the ropes. However, I felt that I was given quite a bit of latitude to try things out, and in retrospect, I feel that this opportunity to really "sink or swim" was an invaluable experience during which I grew twice as much professionally than I probably would have otherwise.

Although not perfect, Miami University Libraries should be commended that it began a program that has given over thirty librarians of color the opportunity to explore the library profession. The residency program has changed from its infancy when it focused on librarians of color and has evolved into a program for recent library school graduates who may not be of a certain ethnicity. We should continue to promote these programs and work to make them a vital part of the library structure. Opportunities such as these are valuable to the library profession, so we should continue to promote residency program to avoid their demise.

Retention and Career Development: Promotion and Tenure

Residence programs are an important method of bringing minorities into the field of librarianship, but in themselves they are not enough to ensure that librarians of color remain in the profession or move into leadership roles. Early- and mid-career retention should be an instrumental component in libraries that plan not only to hire and retain talented librarians but also—and perhaps most importantly—for those that see transition in leadership as a fundamental component of strategic planning. Although good recruitment and retention programs should co-exist and complement each other, in the words of Linda Musser: "there is much concern about recruitment and retention of diverse employees but usually the focus is on the former with little or no discussion of the latter."[8] According to the 2007 ACRL white paper on the recruitment, retention, and advancement of librarians of color, a solid retention plan in academic libraries should include elements such as orientations, fostering a positive environment, programming to address work culture in a nonthreatening way, rewards and recognition, mentoring, support for promotion and tenure, and challenge through increased responsibilities, committee activities, research, and grant writing.[9]

While Miami University Libraries does not have a formalized retention plan for minority librarians, it does support a number of initiatives that attempt to ensure that conversations about diversity and inclusion are woven into the culture and fabric of the organization, and help to create a supportive environment to retain librarians of color. In addition, a number of the factors identified as key elements of a solid retention plan are included as part of the promotion and tenure system for librarians: we are encouraged to participate in a wide range of committees within the libraries as well as in the university, we are supported in creative and scholarly endeavors, and we receive funding to participate in professional development activities.

Promotion and Tenure System

Miami University implemented a promotion and "continuing contract" (tenure) system called the Libraries' Appointment, Rank, and Promotion System (LARPS) in 2003, passed by a vote among librarians and then approved by the University Provost, Senate, and Board of Trustees. Although librarians at Miami University are considered professional staff and not faculty, LARPS was designed to parallel the promotion and tenure process for faculty, and is included in the

---

8. Linda R. Musser, "Effective Retention Strategies for Diverse Employees," *Journal of Library Administration* 33, no 1/2 (March 2001): 63.

9. Teresa Y. Neely, and Lorna Peterson, "Achieving Racial and Ethnic Diversity among Academic and Research Librarians," in The Recruitment, Retention, and Advancement of Librarians of Color: A White Paper, *College & Research Libraries News* 68, no. 9 (2007), 562-565.

University's governance documents as a separate but parallel track. Like tenure-track faculty, librarians hired after 2003 are evaluated on their Primary Professional Responsibilities (which may include teaching), their Scholarly and Creative Activity, and their Service. Evaluations are made by the librarian's supervisor, a Personnel Committee in the Libraries, the Dean of Libraries, external reviewers, the University Provost, and finally approved by the Board of Trustees. Librarians are typically hired in as Assistant Librarians, and can be promoted to Associate Librarian and Principal Librarian.[10]

There are a number of benefits to having a formalized system such as LARPS in terms of retention. The timetable set by LARPS—a full review for promotion and continuing contract in the sixth year of qualifying service, with an additional formal review by a Personnel Committee and the Dean of Libraries in the third year, and annual reviews by one's Department Head—can help librarians establish short and long term goals. The annual reviews also require librarians to include a section of yearly goals with concrete outcomes and timeframes for completion. These goals are discussed with one's supervisor, who can help young librarians better define these goals, and who can be an ally in helping the librarian to achieve them. This process of goal setting and evaluation can be beneficial to librarians in order to see tangible progress in their careers on an annual basis.

At Miami University, most librarians are extremely motivated by LARPS to become active in service and scholarship. Many librarians take on roles in regional and/or national committees in addition to contributing to committees within the libraries or within the university. Likewise, most librarians also engage in research and creative work, often in collaboration with others. Miami University is a mid-size institution, and because creative work is encouraged, many librarians have found it possible to receive the latitude and support to take on a variety of projects without much bureaucracy. It has also been our experience that

---

10. Miami University Libraries, "Appointment, Rank, and Promotion System (LARPS)," accessed June 26, 2014, http://www.lib.miamioh.edu/about/larps. pdf.

many librarians who have gone through the LARPS system and achieved promotion and continuing contract actively try to help out newer librarians by inviting them to participate in committees or research projects.

> ELIAS: A promotion system can be an excellent guide for setting up and working towards professional goals in the areas of service and scholarship. Overall, LARPS is a good way to think beyond one's Primary Professional Responsibilities, and it can also help one to think about contributions at the regional, national and international levels. Perhaps better support for attending professional development programs and time off for research can make it a little bit more effective and productive.

> KWABENA: The LARPS process was a valuable exercise that assisted me in developing professional skills. It was challenging as well.

> STACY: I felt that I continually received a good deal of feedback on my progress throughout my experience as a librarian at Miami. However, I do think I had an advantage in that I had about 1.5 years as a resident in the system during which I was able to observe how LARPS really worked before I was really subject to evaluation under that system.

Of course, any tenure and promotion system also has challenges. For some, the LARPS system creates a tremendous amount of stress, and some librarians do not fully understand the tenure system when they are hired. The dark side of a tenure system can create an environment where librarians may feel like they are in competition with their colleagues. At Miami University, librarians are not officially given time off for research during the week,[11] and funding for travel to conferences has dwindled as the Libraries have experienced budget constraints. As a result, many librarians found themselves paying for conferences out of pocket. Finally, for librarians who were hired prior to the establishment of LARPS, but who elect to go through the process anyway in order to attain promotion, the process and timetable is less clear than it is for those who were hired directly into the LARPS system. LARPS may also

---

11. Some university libraries designate set percentages, such as 20% of one's work week, for research.

pose additional challenges for minority librarians, especially for those who do not write in English as their native language:

> KWABENA: Satisfying the scholarship criterion was especially challenging for me. In order to go through the system one is supposed to have a number of articles published. As an African coming from a physical science background where I didn't do much writing, it was daunting for me to identify research topics that interested me let alone write multiple papers in a second language. With the encouragement and support of supervisors and colleagues I eventually did find topics that I researched and published on.

The financial burden of having to pay for one's own travel to attend conferences can also hinder participation in committees or presentation of papers, particularly if those conferences are international:

> ELIAS: For me, service was a bit of challenge, especially because of budget limitations; however, this situation also led me to concentrate on scholarship, which translated into grant funded projects, several peer-reviewed publications, and software development.

> KWABENA: The LARPS system also had challenges when considering professional travel. It was difficult to find money to supplement what the library offered for professional development. I did have a proposal that was accepted for an international conferences (IFLA) in 2007 and 2008 but cancelled because of limited funding. The administration has provided me with many positive career successes though.

Leadership and Mentoring

In addition to providing support through the promotion and continuing contract process, Miami University Libraries has invested in retaining and developing minority librarians by providing funding and time for librarians to participate in career development programs. While career development may be important for all librarians, these types of programs are particularly important for librarians from underrepresented populations; not only are librarians of color underrepresented in the profession and especially in leadership roles, early-career minority librarians are often called upon to "speak for" a group or to take on leadership roles in diversity initiatives.

Two programs that specifically address leadership and career development for librarians of color are the Minnesota Institute for Early Career Librarians and the Association of Research Libraries' Leadership and Career Development Program (ARL-LCDP). Since 1998, three librarians at Miami University have participated in an ARL-LCDP cohort, despite the fact that Miami is not an ARL institution. For all three librarians, Miami University provided encouragement for the application process as well as time and resources to successfully complete the program. Because ARL-LCDP is an 18-month program with a research component, a site visit, two week-long training institutes, regular interaction with a career coach, and travel for programming at ALA Midwinter and ALA Annual, the time commitment is significant. In 2010, Miami University also supported an early career, tenure-track librarian to participate in the Minnesota Institute. Like the ARL-LCDP, the Minnesota Institute required funding from the institution for travel and a participation fee, as well as professional development time off to complete the week-long program.

> STACY: I participated in the ARL-LCDP program from 2013-2014. The program was a unique opportunity to intentionally reflect upon my career, my own strengths and opportunities for growth, and my life goals. LCDP challenged me to take leadership from any level, and to seek out ways to empower others around me. Through discussions with my cohort and through my relationship with my career coach, I gained more clarity of what "leadership" means, and what it means to lead in practice and not just in theory. I felt that I gained a lot of perspective on my own career path as well as my own institution through my interactions with my peers and mentors in the program. My career mentor also happened to be Asian American, and it was very inspiring to me to see someone "like me" taking a position of leadership within the profession. In many ways, I felt that the kind of work in LCDP was similar to the work needed in the field of diversity in general: it requires a lot of self-reflection, it requires you to work through feeling uncomfortable, and it requires you to get a sense of what your own vision is, and the courage to pursue that vision. Since beginning LCDP, I have seen my areas

of responsibilities within the library grow somewhat. Since my current Dean is an alum of LCDP, I have had an opportunity to briefly discuss some of my experiences with the program, and how those experiences might translate at Miami University Libraries.

ELIAS: Attending the MN Institute was a key moment in my professional career. Before the institute I had some real concerns about the best strategy on how to make significant contributions to my department, library, and the profession in general. But after that summer, a lot of things changed positively in my professional life. It was very positive to exchange ideas with such a diverse and committed group of new professionals with a passion about the future of librarianship and its contribution to higher education at different levels. For me, one of the core messages from the program was to understand/accept that every individual has his/her own way of work—based on strengths, culture, values, title, experience, etc.; however, when a group of people need to work for a common project, then it becomes necessary to not only know those (different) qualities but to utilize them in relevant roles in order to achieve excellence at work. In today's ever changing environment, there seems to be a greater need to develop a deep understanding of oneself, learn and apply new skills, and decide how one can best enhance an organization's performance.

Both the ARL-LCDP and the Minnesota Institute incorporate mentoring as a core component to their programs. Having a career mentor outside of one's institution can also be a very helpful way to gain perspective on one's own career, as well as institutional practices and culture. At the same time, any formal mentoring program can be very hit-or-miss depending on the chemistry between mentor and mentee.

STACY: I had a great experience with formal mentoring with my LCDP career coach, but I've also had other formal mentoring experiences that have been less rewarding—in the field of librarianship as well as in higher education in general. For me, if there is no chemistry between two people, the relationship feels forced, and there is not as much trust.

ELIAS: I have not had much experience with formal mentoring. In 2010, as part of the MN Institute I worked with a local mentor and he helped me work and envision a 5-year plan, which included some institutional and personal goals; I thought this was an excellent exercise to visualize a potential mid-career path. However, I have had a few informal mentoring experiences, including ongoing conversations and exchange of ideas with colleagues, friends, supervisor, and former professors.

Miami University Libraries does not have a formal mentoring program for librarians of color, or for any other new librarians. Some within the libraries have asked for such formal mentoring programs. However, our experience has been that informal, organic approaches to mentoring often work better. Developing relationships with other librarians through networking at conferences or professional organizations, or actively participating in leadership roles in the profession can open doors to mentoring type relationships.

> STACY: There are a number of people who I have worked with that I consider "mentors," even though they may not have that title. I consider any person who I can go to who challenges me, or who helps me to gain perspective on an idea or issue, to be a mentor. Once I find a person I can talk to in this manner, I will often re-visit them. Some people are mentors to me even though we don't meet regularly. But I know they are there, and that if I call on them, they will challenge me in a good way.

Retention and Cultural Considerations

Challenges of Location

It can be difficult for minority librarians to be at a predominantly white university in a predominantly white geographic location. Many librarians who contributed to the 2001 publication *Diversity in Libraries: Academic Residency Programs* commented on the challenge of being "far from home" and in an environment where they were perhaps the only librarian of color on staff.[12] Miami University has significantly increased its multicultural student population in recent years: in 2013-14, the student population was 13.3% domestic multicultural, up from 8.2%

---

12. Raquel V. Cogell and Cindy A. Gruwell, eds., *Diversity in Libraries: Academic Residency Programs,* (Westport, CT: Greenwood Press, 2001).

in 2005-06.[13] However, the university still struggles with its image as being an elite, homogenous institution. The city of Oxford (population 27,038) is 12.8% non-white, according to the 2010 US Census.[14] These factors can present challenges in both recruitment and retention.

> JEROME: Recruitment is a challenge … we cannot discount the geographical location of Miami University, where individuals may want a more urban area and may not want to live in southwest Ohio.

> ELIAS: One of the early challenges was probably finding myself in a community with very few Spanish speakers.

Miami University Libraries actually fares well in terms of diversity from a percentages standpoint. With five librarians of color in a staff of 39 librarians, we have a better average (12.8%) than the total percentage of minorities in librarianship in the 2012 ALA Diversity Counts report (11%).[15] However, diversity is not just a numbers game. There are still some real challenges that minorities face, often through the good intentions of others.

> JACQUELINE: Another challenge was the fact that my colleagues believed that any activity that dealt with African Americans was my duty. I organized all tours for African American student, faculty and visitors to the university. While my colleagues believed that this would be advantageous to students and I, it did not allow the students to meet various members of the library community.

When trying to diversify the workplace, it is important to support various programs that attempt to ensure that conversations of diversity and inclusion are woven into the culture and fabric of the organization.

---

13. Miami University, "Fall 2013: Enrollment Management Update," accessed June 26, 2014, http://www.miamioh.edu/documents/oem/Enrollment_Management_Update_Fall_2013.pdf.

14. "Oxford, Ohio Population," Census Viewer, accessed June 26, 2014, http://censusviewer.com/city/ OH/Oxford.

15. American Library Association, "Diversity Counts," accessed June 26, 2014, http://www.ala.org/offices/ diversity/diversitycounts/divcounts.

Diversity Committee

Miami University Libraries has a standing committee for diversity that has been in existence as long as the residence program. Called the "Diversity Cluster," this committee is charged with "promoting diversity through the implementation of academic, cultural and social programs, events, and exhibits that reflect the range of racial, ethnic, religious, geographical, socioeconomic backgrounds, disabilities and sexual orientation within the Miami University community."[16] The Diversity Cluster is comprised of 5-7 members, and sponsors diversity-themed events and programs throughout the year. One regular event is the African-American Read-In, which the library has sponsored for 25 years. Other programs have included films and discussions, external speakers, potlucks, book clubs, online staff profiles, and presentations at regional and national conferences. The Diversity Cluster also strives to create partnerships with other groups on campus that promote diversity.

> JEROME: The thing that made our Diversity Committee different from others was that we had a Dean who was committed to it, she put resources behind it, and she encouraged us to do programming and those types of things.

The goal of the Diversity Clustering is to create community, and to open up a space for people to explore their own similarities and differences through considering topics of diversity and inclusion. A strength of having a standing committee devoted to diversity within the library is that there are continual conversations among staff about how to promote diversity and inclusion. As opposed to having a single "Diversity Librarian" position, a committee by default opens up more possibilities for people to be involved in the planning of and participation in programming.

---

16. Miami University Libraries, "Diversity Cluster Charge," accessed June 26, 2014, https://mulclusters.pbworks.com/w/page/45436445/Diversity%20Cluster.

JEROME: Ultimately, it can't be just one person. People have to be empowered to do it and embrace it globally. If you have one person, then he or she is viewed as the "Diversity Czar," and that's not good for an organization.

Diversity Clustering does have its challenges. Because membership to the Diversity Cluster has in the past been appointed by library administration, there have been members of the committee who do not actually want to serve on the committee. Perhaps not surprisingly, most minority librarians have served on this committee, many times as chair. Some minority librarians have felt that they were named to the Cluster simply because they were minorities and not because they had any particular strength or interest in diversity issues. The Cluster also struggles to distinguish itself and its events from programming for other committees such as Outreach. There is a perception among some within the library staff that the Diversity Cluster is not necessary as a separate committee; rather, they believe that the Outreach Cluster should organize all library programming. However, to its credit, the library administration has strongly supported the Diversity Cluster's continuation, and frequently attends events and programs sponsored by the cluster.

Often, however, the Diversity Cluster struggles with attendance at its programming. Many people will not attend a Diversity event unless there is food provided or another significant benefit (such as staff development credit). Many times, there was insufficient funding available for the Diversity Cluster to invite guest speakers. In addition, the Cluster received reports that some staff would not receive permission from their supervisors to attend Diversity events. In other words, although programming by the Diversity Cluster is "supported" by the University Libraries administration, that support does not always take the form of ensuring that all staff are allowed by supervisors to attend Diversity events, or for funding for things such as external speakers. While all library employees attend a mandatory "Team Member Training" retreat, diversity is not an explicit component of this training. Because there is no requirement for staff to attend Diversity Cluster programming, and because diversity is not a topic included in other mandatory trainings, many of the diversity events in the library are only attended by people who are already interested in or committed to diversity.

Despite its challenges, the Diversity Cluster has been successful in providing multiple opportunities for librarians, staff, and the university community to explore issues related to diversity. While it may be difficult to engage people in asking "hard" questions about diversity and inclusion, there have been many occasions in which participants at Diversity Cluster events have ended up talking about issues that they otherwise would not have considered. Continued conversations about diversity and inclusion of other cultures have enabled librarians who are outside the Diversity Cluster to also pursue grant-funded programs on topics related to diversity such as the ALA/NEH "Let's Talk About It" series on the American Civil War and Muslim Journeys. Therefore, creating a designated, welcoming space where such dialogue can take place is a necessary and valuable step towards creating an inclusive organizational environment.

> JEROME: We always thought that if we could find some basic common denominator for a conversation within the Miami University Libraries on the issue of diversity, that would then allow us to be able to broaden the conversation to those topics that are a little more difficult. But ultimately, what people have to do is that they have to feel comfortable at least talking about it.

Involvement in Campus-Wide Diversity Initiatives

The challenges that the Diversity Cluster faces are indicative of a larger problem that is not unique to this institution. People who work in diversity understand that having a workforce that is more diverse and inclusive of multiple voices and points of view is actually stronger, more creative, more resilient, and more responsive to the changing needs of its environment. Yet for many people who do not come from under-represented backgrounds themselves, it is difficult to see the immediate benefit or relevance of diversity programming for their daily jobs or lives.

Since the campus is predominantly white, in a predominantly white locale, asking non-minorities to address hard questions about diversity is challenging. Several of the authors of this chapter have been active participants in campus-wide diversity initiatives, particularly for faculty and staff, such as the Association of Black Faculty and Staff, the Association for Latino/a Faculty and Staff, and the Asian/Asian-American Faculty and Staff Association.

> JEROME: We didn't have many people of color when I came here to this place. I remember the old adage that my mom used to say: "Jerome, you got to work twice as hard for the same thing." So that's a mindset that I brought with me. And although the program may have been designed for the minority librarian, I was going to be the best young librarian I could be. So we early on began to look beyond the walls of the library profession for opportunities within the university to be able to add value there. So we associated ourselves with the Association of Black Faculty and Staff, we worked with the Diversity Cluster… but we tried to align ourselves with folks who looked like us, but at the same time we tried to expand our horizons a little more.

> ELIAS: I was a member of the Diversity Cluster for four years 2007-2010. In the last two years, I served as the chair, which allowed me to understand a bit better both the opportunities and challenges in organizing diversity-related events. In this role, I also had the opportunity to meet and join other groups on campus who were also working towards a more welcoming and inclusive environment … many of them remain as important and key allies. In fact, one of those contacts is now a partner for one of my current projects: The Center for American & World Cultures Lecture Series Digital Archive; another contact and ally group is the Latino/a Association of Faculty & Staff.

Significantly, our participation in these campus-wide groups has been encouraged by the library administration. These groups frequently discuss issues such as campus climate and its impact on faculty/staff retention, in addition to assisting with cultural events. While most do not perceive the campus to be particularly hostile, many have commented on the need to get past surface-deep discussions on diversity. Creating a more inclusive campus climate requires people to lean into their discomfort, rather than just celebrating differences. The participation of librarians in campus-wide diversity groups has resulted in the library's Diversity Cluster receiving additional recognition on campus, particularly in the purposeful inclusion of library representatives at meetings such as the 2008 President's Summit on Diversity and an Allies Training seminar series in 2010. The Libraries maintains a friendly relationship with Dr. Ron Scott, the university's current Associate Vice President for Institutional Diversity, and individual librarians as well as the Diversity Cluster have partnered with various campus-wide offices on projects and programming related to creating a diverse and inclusive environment.

Conclusion

The experiences and perspectives shared here demonstrate that despite its challenges, Miami University's initiatives to recruit and retain librarians of color have had a positive impact on individuals, the institution, and the profession. The experiences of Stacy Brinkman, Jacqueline Johnson, Kwabena Sekyere, and Elias Tzoc of being promoted to Associate Librarians in the LARPS system after starting as residents are examples of the types of success that occur when a library system demonstrates continued support for residency and diversity programs. The experience of Jerome Conley, who also began as a resident and has been promoted through the library system to be named Dean and University Librarian in January 2014, is an even more extreme example. Dean Conley has expressed his desire to continue Miami University Libraries' commitment to diversity. As librarians of color we have had vast opportunities that have allowed us to collaborate with colleagues, and participate in national projects and professional development experiences. We are excited about the future.

References

Baer, Elizabeth H. *The History of the Miami University Libraries.* Oxford, OH: Miami University, the Friends of the Miami University Libraries, 1997.

Bankhead, Detrice. "The University of California, Santa Barbara Fellowship: A Program in Transition." In *Diversity in Libraries: Academic Residency Programs,* edited by Raquel V. Cogell and Cindy A. Gruwell, 3-6. Westport, CT: Greenwood Press, 2001.

Brewer, Julie. "Reflections of an Academic Library Residency Program Coordinator." In *Diversity in Libraries: Academic Residency Programs,* edited by Raquel V. Cogell and   Cindy A. Gruwell, 7-16. Westport, CT: Greenwood Press, 2001.

Cogell, Raquel V., and Cindy A. Gruwell, eds. *Diversity in Libraries: Academic Residency Programs.* Westport, CT: Greenwood Press, 2001.

Dawson, Patrick and Llamas, Nerea A. "From Innovative to Controversial: The UCSB Library Fellowship." In *Diversity in Libraries: Academic Residency Programs,* edited by Raquel V. Cogell and Cindy A. Gruwell, 143-153. Westport, CT: Greenwood Press, 2001.

Emery, Kathy, Linda Reid Gold, and Sylvia Braselmann. *Lessons from Freedom Summer: Ordinary People Building Extraordinary Movements.* Monroe, ME.: Common Courage Press, 2008.

Hu, Sylvia S., and Demetria E. Patrick. "Our Experience as Minority Residents: Benefits, Drawbacks, and Suggestions." *College & Research Libraries News* 67, no. 5 (2006): 297-300.

Lyles, Toby A., Charmaine Henriques, and Lamara Williams-Hackett. "The Three-Year Experience: The Minority Research Residency Program at the University of Iowa Libraries." In *Diversity in Libraries: Academic Residency Programs,* edited by Raquel V. Cogell and Cindy A. Gruwell, 79-88. Westport, CT: Greenwood Press, 2001.

Musser, Linda R. "Effective Retention Strategies for Diverse Employees." *Journal of Library Administration* 33 no 1/2 (March 2001): 63-72.

Neely, Teresa Y., and Lorna Peterson. "Achieving Racial and Ethnic Diversity among Academic and Research Librarians: The Recruitment, Retention, and Advancement of Librarians of Color: A White Paper." *College & Research Libraries News* 68, no. 9 (2007): 562-565.

Sugarman, Tracy. *Stranger at the Gates: A Summer in Mississippi.* New York: Hill and Wang, 1966.

————. *We Had Sneakers, They Had Guns: The Kids Who Fought for Civil Rights in Mississippi.* Syruacuse, NY: Syracuse University Press, 2009.

Watson, Bruce. *Freedom Summer: The Savage Season That Made Mississippi Burn and Made America a Democracy.* New York, NY: Viking, 2010.

Chapter 12

BUILDING DIALOGIC BRIDGES TO DIVERSITY: ARE WE
THERE YET?

Roland Barksdale-Hall

Introduction

According to Martin Buber, dialogue is central to maintaining the delicate balance between relationship and principle, wherein democratic communities prosper. In recent years the perception of limited economic resources has heightened cultural tensions in the workplace, exacerbating "the polarization already implicit in poverty and racism."[1] These trends are dangerous, as they promote "group protection from others."[2] Such times bring forth a shift from true democratic society to autocratic groups, where dissenters are excluded from relationship. Conversely, autocratic groups thwart the development of dialogue as espoused by Martin Buber.

As an African American culture keeper, library educator, and academic library administrator, I look at the professional literature, oral histories of African Americans in academia, librarian practitioner journals, and

---

1. Maurice Freedman, foreword to *Communication and Community: Implications of Martin Buber's Dialogue,* by Ronald Arnett, (Carbondale, IL: Southern Illinois University Press, 1986), xiv.

2. Ronald Arnett, *Communication and Community: Implications of Martin Buber's Dialogue.* (Carbondale: Southern Illinois University Press, 1986), 81.

leadership theory in this essay. I would like to thank Dr. Jane Moore McGinn, Dr. Clarence J. Cotton, Jr., Dr. James B. Stewart, Dr. Anthony B. Mitchell, Dr. James Henderson, Karim Rand, George H. Updegrove, Anna Steinbach, Tiffeni Fontno, Jocelyn Poole; Georgia Southern University for a grant in support of the Oral History of Black Librarians Pioneers Project; Dr. John Kaiser, retired librarian at Penn State University, who recommended that I consider writing a case study to gain insights from colleagues at an Association for Research Libraries (ARL) Management Training; and the membership of the Black Caucus of the American Library Association (BCALA) for support of this research inquiry. I wrote earlier versions of this case study, based upon experiences at Penn State University, under the fictitious name Spingarn University, for coursework in partial fulfillment of the requirements for a master's degree in leadership and liberal studies from Duquesne University, and solicited feedback from national diversity experts and African American library practitioners through the *Newsletter of the Black Caucus of the American Library*. Minority librarians view themselves as being acted upon and not being in control, and their recruitment receiving priority over retention.[3] Findings indicate potential for empowerment, problem-solving, and critical communication skills. This chapter is dedicated to the memory of Ms. Ida Mary Lewis (1924-2011), mentor, civil rights activist and Head of the African American Collection at the University of Pittsburgh, and Dr. E. J. Josey (1924-2009), mentor, civil rights activist, and founder of the BCALA.

Are We There Yet?

In the twenty-first century great strides have been made. In 2015, the eagerly anticipated and agitated for Smithsonian Museum of African

3. Patricia Ball, "African American Male Library Administrators in Public and Academic Libraries," *College and Research Libraries* 56, no. 6: 531-45, 543; Roland Barksdale-Hall, "Dialogic Bridges in the Workplace," *Newsletter of the Black Caucus of the American Library Association* 30, no. 6 (June 2002): 9-10; Tiffeni Fontno, "Reinventing Diversity," *Newsletter of the Black Caucus of the American Library Association* 30, no. 6 (June 2002): 8.

American History and Culture is scheduled to open on the National Mall in Washington, D.C. To imagine that someone by the name of Barack Hussein Obama would be elected the first African American president would have been unfathomable to prior generations, given the long shadow of inequality and social exclusion people of color faced in America. For sure, these are momentous times.

Granted progress has been made, it still remains inconclusive what exactly history will say about the role of a diverse professional information workforce during an Information Era. Almost a decade has passed since ALA President Mitch Freedman pledged to fight for initiatives for minorities, including recruitment and retention.[4] "Are we there yet?" Ice Cube appears in a popular movie by that name, in which he travels with two youth on a journey. The youth periodically ask, "Are we there yet?" This question beckons us to explore the ongoing journey to freedom. Let's take a few minutes to explore that question—"Are we there yet?"

Literature Analysis

The professional literature reports an alarming trend of marginalizing the role of minority leaders in the workplace. Josey and Shockley chronicle the history of racism in American libraries.[5] Morrison cites "the lack of enforcement of affirmative action guidelines under the Reagan administration" as a barrier to the hiring or promoting of nontraditional managers.[6] Ball examined the characteristics, status, and perceptions of discrimination in the workplace of African American library administrators in public and academic libraries, and found academic library administrators at Black institutions had fewer problems

---

4. Plummer Jones, *Still Struggling for Equality: American Public Library Services with Minorities*, (Westport, CT: Libraries Unlimited, 2004), 196.

5. E.J. Josey, *What Black Librarians Are Saying*, (Metuchen, NJ: Scarecrow Press, 1972); eds. E.J. Josey and Ann Shockley, *Handbook of Black Librarianship*, (Littleton, CO: Libraries Unlimited, 1977).

6. Ann Morrison, "Challenging the Barriers to Opportunity," in *The Leader's Companion: Insights on Leadership Through the Ages*, ed. Thomas Wren, (New York: Free Press, 1995), 234.

than those in predominantly white institutions, where perceptions of isolation and alienation were reported.[7] Thornton identified job satisfaction as a significant issue in a study of African American female librarian practitioners.[8] Jackson, Jefferson, and Nosakhere showed the challenges faced by minority leaders are more subtle but similar to those of past generations.[9] Hirsch and Lyons identified the workplace context as a factor for understanding the process of how people applied legal concepts of discrimination to their work experiences.[10] Abif and Neely showed that persistent challenges exist for a newer generation of people of color recruited to the library profession.[11] Howland identified six challenges to working in a multicultural environment: 1) fluctuating power dynamics; 2) merging a diversity of opinions and approaches; 3) tokenism, reality or perception? 4) overcoming a perceived lack of empathy; 5) accountability; and 6) transforming challenges to opportunities.[12] The professional literature also identified benchmarking, training, and communication as effective tools for employers interested in increasing diversity.[13]

---

7. Patricia Ball. "African American Male Library Administrators in Public and Academic Libraries." *College and Research Libraries* 56, no. 6: 531-45.

8. Joyce Thorton, "Years at Present Institution and Job Satisfaction African American Female Librarians: A Study of Job Satisfaction," in *Diversity Now: People, Collections, and Services in Academic Libraries: Selected Papers from the Big 12 Plus Libraries Consortium Diversity Conference*, ed. Teresa Neely (New York: Haworth Press, 2001), 159-60.

9. Andrew Jackson and Julius Jefferson, eds., *The 21st Century Black Librarian in America: Issues and Challenges*, (Lanham, MD: Scarecrow Press, 2012).

10. Elizabeth Hirsh and Christopher Lyons, "Perceiving Discrimination on the Job: Legal Consciousness, Workplace Context, and the Construction of Race Discrimination," *Law and Society Review* 44, no. 2 (June 2010), 269-98.

11. Teresa Neely, and Khafre Abif, eds., *In Our Own Voices: The Changing Face of Librarianship*, (Lanham, MD: Scarecrow Press, 1996).

12. Joan Howland, "Challenges of Working in a Multicultural Environment," in *Diversity Now: People, Collections, and Services in Academic Libraries: Selected Papers from the Big 12 Plus Libraries Consortium Diversity Conference*, ed. Teresa Neely, (New York: Haworth Press, 2001), 105-23.

13. *Newsletter of the Black Caucus of the American Library* 30, no. 4 (June 2002).

Norlin and Morris identified collaboration between historically Black colleges and universities (HBCU) libraries, Association for College and Research Libraries (ACRL) libraries, and other libraries as critical.[14] Unaeze lists required competencies of HBCU library directors: strategic planning, budgeting, collaboration, communication, technology, and emotional intelligence; and emphasized the importance of leadership development in future success.[15] Hardy and Stiff identified the role of HBCU librarians as mentors for students, visibility from faculty-librarian cooperation, technology utilization, strategic planning, and performance standards as beneficial factors.[16]

Oral History of Black Librarian Pioneers Project

In commemoration of the 50th Anniversary of Brown v. Board of Education and other pending Civil Rights Era milestones, the Oral History of Black Librarians Pioneers sought to document the educational, working, and social conditions of black librarians who participated in the struggle for civil rights, held leadership positions and/or engaged in professional or civic activities. Virginia Proctor Powell Florence (1897-1991) was the second African American professionally trained librarian, following Edward Christopher Williams (1871-1929). She graduated from the Pittsburgh Carnegie Library School in 1923. Lee and Gunn document the struggle of Virginia Proctor Powell Florence, the first

---

14. Elaina Norlin and Patricia Morris, "Historically Black College and University Libraries in the 21st Century: Accomplishments, Challenges and Recommendations" in *Diversity Now: People, Collections, and Services in Academic Libraries: Selected Papers from the Big 12 Plus Libraries Consortium Diversity Conference*, ed. Teresa Neely, (New York: Haworth Press, 2001), 183-97.

15. Felix Unaeze, "Managing Historically Black Colleges and University Libraries during Economic Recession: Challenges and Expectations for Library Deans and Directors," in *Handbook of Black Librarianship*, eds. E.J. Josey and Marva DeLoach (Lanham, MD: Scarecrow Press, 2000), 97-104.

16. Floyd Hardy and Renee Stiff, "The Future of the Black College Library," in *Handbook of Black Librarianship*, eds. E.J. Josey and Marva DeLoach (Lanham, MD: Scarecrow Press, 2000),, 387-96.

professionally trained African American female librarian.[17] In 1968, Florence stated the following about her participation in the struggle for civil rights: "My husband and I, being negroes, are especially interested in Civil Rights and better race relations. We work with our church, YWCA, and the Richmond Crusade for Voters toward that end."[18] The Oral History of Black Librarians Pioneers Project was created to show how these librarians saw their role in providing access to information during the age of segregation. A comparative analysis was planned for these interviews and those done earlier by Ann Allen Shockley, former Head of Special Collections at Fisk University, in the early 1970s.

The civil rights struggle of African American librarian Ida Mary Lewis (1924-2011) was brought to public attention in 1976, when the activist filed an Equal Employment Opportunity Commission (EEOC) class action suit against the University of Pittsburgh Book Center, which lasted about eight years. In the early 1990s, I interviewed the silver-haired Lewis, then Head of the African American Collection at the University of Pittsburgh. Ida Mary Lewis was born on September 28, 1924 to Maurice Fulton, an African American postal worker and May Anderson Lewis in Bellvue, Pennsylvania.[19] In 1945, she became the first African American apprentice librarian hired at the Carnegie Allegheny Library on Pittsburgh's Northside. She came highly qualified with three years of college at Carnegie Tech, now Carnegie Mellon University, at a time when the majority of whites who qualified for the apprentice librarian position had only a high school diploma. George Seible, then the library director, commended Lewis as "the best educated librarian that

---

17. Grant Lee, "Honoring Virginia Florence," *American Libraries* 18, no. 4 (April 1987), 250; Arthur C. Gunn, "The Struggle of Virginia Proctor Powell Florence: A Black Woman Wants to Be a Professional..." *American Libraries* 20, no. 2 (February 1989), 154-57.

18. "Virginia Proctor Powell Florence: A Remarkable Oberlin Alumna Librarian," *Library Perspectives: Newsletter of the Oberlin College Library,* 32 (Spring 2005), 5, accessed December 6, 2014, http://www.oberlin.edu/library/friends/perspectives/32.pdf.

19. "Ida M. Lewis: Obituary," RememberingPa.us, accessed August 9, 2012, http://www.legacy.com/ obituaries/publicopiniononline/obituary.aspx?n=ida-m-lewis&pid=155250820&fhid=8387.

he ever met." She worked as an apprentice librarian until 1956, while she pursued additional studies. She earned a B.S. from Carnegie Institute of Technology (Margaret Morrison Carnegie College), a Master's from the University of Pittsburgh, and a Master's in Library Science from Carnegie Mellon University over a fifteen-year period. She was a member of the last graduating class of the Pittsburgh Carnegie Library School in 1961. She was a member of the NAACP, Fineview Citizens Council, Aurora Reading Society of Pittsburgh, and the Pittsburgh Chapter of the Afro-American Historical and Genealogical Society (AAHGS).

Today the annual Ida Mary Lewis Memorial Lecture at the Carnegie Library of Pittsburgh, Hill District Branch, commemorates her life and advocacy as a "trailblazer for women and minorities in the Pittsburgh educational, historical and cultural arena." For her civil rights struggle and contributions to the African American community, she received awards from the University of Pittsburgh Black Action Society and the School of Social Work, as well as communitywide recognition. In her lawsuit, she alleged that she was passed over for a promotion to assistant book buyer because of a combination of her race and nepotism. A jury found that she was more than qualified for an assistant book buyer's position. However, it was her poor work performance that disqualified her for the position. Lewis, represented by attorney James H. Logan, appealed the decision to the 3rd U.S. Courts of Appeals in Philadelphia. Lewis petitioned for review by the U.S. Supreme Court and argued that the standard for proving discrimination was too high and that the evidence concerning nepotism did not receive consideration. A decision that she deserved a new trial led to negotiations that resulted in her hire as Head of the African American Collection.[20] The life story of this librarian practitioner pioneer sheds light on the early twentieth century struggles of African American librarian practitioners.

As part of the Oral History of Black Librarians Pioneers, the following is an interview about her litigation that I conducted with Ida Mary

---

20. Lewis v. University of Pittsburgh, 725 F2d 910, Open Jurist Website, accessed November 28, 2014, http://openjurist.org/print/273492.

Lewis at the University of Pittsburgh's William Pitt Student Union on April 8, 2006:

Barksdale-Hall: Well, tell us about your career as a librarian. Did you stay in Pittsburgh?

Lewis: Yes, I did stay in Pittsburgh after I got my Master of Science in Library Science in 1962. Then I worked for a while, about two years in the Main Carnegie [Library] in Pittsburgh. But, I left there after a while because I found there was a lot of prejudice.

Barksdale-Hall: Was that in 1964?

Lewis: Yes, that was in 1964. I really wanted to work on my doctorate. I really had to save. I decided that that wasn't feasible. So what I did I worked in Kauffmann's Store in the bookstore, which was quite enjoyable. I enjoyed the fact that I was selling books and competing with other clerks, doing the same thing whereas before I was giving out books, free naturally to the public. But I found it was a pleasure to sell books to people that were interested in buying them and making them part of their own private collection.

Barksdale-Hall: Well, then you went to...

Lewis: I went to Kauffmann's and worked there... [T]he Vietnam War was going on. Many of the men weren't at the University of Pittsburgh Bookstore. There were openings then. I was still searching. I wanted a position as a librarian at the University of Pittsburgh but I found there were not going to be any openings for Negroes. I went... many times [the employment process dictated] going through partial procedures. Once you found one or two people you met [you learned] they had no Negroes in their department and they had no Negro librarians in the library system I decided very well then I would stay [in the Bookstore.]
    I then stayed for 22 years as a clerk at the University of Pittsburgh Bookstore. And then I became a buyer and then I was reduced to a clerk. And then it was I decided racial discrimination, failure to promote and nepotism was being practiced in such a scale that I decided to sue the University of Pittsburgh and the University of Pittsburgh Book Center under the 1964 Civil Rights Act for those three things—racial discrimination, failure to promote and the nepotism.

Barksdale-Hall: And when was that?

Lewis: I filed the charge in 1976. I think that was the two hundredth anniversary history of our great republic. Because I felt that I had been mistreated and suffered these wrongs and because there was this 1964 Civil Rights Act in place, brought forth by the Democratic Party and in particularly... the whole process of being able to charge racial discrimination was part of Lyndon Johnson's new administration, I felt that I was in that position and I wanted a remedy. I didn't want to... I just felt this was a position that I had to take...did so in November of 1976.

It is quite a long time... You file a charge then you go through a period of reconsideration. It is mainly one in which you have to achieve the right to sue. The right to sue came three years after 1976 and that put in motion [my] charge and [I] was more in the legal system. There was a trial. Then I [think] I had in 1982 because I was in interrogatories.

I was advised by my attorney to take it to the U.S. Supreme Court to review the whole situation. From this I perhaps could have two or three Justices, who having seen and heard my case; I would get some recommendations, some consideration. What happened was of the Justices there I was particularly interested in Thurgood Marshall. And I knew Blackmun and Brennan were progressive judges. As it turned out I don't believe Thurgood Marshall saw my case, as I believe he was ill at the time. But judges Blackmun and Brennan said that I deserved a new trial based upon the 22 pages affirming my position that I had received from the 3rd Circuit Court, which I took it to in Philadelphia. There they had reviewed [my case] and felt well that the court in Western Pennsylvania had erred and it was their 22 pages affirming my position that helped me and my attorney make the decision that well if we take it to the Supreme Court they would review [my case] and win some merit. And what happened [was] two great Justices, Blackmun and Brennan, said I deserved a new trial.

Taking this information back to the Legal Department at the University of Pittsburgh I and my attorney pressed them for whatever openings that there ever came in the library field for me... I did not want a new trial... that to me would be so costly. I just did not wish that. But what happened was because they had an African American Studies Department at the University of Pittsburgh and at Hillman Library, and part of that on the first floor was an African American Collection, I was transferred there and then started to work as a librarian, as the Head Librarian of the African American Collection of Hillman Library in November of 1987 and stayed there until November of 1990 when I retired, because I felt I was of an age that felt I should.

Barksdale-Hall: So after the litigation you then became Head of the African American Collection at Hillman Library of the University of Pittsburgh.

Lewis: Yes.

Barksdale-Hall: And what year was that?

Lewis: That was in 1987 and I stayed there until 1990.

Barksdale-Hall: There are two articles—one that appears in the *University Times* (January 13, 1983); the heading is "Discrimination Suit is Heard." Subsequently, the *Post-Gazette* in its Wednesday, October 10, 1984 wrote "Promotion is Upheld in Pitt Rights Case," which followed suit on that. What reflections do you have on that great Civil Rights struggle?

Lewis: Well, it was a long ordeal. There were many disappointments and difficulties. I am very glad that I survived them all. And I will never forget the impact upon my life, going through it all. It was such a waste in a way in my life. With my qualifications and skills I had to spend out an enormous amount of my time, carrying out a legal battle in which really innervated me at times discouraged me. But I was asked from time to time to drop the case or to... [locate] employ[ment] in other places... none which I wanted. I think it was damaging physically and to my mental attitude towards... educational institutions that put you through this... and find out you are misrepresented. [21]

As this interview reflects, in the late twentieth century, African Americans organized professional groups and addressed various concerns. In 1970, African American librarians "concerned about the effects of institutional racism, poverty, the continued lack of educational, employment and promotional opportunities upon [us] and other minorities," led by E.J. Josey, organized the BCALA. In 1981, Wendell L. Wray (1926-2003), then professor at the School of Library and Information Science, University of Pittsburgh, and Jeff Jackson, then head of the Afro-American Collection at the University of Pittsburgh's Hillman Library, organized the American Library Association (ALA) African American Studies Librarians Section (AFAS) of the Association of Research Libraries (ACRL) with an emphasis upon Black Studies. Organizers identified

---

21. Ida Mary Lewis, interview by Roland Barksdale-Hall. William Pitt Student Union, University of Pittsburgh, April 8, 2006.

twelve relevant discussion topics.[22] Many of these topics remain "as relevant today as they were [more than] twenty years ago," according to Dr. Stanton F. Biddle in an address at the ALA ACRL AFAS Twentieth Anniversary Program, held at the Westin St. Francis Hotel, San Francisco, California, on June 16, 2001.[23]

My Career as an Academic Librarian

Over the course of more than a decade, Ida Mary Lewis candidly shared conversations with me on many topics, ranging from race matters to librarianship. My first impression of her was of an amiable, soft-spoken, reserved, and intelligent person. Her dress was conservative: a skirt, dark jacket, and white blouse. However, I was not misled by her meek-and-mild demeanor, as her reputation as a civil rights activist preceded her. Lewis and I earlier applied for the same position of Head of the African American Collection at the University of Pittsburgh. Professor Wendell L. Wray, my mentor, later explained to me that I would have been hired, if it were not for her lawsuit. I did not hold anything against her. Moreover I was intrigued by her experiences.

I first met Lewis in the University of Pittsburgh's Hillman Library when, at my invitation, she became a charter member and Vice President of the AAHGS Pittsburgh Chapter. I, too, was a charter member and first president and executive director of the AAHGS Pittsburgh Chapter. At Society programs she gave presentations on the art of Romare Bearden and Henry Ossawa Tanner. We developed a model school/community partnership at the Martin Luther King Elementary School in her neighborhood. We traveled together to cultural programs throughout the Pennsylvania and Ohio region.

22. Roland Barksdale-Hall, "Wendell Leonard Wray, Co-founder of ALA AFAS Section of ACRL," *Newsletter of the Black Caucus of the American Library Association* 32, no. 2 (October 2003): 35.

23. Roland Barksdale-Hall, "Preparing for the Future: Strategic Planning and Leadership in Special Collections," *Against the Grain* 16, no. 1 (February 2004): 30-32; Stanton Biddle, e-mail message to Roland Barksdale-Hall, September 18, 2003.

Granted our difference in age and backgrounds, some might have assumed us to be unlikely friends. She came from a typewriter generation; I came from a computer generation. Her father was employed as a postal service worker, while my father, a southern migrant, was employed as a chipper in the mills.

I was drawn to Lewis. I recognized a kindred spirit with an insatiable love of books and learning. We enjoyed lunch and a visit to the antiquarian bookstore. At her fingertips she held a vast array of knowledge about Pittsburgh history, politics, law, and the arts.

Lewis and I developed a close friendship centered on shared values. Fair-skinned Lewis came from, for lack of a better term, an "Old Pittsburgh" family, where skin color meant something. Consequently, I was not totally caught off-guard when she remarked about my exceptional confidence, leadership skillset, and how much I achieved with the added burden of being dark-skinned in Pittsburgh. My mother's family stories of educators and graduates from HBCUs provided my confidence.

She later would say that what she liked about me was my family ties. When she first saw me I was carrying my son in my arms into the library. Over the years she tracked my son's academic progress. She valued family ties in her own life.

Lewis and I shared a mutual respect for one another. She interrupted her doctoral studies to care for her parents. When her mother passed she invited me to speak at the Brown Chapel A.M.E. Church memorial service.

Our mutual respect was based upon something unstated. The courage of our convictions perhaps bonded us. During my freshman year and later as a graduate library student, I was employed in the Langley Biological Sciences and Psychology Library, where I had pleasant experiences. I am indebted to the head of the Langley Library, Drynda Lee Johnston, who played a significant role in my recruitment to the library profession through exhibiting courageous conversation, forthrightness, fairness, and emotional intelligence; moreover she provided valuable insights about personal character traits I possessed. In what was my first professional letter of reference, she described me as handling "all with aplomb," "soft-spoken and easy-going, yet… assertive in a non-threatening way," "reliable," "intelligent," "trustworthy," "well-liked by co-workers," "participates fully in cooperative efforts," possesses "a sense of humor that is refreshing and unique" and "excellent interpersonal skills" that should "stand him in good stead in a public service position."[24]

Lewis similarly recalled her first impression of libraries as "pleasant" places. Factors that contributed to her recruitment into the library profession included: 1) positive library environment; 2) love of learning and reading; and 3) paraprofessional library experience. She initially aspired to be a writer. However, an interest in history and books attracted her to librarianship. We both followed an indirect path to an academic leadership track. I shared with Lewis an interest in writing.

I wondered what similarities and differences existed in our professional career paths. Core to my inquiry was a question: What difference, if any, existed between a post-Civil Rights Era librarian like me and a pre-Civil Rights Era librarian Ida Mary Lewis? In contrast to Lewis, I held a B.S. in biological sciences from the University of Pittsburgh. My first career choice was in the field of science and health care. I identified the acquisition of research skills as the primary reason for my choice of academic librarianship. The possibility of acquiring a multidisciplinary research skillset in the fields of science and humanities, along with acquiring knowledge to benefit the African American community was viewed favorable. Factors that contributed to my recruitment into the library profession included: 1) positive mentor/mentee relationship; 2) employability; 3) paraprofessional library experience; and 4) availability of funding. Core components of anticipated professional advancement included: 1) subject specialty in "history;" 2) writing; and 3) teaching.

There is some yet unexplainable evidence of Lewis' geographical mobility. This is an area where more research is needed. However, what is known that she "spent four years in New York City working in two libraries, two bookstores and the French Embassy," though it is not

---

24. Drynda Lee Johnston, letter to Roland Barksdale-Hall, October 17, 1984.

clear "why she changed jobs so much and so often."[25] The majority
of her work apparently was not as a library practitioner and was not
mentioned during the interview. She held these positions early in her
career and they might represent a search for entry-level positions or
alternative career choices. She possibly might have forgotten her stint
in New York City.

In contrast, I benefitted from the availability of entry-level positions
in the Washington, D.C. Metropolitan Area (not available in Pittsburgh).
Two African American females, Gloria J. Reaves and Barbara Williams,
provided me with entry-level positions. I found part-time employment at
the Capitol Institute of Technology, followed by full-time employment
at the National Aeronautics and Space Administration Headquarters'
(NASA HQ) Library.

Goleman reported "sensing others' development needs and bolstering
their abilities" as an important social competency of emotional intelligence.[26] I benefitted from these women's empathy and through their
participation in the National Conference of African American Librarians
(NCAAL). Upon publication of my first essay, my mentor, an African
American academic library administrator at the Capitol Institute of
Technology in Laurel, Maryland, Gloria J. Reaves, showered me with
encouragement: "Now that you're over the first hurdle, other publications are sure to follow." She said this in a quiet matter-of-fact voice.
I also presented papers at the NCAAL and achieved in other professional areas. Manz referred to this leadership style as SuperLeadership,
because it focuses largely on developing the self-leadership abilities
of constituents.[27] When I entered library administration, I aspired to
emulate Gloria's wonderful example.

---

25. Lewis v. University of Pittsburgh, 725 F2d 910, Open Jurist website,
accessed November 28, 2014, http://openjurist.org/print/273492.

26. Daniel Goleman, *Working with Emotional Intelligence* (New York: Bantam
Books, 1998), 27.

27. Charles C. Manz, "SuperLeadership: Beyond the Myth of Heroic Leadership," in *The Leader's Companion: Insights on Leadership Through the Ages*, ed.
Thomas Wren (New York: Free Press, 1995), 216.

My path to a library administrator position was not without challenges. Some problems that Lewis and I faced in the workplace might have had some racial undertones. In the 1960s, Lewis recalled unfair assignment of duties time. Twenty years later, at Johns Hopkins University, an institutional member of the Association of Research Libraries (ARL), I faced a slight by a white patron or two, who preferred to talk to the white female library assistant rather than me. At the time I was employed as a science/engineering reference librarian. I was the sole African American in my department and one of only two African American librarians on campus. The other African American librarian was a senior level administrator. I never had the perception of outright racial discrimination and the evaluations were objective.

I was twenty-something when I applied for a library administrator position at the Montgomery, Maryland, Regional Campus and the white female head of library personnel immediately expressed that I was "ambitious." "Why would I not expect to improve myself?" I thought.

Lewis and I faced challenges of varying degree. In the 1940s, Lewis perceived the entrenched character of white librarians as barriers to dialogue. She faced prejudice and blatant resistance. These challenges produced alienation and isolation. In contrast, I faced challenges more ethical in nature, which had to do with flawed human interactions and misunderstanding of values, both cultural and common to the business sector, more than race. Forty years later, communication barriers persisted.

In my second year at Johns Hopkins I began to feel somewhat alienated and isolated, due to an event around a family tie and the following incident: Science, social science, and humanities literature searches routinely were placed in one drop box at the reference desk before being assigned to prospective units. A white male faculty member complained that his literature search request on life forms in the benthic area was not exhaustive and this error might adversely affect his research funding. I redid the search and found additional sources. The faculty member already knew of an existing article that was not present in the prior search. I was surprised to discover that one white male, a peer on my same level, was surreptitiously was doing the computer literature searches in my subject field.

"Why would someone, who I would go lunch with regularly, be pumping me for information, doing my work, and had never taken the opportunity to mention this?" I pondered. There likely was some personal advancement that my white male colleague was pursuing at my personal expense. My opinion of my librarian colleague changed following this event. To be candid, I curtailed going to lunch with this peer, because I lacked trust in him and felt his actions were disrespectful.

My departure from Johns Hopkins University came swiftly. Another white male lunch buddy disappointedly asked me, "Why did you not tell me you were looking for a job?" I really was not looking for a job, yet I was at a loss for words and felt sort of bad. I felt what occurred might have been handled differently, because I did not hold any malice toward him. The primary reason for my departure was a better salary and a more challenging employment opportunity at a Historically Black Colleges and Universities (HBCU) institution. Like Lewis, during my years as librarian practitioner, compensation and family ties ranked high in job satisfaction and the decision to move to other jobs. However, Lewis and I both recognized work climate, alienation, and isolation as secondary factors in job satisfaction.

HBCUs

Lewis did not reference any family tradition of HBCU involvement in her interviews. I wondered how she might have fared in this environment. In contrast I benefitted from employment at both Hampton University and Howard University. At HBCUs, time and again I found collegial environments where collaboration with professors, engaging discourse with students, and recruitment of minorities to the library profession occur. As Peabody Special Collections Librarian at Hampton University, I wrote an essay that addressed proactive leadership, strategic planning, forecasting, the need to explore cooperative learning, and teaching programs on the campuses of HBCUs.[28] In a letter to me, Dr. Clarence J. Cotton, Jr. identified the benefits of a collaborative teaching initiative between classroom-instruction and the library's Peabody Special Collection for a research-oriented course on the Civil Rights Era. The benefit of relationships established with minority mentors: Loretta O'Brien Parham and Gladys Smiley Bell, both of Hampton, and Bobby Player, Sr., of Howard, played a significant role in my professional advancement through a record of professional publication and involvement in national professional library associations, such as the BCALA, ALA, ACRL, and AFAS.

In the 1980s Salvador B. Waller, who had gone on to become an African American director, recruited me from Johns Hopkins University to join the biomedical library team as an assistant librarian at Howard University Health Sciences Libraries. I earlier worked with him at the NASA HQ Library. Recognized as a "visionary," Salvador B. Waller taught me a lot about project management through the design, planning and "manifestation" of the "state-of-the-art Louis Stokes Health Sciences Library on Howard University's campus."[29] As part of my responsibilities, I initiated an international resource-sharing project between the Howard University biomedical research center and centers in West Africa and the Caribbean and marketed libraries via special publications, programming and exhibits. With assistance from Howard University researchers I published a paper, "Breast Cancer: Does Lightning Strike Twice?" in *Sisters*, the magazine of the National Council of Negro Women, circulated at an international women's conference in Cairo, Egypt.

---

28. Roland Barksdale-Hall, "Preparing for the Future: Strategic Planning and Leadership in Special Collections," *Against the Grain* 16, no. 1 (February 2004), 30-32.

29. Karim Rand, "The Meeting of Minds," *Newsletter of the Black Caucus of the American Library Association* 31 no. 1 (August/September 2002): 16-17; Salvador Waller, "The Louis Stokes Health Sciences Library Howard University, Washington, D.C.," *Newsletter of the Black Caucus of the American Library Association* 33, no. 1 (August/September 2004): 17-18.

I shared the empowering story of HBCU recruitment as a panelist for a session, "Recruitment of Minority Librarians: An African American's Perspective," at the National Conference of African American Librarians in Milwaukee, Wisconsin.[30] The story of former library page Karim Rand, who expressed appreciation for my sharing research skills in black genealogy and noted me as one of four "primary drivers" in his "decision to attend library school," was shared. Rand credited other drivers, all African-American males at Howard University Health Sciences Library: Mr. Sekou Boni-Awotwi and "technocrat" and chief interlibrary loan officer, Mr. Herbert Hunter. Ethnic studies interests are identified as research interests for many minority librarians, and ethnic studies, cultural interests, and black genealogy have been entrees for recruitment. Mentees identified my mentoring qualities as: 1) full leadership skills; 2) goal and or purpose-oriented; 3) self-starter; 4) commitment; and 5) non-judgmental.[31]

My departure from Howard University came about due to a work-related accident, which precipitated a move back home to Western Pennsylvania. Family responsibilities (the arrival of our second child and care of elders in our family) and community ties were factors that also contributed to the choice to leave there.

In the 1990s I was one of 65 African American male academic and public librarian administrators in the nation[32] when I became a head librarian at Penn State Shenango. Upon my arrival, the library staff and director's office, and the library in general lacked personal computers, except for a few dedicated online public access catalogs. This was

---

30. Sterling Coleman, Jr., "It's No Longer about Black and White, It's All about Power," *Newsletter of the Black Caucus of the American Library Association* 31 no. 4 (January/February 2003), 2, 5.

31. Rand, "The Meeting of Minds," 16-17.

32. "Penn State Head Librarian Resigns Filing Discrimination," Buckeye Review (May 31-June 6, 1996), 6-7; Joyce K. Thorton, "Years at Present Institution and Job Satisfaction African American Female Librarians: A Study of Job Satisfaction," in *Diversity Now: People, Collections, and Services in Academic Libraries: Selected Papers from the Big 12 Plus Libraries Consortium Diversity Conference*, ed. Teresa Neely (New York: Haworth Press, 2001), 146.

because the former director, who had been there for 25 years, "did not like technology." The library, viewed as the worst at Penn State, was located in several classrooms on the third floor of a former public school and had an old wooden manual circulation desk in the hallway. There was minimal signage and no finding aids. I had my work cut out for me.

In my role as library leader, I planned for results. I introduced regular team meetings, and ordered personal computers for the staff. I advanced diversity through staff hiring, education, programming, and publications. I collected data for a library needs assessment, distributed a library survey to 140 staff, students, faculty, and administrators on campus, and developed a library program and space utilization plan. I got a library mission statement approved, marketed the library through flyers, and provided oversight for a one million dollar state-of-the-art newly renovated library facility with computers for staff and library users. I taught a three-credit African American History course, served on library committees, and attended an ARL, Office of Management Studies Training Institute: The Manager in Denver, Colorado. I conducted a survey on collaboration in 100 institutions. I presented papers at national conferences, published my research in refereed journals, encyclopedias, library conference proceedings, book chapters, and books, and garnered numerous national awards for my scholarly research.[33]

My community looked to me as a native son, scholar, and "their historian," though I had an unusual social responsibility as celebrated native son and my deceased father's son. In the same northern industrial town where Penn State Shenango was located, I grew up and exhibited leadership skills. When "Roots" aired, there was racial unrest at my majority white public school. I was elected president of the newly formed Human Relations Council and created programming to promote tolerance, because I was friendly and got along with both whites and blacks, as well as the international students. I was one of two African Americans in the majority of my honor classes and I presided over the

33. Judy Reynolds, "There Must Be 50 Ways to Be a Leader," *College and Research Libraries News* 57, no. 4 (April 1996), 208-209.

induction of the honor society and won national leadership awards. I was selected editor of the school newspaper because I possessed the strongest writing skills.

The ugly specter of racism lifted its head when I was elected over a strong field of white candidates from surrounding communities as president of my Junior Achievement Company. I possessed experience and leadership skills. The prior year I served as treasurer of the company, attended the leadership conference, and had perfect attendance. At departure time I came outside and one of the white males, who lived out in the county district, called me "nigger" and ran across the street. I had two advisors for my company; one was a white male and the other an African American male. The white male advisor, who I had the prior year, acted differently now that I was president and told me behind closed doors that "you are not going anywhere in life." I got up and responded, "Thank you, but that's just your opinion." I was shocked, but I never told my parents about these two incidents. I did not want them to be upset, but I took home a new valuable life lesson: success has the potential to bring out latent racist behaviors.

I came from a family of successful scholars and activists. "Everyone is not your friend," my mother always warned me, because I was the friendly child. My parents, through precept and example, taught: "It is better to be respected than liked." My mother was a proponent of education, served as treasurer of the band boosters, and made site visits to schools to ensure fair treatment for her children. The work paid off, with all of my brothers holding masters degrees. I had an older brother, who was a math teacher at the suburban high school and who worked with the wife of the campus Director of Academic Affairs. I knew my working-class community looked to me as the son of a United Steel Workers of America (U.S.W.A.) labor leader. My father, a native of Alabama, had a fourth grade education, yet he possessed the keen analytical mind of a Thurgood Marshall. My father served as a respected chairman of the grievance committee and fought to protect working class people, both black and white, from unfair employment practices. At my father's funeral a white male stood up and talked about how my father had helped him to keep his job. Well, I played secretary for my father sometimes and knew there were plenty of people of all colors that he helped to not only keep their jobs but to obtain promotions.

My homecoming was covered in the newspaper and reminiscence of elders. I initiated a successful community-based African American history project between an academic institution, a public historical society, and a minority cultural organization, highlighted in both the *College and Research Libraries News* and *American Libraries*.[34] I presented papers on components of this project at national conferences. Drawing upon primary and secondary historical materials, the finished project involved continuing education courses, a traveling exhibit, and a companion text.

In my role as community leader I brought together various stakeholders, formed a diverse focus group, and advocated for community pride. I received letters of endorsement from the local newspaper, the Urban League, the local economic development corporation, a unit of the National Association for the Advancement of Colored People, a genealogical society, and various public schools. A diverse interracial group of schoolteachers, retirees, traditional aged college students, blue collar workers, and civic leaders enrolled in a six-session course that I developed about local African American history. 100% of the survey respondents ranked the stimulation of thinking as excellent. 8 out of 9 ranked the overall program, instructor, and organization of content as excellent. Dr. Dewitt explains, "Tolerance for diversity must be internalized before [teachers] can teach tolerance to others."[35] A significant goal of the program was to promote tolerance.

As a follow-up, I met with graduates of the adult continuing education course, social workers, educators, civic leaders, and genealogists in a focus group to examine the feasibility of summer cultural enrichment program for youth. The group arrived at the following program format:

---

34. "When Opportunity Knocks," American Libraries 26, no. 10 (November 1995), 997; D. Abston, "Building Bridges to Unity," *College and Research Libraries News* (January 1995), 31.

35. Debbie Dewitt, "Thinking about Diversity, Some Critical Issues," *National Forum* 74, no. 1 (Winter, 1994), 16-18.

a week-long summer cultural camp on local African-American history.
I taught the course, which was offered to coincide with the free lunch
program at an elementary school. Course fees were waived to encourage
active participation. The companion text about the local community,
*People in Search of Opportunity: The African American Experience in Mercer
County*, now out of print, has since been updated by newer publications:
African Americans in Mercer County and Farrell.[36] When the Ku Klux Klan
held a rally at the courthouse, the traveling exhibit was hosted by the
newly formed Anti-Discrimination Committee at the rotunda of the
courthouse.

My roles as community leader and tenured librarian sometimes were
at odds. Through lack of proper diversity training, "dysfunctional conflicts" occurred. Some community members, staff, and faculty were
portrayed as virtuous and honorable, while I was portrayed by pervasive
myths about African Americans rooted in racial stereotypes, ranging
from "unapproachable," "the brute—mean if not abusive to white
female subordinates" to "sensitive—wearing my heart on my shoulder,"
"victim," and "vociferous." I wrote letters to the editor, appeared in leadership columns and developed a following. Topics ranged from "More
Women Needed As Elected Officials"[37] to "Don't Blame All Social Ills
On African Americans" and "Confederate Battle Flag Displayed as a
Statement."[38] I received messages: Everybody was "not happy..." "got
along just fine before you arrived" and "feel sorry for you."

I became a whistleblower when these events that transpired at Penn
State Shenango took a toll on my health. I possessed the courage of my
convictions and the resolve to fight back. I wrote then President William
Clinton, contacted the media and the American Library Association,

36. Reynolds, "There Must Be 50 Ways To Be A Leader," 208-9.

37. Roland Barksdale-Hall, "More Women Needed As Elected Officials,"
The Herald (May 15, 1997), A-6.

38. Roland Barksdale-Hall, "Don't Blame All Social Ills On African Americans," Herald Forum, *The Herald* (March 24, 1994), 12; Roland Barksdale-Hall,
"Confederate Battle Flag Displayed As A Statement," *The Herald*, (August 5,
1994), 10.

filed complaint with the U.S. Equal Employment Opportunity Commission, and received the right to sue under Title VII. Coverage of my departure was carried on the front of both minority and majority newspapers.[39] After my departure "the Dean of the Pennsylvania State (Penn State) University Libraries formed a task force to examine issues and recommend methods to improve recruitment and retention of underrepresented groups in the University workforce."[40] Upon my departure I had strong support in various segments of the community.[41]

Diversity Box

Some library organizations seemed to lost interest in retention, once the diversity box was checked. The African American Caucus at Clarion University of Pennsylvania voiced concerns about the "commitment to recruitment and retention of African American and Hispanic faculty" in the early 2000s when I was one of two African American faculty members at the Clarion University of Pennsylvania's Library School.[42] During the five prior years, Clarion University promoted having the largest enrollment of African Americans in the State System of Higher Education.

Factors in job satisfaction included: 1) contract terms, 2) health care coverage, and 3) climate. I was hired for a fixed term one teaching position, and taught an overload for two consecutive semesters. I found that signing separate contracts for the fall and spring semesters impacted my benefits and faculty status. The other African American faculty member informed me of my eligibility for health care, addressed my

39. "Penn State Head Librarian Resigns Filing Discrimination," 6-7.

40. Linda Musser, "Effective Retention Strategies for Diverse Employees," in *Diversity Now: People, Collections, and Services in Academic Libraries: Selected Papers from the Big 12 Plus Libraries Consortium Diversity Conference*, ed. Teresa Neely (New York: Haworth Press, 2001), 63-72.

41. Marlene Torrence, "Community, Campus Losing Valuable Member," *The Herald* (May 22, 1996), A-6.

42. Solomon Obotetukudo (Chair of African American Caucus), letter to Joseph Grunenwald (Provost), September 29, 2000.

exclusion from faculty departmental meetings, and lack of other critical information. With four young children at home, this had the potential to create undue hardship. I spoke up, and received retroactive health care. However, I never was invited to attend a faculty meeting and perceived my exclusion as a tactic to diminish the minority voice.

At the end of the school year, I interviewed for my contract renewal. The search committee chose another candidate, though I had received a glowing letter of evaluation, and held a reasonable expectation of continuous employment. I was disappointed to hear that if only I had possessed a Ph.D. (rather than 3 master's degrees), my contract would have been renewed and I would have been placed on a tenure track.

In recent times I became a fulltime teacher at a for-profit academic institution, Bryant and Stratton, where I assisted in developing and taught a three-credit undergraduate course targeting marginalized communities. After several years, my full-time course-load was drastically reduced to make way for non-librarians to teach information literacy courses.

Are We There Yet?

The experiences of post-Civil Rights Era librarians pale in light of the "unabated resistance" that their predecessors faced. The pre-Civil Rights Era generation produced Ida Mary Lewis and other stalwart "soldiers of a caliber" and the post-Civil Rights Era generation are "challenged by their stories," inspired to "straighten up their acts," and assume more responsible leadership roles.[43] The shared experiences of Lewis and myself show persistence of employment inequities, perhaps in a subtler form yet producing similar end results. Granted some perceptions rooted within America's history of drawing lines of separation might be inescapable in the workplace, thus courageous conversations about race for transformation to an inclusive society will be required. A commitment to authentic dialogue and transparency in the tenure process on the part of majority institutions will be one step toward establishing a creative

43. Rand, "The Meeting of Minds."

balance between relationship and principle found in well-functioning dialogic organizations.[44] Democratic communities grounded in dialogue will make room for people from various backgrounds.

The accounts of successive generations beginning with Virginia Proctor Powell Florence, through Ida Mary Lewis to myself have been in keeping with those recorded in the professional literature. Collins observed that "discrimination manifests itself in a variety of ways," ranging from social ostracism to harassment.[45] Pillow voiced concern about "schmoozing" and "socializing with certain people" as requirements for ongoing appointments, promotion, and tenure, because "subjectivity" and "capricious" nature engender a toxic environment.[46] Senior-level Black administrators, as evidenced by Yate's observations, are experiencing increased opposition by "dissident staff which totally undermine [their] authority."[47] Yates reported that some are pursuing legal redress.[48] Fighting back, according to Collins, may involve, "grieving with the employing agency or bargaining unit, settling outside of court, suing in state and federal courts, and using the political process to bring about change. Others [simply] are choosing to move to new jobs or occupations."[49]

Why do these problems persist? Many present-day "employment problems, which employees may believe are based on prejudice, sometimes are mistakenly seen in reality as a result of flawed human

---

44. Ronald C. Arnett, *Communication and Community: Implications of Martin Buber's Dialogue.* (Carbondale: Southern Illinois University Press, 1986), 97.

45. Margaret Collins, "Employment Discrimination Faced by Black Librarians," in *The Black Librarian in America Revisited*, ed. E.J. Josey (Metuchen, NJ: Scarecrow Press, 1970), 257.

46. Lisa Pillow, "Academic Librarianship: A Personal Perspective," in *In Our Own Voices: The Changing Face of Librarianship*, eds. Teresa Neely and Khafre (Lanham, MD: Scarecrow, 1996), 98.

47. Ella G. Yates, "Reflections of a Former State Librarian," in *The Black Librarian in America Revisited*, ed. E.J. Josey (Metuchen, NJ: Scarecrow Press, 1970), 273.

48. Ibid., 273.

49. Ibid., 255-62.

interactions, bureaucratic structures," or cultural biases,[50] which has resulted in "capricious and biased behavior" based upon "schmoozing" and "likability rather than meritorious work." However, the majority has taken for granted white privilege.[51] "The majority may feel more threatened by Blacks than by other minority groups because Blacks, up until recent times, have represented the largest minority group in the United States and compete more intensely in all areas with the majority," Fernandez postulates; Blacks consequently "face more types of discrimination and more severe discrimination."[52]

"So are we there yet?" I say we're on the road to slow progress, yet we need to be vigilant and remain activist librarians. Some areas of the country have been slow in progress. Byrd recognized that "the ARL's Leadership and Career Development Program and the ALA Spectrum Initiative are preparing the next generation of minority librarian leaders."[53]

"Are we there yet?" In recent times I have reapplied for the position of head librarian at Penn State Shenango when I have seen the job posting. The old guard now has retired with full benefits and a question of equity and fairness remains to be asked: Will past inequities be corrected?

In addition to recruitment, libraries will need to focus on retention, practice transparency, acknowledge that past mistakes have been made, and take action to hire back those that they have avoided. I humbly close out my narrative with a few recommended solutions: ARL, ALA ACRL, and BCALA need to consider social justice awards in two categories: 1) libraries with outstanding minority recruitment and retention records; 2) contemporary minority librarians who have advocated for change to break down barriers in the profession; 3) the majority need to address

---

50. John P. Fernandez, *Managing a Diverse Work Force: Regaining the Competitive Edge* (New York: Lexington Books, 1991), 239.

51. Theresa S. Byrd, "Managing the Academic Library: the Role of the Black Librarian Leaders in Three Different Institutional Environments," in *The 21st-Century Black Librarian in America: Issues and Challenges,* eds. Andrew P. Jackson, Julius Jefferson and Akilah Nosakhere (Lanham, MD, Scarecrow, 2012), 108.

52. Fernandez. *Managing a Diverse Work Force,* 157.

53. Ibid., 108.

institutional barriers and practice courageous conversations about race; and 4) as mentioned earlier, in the 21st century minority librarian practitioners will need to focus more on enhancing their communication skills and connections to the pipelines of power and authority.

Future Implications

In the 21st century, courageous conversations will be required to support the growth and development of democratic work communities, though the majority up to this point has displayed an unwillingness to participate in courageous conversations about race as most benefit from the practice of "silent racism." Winston expressed that "communication norms and rules, communication taboos" and the "social phenomenon of embarrassment" possibly work to deter open dialogue about race, maintain the status quo, and "preserve the expressive order."[54] Trepagnier's brilliant analysis showed that many whites, who might not be classified as racists, have benefited from their "silent racism."[55] An African American ARL librarian administrator, Theresa S. Byrd, furthermore acknowledged institutional racism, that "racism still exists," and offered a clarion "challenge to all library leaders to be courageous enough to address these issues."[56]

What happens when the silence about oppression and racism is ended? Authentic dialogue can help to build trust and restore confidence in the workplace. An Hispanic Head of Archives and Special Collections at Hunter College, Julio Luis Hernandez-Delgado, recalled how an African

---

54. Mark D. Winston, "Communication and Teaching: Education About Diversity in the LIS Classroom," in *Diversity Now: People, Collections, and Services in Academic Libraries: Selected Papers from the Big 12 Plus Libraries Consortium Diversity Conference*, ed. Teresa Neely (New York, Haworth Press, 2001), 204.

55. Barbara Trepagnier, *Silent Racism: How Well-Meaning White People Perpetuate the Racial Divide.* (Boulder, CO: Paradigm Publishers, 2006).

56. Theresa S. Byrd, "Managing the Academic Library: The Role of the Black Librarian Leaders in Three Different Institutional Environments" in *The 21st-Century Black Librarian in America: Issues and Challenge*, eds. Andrew P. Jackson, Julius Jefferson and Akilah Nosakhere (Lanham, MD, Scarecrow, 2012), 108.

American librarian supervisor, Professor Lee E. Sellers (1937-2004), exhibited the courage found in the harmony of principle-centered leadership and relationship. Professor Hernandez-Delgado memorialized his colleague as an adherent of courageous conversation:

"Professor Sellers was direct, sincere, witty and compassionate with all types of people. He had a wonderful sense of humor and took delight in bringing joy and happiness to others… On a more serious note, he was not one to put up with injustice and the double-standard treatment of non-whites in America. He detested racism and wasn't afraid to confront those who engaged in racist behavior… [He] helped me in so many ways. "[57]

In another example, a healthy relationship of supervisor/subordinate evolved to mentor/mentee and developed into friendship over the course of eleven years. Singleton and Linton persuasively argued that a need for courageous conversations about culture and race existed among most white participants, who avoided such conversation because they did not feel comfortable with the concept of whiteness as a base for empowerment and entitlement.[58] Let us end the silence.

Let us now momentarily pause to remember the noble efforts of heroic ancestors, such as Professor Lee E. Sellers, Dr. E.J. Josey, Dr. Arnulfo D. Trejo (1922-2002), Professor Wendell Wray, the first professional trained African American female librarian Virginia Proctor Powell Florence, and the former Head of the African American Collection Ida Mary Lewis, many of whom were highly qualified and waited outside the door for over twenty years for challenging professional academic library practitioner or educator positions. "How much has changed in some places in twenty years?" "Where are the African American male librarian practitioners?" So I ask twenty years later, "Are we there yet?"

---

57. Julio Luis Hernandez-Delgado, "Reflections on Professor Sellers," *Newsletter of the Black Caucus of the American Library Association* 33, no. 2 (October/November 2004), 5.

58. Glenn E. Singleton and Curtis Linton, *Courageous Conversations About Race: A Field Guide for Achieving Equity in Schools* (Thousand Oaks, CA: Corwin Press, 2006), 61, 189-91.

References

Abston, D. "Building Bridges to Unity." *College and Research Libraries News* (January 1995): 31 .

Arnett, Ronald. *Communication and Community: Implications of Martin Buber's Dialogue.* Carbondale, IL: Southern Illinois University Press, 1986.

Ball, Patricia. "African American Male Library Administrators in Public and Academic Libraries." *College and Research Libraries* 56, no. 6: 531-45.

Barksdale-Hall, Roland. "Confederate Battle Flag Displayed as a Statement." *The Herald,* August 5, 1994, 10.

———. "Dialogic Bridges in the Workplace." *Newsletter of the Black Caucus of the American Library Association* 30, no. 6 (June 2002): 9-10.

———. "Don't Blame All Social Ills On African Americans." Herald Forum, *The Herald,* March 24, 1994, 12.

———. "More Women Needed As Elected Officials," *The Herald,* May 15, 1997, A-6

———. "Preparing for the Future: Strategic Planning and Leadership in Special Collections." *Against the Grain* 16, no. 1 (February 2004): 30-32.

———. "Wendell Leonard Wray, Co-founder of ALA AFAS Section of ACRL." *Newsletter of the Black Caucus of the American Library Association* 32, no. 2 (October 2003): 35.

Byrd, Theresa. "Managing the Academic Library: The Role of the Black Librarian Leaders in Three Different Institutional Environments." In *The 21st-Century Black Librarian in America: Issues and Challenges,* edited by Andrew P. Jackson, Julius Jefferson and Akilah Nosakhere, 105-109. Lanham, MD, Scarecrow, 2012.

Coleman, Sterling, Jr. "It's No Longer about Black and White, It's All about Power." *Newsletter of the Black Caucus of the American Library Association* 31 no. 4 (January/February 2003): 2, 5.

Collins, Margaret. "Employment Discrimination Faced by Black Librarians." In *The Black Librarian in America Revisited*, edited by E.J. Josey, 255-62. Metuchen, NJ: Scarecrow Press, 1970.

Dewitt, Debbie. "Thinking about Diversity, Some Critical Issues." *National Forum* 74, no. 1 (Winter, 1994): 16-18.

Fernandez, John. *Managing a Diverse Work Force: Regaining the Competitive Edge*. New York: Lexington Books, 1991.

Fontno, Tiffeni. "Reinventing Diversity." *Newsletter of the Black Caucus of the American Library Association* 30, no. 6 (June 2002): 8.

Freedman, Maurice. Foreword to *Communication and Community: Implications of Martin Buber's Dialogue*, by Ronald Arnett, i-xiv. Carbondale, IL: Southern Illinois University Press, 1986.

Goleman, Daniel. *Working with Emotional Intelligence*. New York: Bantam Books, 1998.

Gunn, Arthur C. "The Struggle of Virginia Proctor Powell Florence: A Black Woman Wants to Be a Professional…" *American Libraries* 20, no. 2 (February 1989), 154-57.

Hardy, Floyd and Renee Stiff, "The Future of the Black College Library." In *Handbook of Black Librarianship*, edited by E.J. Josey and Marva DeLoach, 387-96. Lanham, MD: Scarecrow Press, 2000.

Hernandez-Delgado, Julio Luis. "Reflections on Professor Sellers," *Newsletter of the Black Caucus of the American Library Association* 33, no. 2 (October/November 2004): 5.

Hirsh, Elizabeth and Christopher Lyons. "Perceiving Discrimination on the Job: Legal Consciousness, Workplace Context, and the Construction of Race Discrimination." *Law and Society Review* 44, no. 2 (June 2010): 269-98.

Howland, Joan. "Challenges of Working in a Multicultural Environment." In *Diversity Now: People, Collections, and Services in Academic Libraries: Selected Papers from the Big 12 Plus Libraries Consortium Diversity Conference,* edited by Teresa Neely and Kuang-Hwei Lee-Smeltzer, 105-23. New York: Haworth Press, 2001.

"Ida M. Lewis: Obituary." RememberingPa.us. Accessed August 9, 2012. http://www.legacy.com/ obituaries/publicopiniononline/obituary.aspx?n=ida-m-lewis&pid=155250820&fhid=8387.

Jackson, Andrew and Julius Jefferson, eds. *The 21st Century Black Librarian in America: Issues and Challenges.* Lanham, MD: Scarecrow Press, 2012.

Jones, Plummer. *Still Struggling for Equality: American Public Library Services with Minorities.* Westport, CT: Libraries Unlimited, 2004.

Josey. E.J. and Ann Shockley, eds. *Handbook of Black Librarianship.* Littleton, CO: Libraries Unlimited, 1977.

Josey, E.J. *What Black Librarians Are Saying.* Metuchen, NJ: Scarecrow Press, 1972.

Lee, Grant. "Honoring Virginia Florence." *American Libraries* 18, no. 4 (April 1987), 250.

Lewis v. University of Pittsburgh. 725 F2d 910. Open Jurist website. Accessed November 28, 2014. http://openjurist.org/ print/273492.

Manz, Charles and Henry Sims. "SuperLeadership: Beyond the Myth of Heroic Leadership." In *The Leader's Companion: Insights on Leadership Through the Ages,* edited by Thomas Wren, 207-11. New York: Free Press, 1995.

Morrison, Ann. "Challenging the Barriers to Opportunity." In *The Leader's Companion: Insights on Leadership Through the Ages,* edited by Thomas Wren, 231-42. New York: Free Press, 1995.

Musser, Linda. "Effective Retention Strategies for Diverse Employ-
    ees." In *Diversity Now: People, Collections, and Services in Academic
    Libraries: Selected Papers from the Big 12 Plus Libraries Consortium
    Diversity Conference,* edited by Teresa Neely and Kuang-Hwei
    Lee-Smeltzer, 63-72. New York: Haworth Press, 2001.

Neely, Teresa and Khafre Abif, eds. *In Our Own Voices: The Changing
    Face of Librarianship.* Lanham, MD: Scarecrow Press, 1996.

Norlin, Elaina and Patricia Morris, "Historically Black College and
    University Libraries in the 21st Century: Accomplishments,
    Challenges and Recommendations." In *Diversity Now: People,
    Collections, and Services in Academic Libraries: Selected Papers from
    the Big 12 Plus Libraries Consortium Diversity Conference,* edited
    by Teresa Neely and Kuang-Hwei Lee-Smeltzer, 183-97.
    New York: Haworth Press, 2001.

"Obituary of Ida Mary Lewis." Accessed August 9, 2012. http://
    www.legacy.com/obituaries/publicopiniononline/obituary.
    aspx?n=ida-m-lewis&pid=155250820&fhid=8387#fbLogge
    dOut.

"Penn State Head Librarian Resigns Filing Discrimination." *Buckeye
    Review* (May 31-June 6, 1996): 6-7.

Pillow, Lisa. "Academic Librarianship: A Personal Perspective." In
    In Our Own Voices: The Changing Face of Librarianship, edited
    by Teresa Neely, and Khafre Abif, 190-204. Lanham, MD:
    Scarecrow, 1996.

Rand, Karim. "The Meeting of Minds." *Newsletter of the Black Caucus
    of the American Library Association* 31, no. 1 (August/Septem-
    ber 2002): 16-17.

Reynolds, Judy. "There Must Be 50 Ways To Be A Leader." *College and
    Research Libraries News* (April 1996): 208-209.

Singleton, Glenn and Curtis Linton. *Courageous Conversations About
    Race: A Field Guide for Achieving Equity in Schools.* Thousand
    Oaks, CA: Corwin Press, 2006.

Starkey, Shawn. "Librarian Quits Job At PSU Campus." *The Herald,* May 17, 1996. 1, A-6.

Thorton, Joyce. "African American Female Librarians: A Study of Job Satisfaction." In *Diversity Now: People, Collections, and Services in Academic Libraries: Selected Papers from the Big 12 Plus Libraries Consortium Diversity Conference,* edited by Teresa Neely and Kuang-Hwei Lee-Smeltzer, 141-64. New York: Haworth Press, 2001.

Torrence, Marlene. "Community, Campus Losing Valuable Member," *The Herald* (May 22, 1996): A-6.

Trepagnier, Barbara. *Silent Racism: How Well-Meaning White People Perpetuate the Racial Divide.* Boulder, CO: Paradigm Publishers, 2010.

Unaeze, Felix. "Managing Historically Black Colleges and University Libraries during Economic Recession: Challenges and Expectations for Library Deans and Directors." In *Handbook of Black Librarianship,* edited by E.J. Josey and Marva DeLoach, 97-104. Lanham, MD: Scarecrow Press, 2000.

"Virginia Proctor Powell Florence: A Remarkable Oberlin Alumna Librarian." *Library Perspectives: Newsletter of the Oberlin College Library* 32 (Spring 2005), 5. Accessed December 6, 2014. http://www.oberlin.edu/library/friends/perspectives/32.pdf.

Waller, Salvador. "The Louis Stokes Health Sciences Library, Howard University, Washington, D.C." *Newsletter of the Black Caucus of the American Library Association* 33, no. 1 (August/September 2004): 17-18.

"When Opportunity Knocks." *American Libraries* 26, no. 10 (November 1995): 997.

Winston, Mark. "Communication and Teaching: Education About Diversity in the LIS Classroom." In *Diversity Now: People, Collections, and Services in Academic Libraries: Selected Papers from the Big 12 Plus Libraries Consortium Diversity Conference,* edited by Teresa Neely and Kuang-Hwei Lee-Smeltzer, 199-12. New York: Haworth Press, 2001.

Yates, Ella. "Reflections of a Former State Librarian." In *The Black Librarian in America Revisited*, edited by E.J. Josey, 273-82. Metuchen, NJ: Scarecrow Press, 1970.

Chapter 13

MAKING DIVERSITY WORK IN ACADEMIC LIBRARIES

Miguel Juárez

As a second generation Mexican-American from a working class background, the academic library profession has proven to be a vast experience, filled with numerous opportunities and possibilities for learning, networking,[1] working with students, and learning how university environments, special collections, research, teaching, information, and the publishing world converge. But in my experience as a librarian of color, at times it has also been a challenging and sometimes hostile environment. I have always been a big picture and out-of-the-box thinker and in this essay, I write about issues all librarians of color face, may have faced, or may continue to face in the profession, but that no one really discusses.

Librarianship is more than shelving books, as librarians in the academic environment are typically defined and depicted; we know differently, but the general community doesn't. The profession also gets short-shrift from academe: teaching faculty often don't have an idea what we as academic librarians do and because they are often just as busy

---

1. Networking or the building of cultural and social capital is pivotal for librarians of color. Networking is the informal process that librarians utilize to hear of upcoming positions, changes inside libraries, and other issues that can seldom be disclosed publicly. Networking levels the playing field for librarians of color.

as we are in their positions, they do not have the time or the interest
to find out what we do unless they develop a close working relationship with us. As an activist and community scholar in El Paso, Texas
prior to attending library school as part of the Arthur A. Schomburg
Fellowship Program,[2] I was not aware of what academic librarianship
entailed or what it meant to become a librarian/archivist. My interests
in information and building collections, coupled with the opportunity
to obtain my library degree to work in various positions that aligned
with my skills sets, positioned me to become an academic librarian and
enjoy a productive, although at times, rocky career.

My experiences in the SUNY Buffalo library residency program
are detailed in an article I wrote as a requirement of the residency. It
described my experiences relocating from one geographical border to
another, from the U.S./Mexican border to the U.S./Canadian border,
to take advantage of the fellowship. This program was a forerunner
of ALA's Spectrum Program.[3] Relocating to Buffalo, New York from
El Paso, Texas in 1997 to attend graduate school, where I was the only
Latino library science student in the program, was somewhat of a culture shock. I quickly acclimated and made life-long friends, although
I was subjected to some rather peculiar questions.[4] It took me nine
months to finish my coursework, obtain my MLS, and then begin my
position as a Visiting Reference Librarian at the Oscar A. Silverman
Undergraduate Library.

Luckily, at SUNY Buffalo, I had a strong mentor who guided me
through my first months as an academic librarian and who stayed with

---

2. University at Buffalo, The State University of New York, "Arthur A.
Schomburg Fellowship Program," accessed December 10, 2014, http://grad.
buffalo.edu/FinancialSupport/Scholarships_ Fellowships/schomburg.html.

3. Miguel Juárez, "De Frontera A Frontera/From Border to Border: The UB
Library Internship/Residency Program," in Diversity in Libraries: Academic
Library Residency Programs, ed. Raquel V. Cogell and Cindy A. Gruwell
(Westport, CT: Greenwood Press, 2001), 29-34.

4. A few semesters prior to my arrival at SUNY Buffalo, Dr. Filiberto Martínez had been a doctoral student in the Library Science program, but by the
time I got there he had graduated. Upon my arrival in Buffalo, some of the
librarians asked me if I knew him. I didn't.

me as I transitioned to a full-time professional position one year later.[5] I had also developed a great working relationship with one of my LIS professors whom I would often call and who always offered me sound advice as I contemplated new opportunities and even invited me to participate as a virtual guest in his online classes.[6] At SUNY Buffalo, I engaged in outreach to student organizations and presented talks at career day at local elementary schools, where I asked students of color to envision themselves as future librarians. At a local career day, I told multicultural elementary students that if they were fanatical about organizing their CD collections, they could become librarians.

A brief discussion of my work in diversity efforts in academic libraries is needed, so that readers can have an idea of the range of my efforts in this rich area. After leaving the Undergraduate Library at the University at Buffalo, I took a position as the Fine Arts Librarian at the University of Arizona. At the University of Arizona library, I was one of the few Latino art librarians in the country and I strove to make a difference in diversity as part of the ARLIS, the Art Libraries Society of North America. I arrived at the University of Arizona at a time of turmoil in the Center for Creative Photography and again, I was one of a handful of Latino photography librarians, if not the only one, at a major university from 2000-2005. While at the University of Arizona, I was active in the group "Allies of LGBT Staff at the University of Arizona Library," worked on programming with this group from 1999 to 2005, and helped identify local funding to support a lecture by the late Leslie Feinberg at the Jewish Community Center.[7]

---

5. Thank you Glendora Johnson-Cooper (now an Associate Librarian/ Social Sciences Librarian at SUNY Buffalo) for making my experience at SUNY Buffalo a great experience! Johnson-Cooper managed the Library Residency Program.

6. Thank you Dr. John Ellison for guiding me throughout my academic library career.

7. When I began my position as Fine Arts Librarian in 1999 at the University of Arizona Library, there was already an LGBT Employees group in existence. The Allies Group of LGBT Staff formed in 1996 after a library workshop, facilitated by Amy Zuckerman, called "Not So Straight II: A Continuing Dialogue with your Lesbian, Gay & Bisexual Colleagues. A result of

At Texas A&M, from 2005-06, as a new librarian, I was selected as chair of the Diversity Committee at the Sterling C. Evans Memorial Library, where I resurrected a languishing diversity committee. As part of our work, we increased attendance, participation. and interest in events, and I received letters of commendation for exceptional performance in chairing the committee. At Texas A&M a group of librarians took the exam and participated in the workshop for the book *Now Discover Your Strengths* and I was identified as being the only Woo[8] in the library. The workshop leader told me someone else in another workshop had the same characteristic of being the only Woo in the library, and shortly thereafter left her institution. Even though I discounted it at the time, the same thing would eventually happen to me. I left Texas A&M in 2007.

While at UCLA, I was involved in diversity efforts in many of my professional positions and via service opportunities during the time period of 2007-2010. I served on the ALA Committee on Diversity (COD) from 2007-09, and was the Inaugural Chair of the Diversity Research Grant (DRG) Advisory Committee from 2007-09, when we designated the first research grant that was awarded to LGBT diversity research for the 2008-09 cycle. I also served as Juror for DRG Grant

---

this workshop was to continue working towards creating a more positive environment in the library. The Allies Group of LGBT staff organized yearly book exhibits during Pride Month, participated in the annual Pride March and promoted GLBT activities in the library. The group also maintained a listserv that included supportive staff and librarians, as well as support the Dean of Libraries and the Center for Creative Photography. In 2001, the core group of Allies members was mostly comprised of classified staff members. Although there were other LGBT librarians and managers on staff, these individuals did not seek to openly identify with the Allies Group, but were supportive of Allies' efforts. Having a background in programming and organizing exhibits in the past, and having an interest in LGBT issues in art, photography, and material culture, I was eager to work with the Allies Group in developing exhibits and programming. The group had not done as much programming associated with exhibits in their past.

8. According to the Clifton StrengthsFinder Themes that measures the presence of 34 talent themes: "People strong in the Woo love the challenge of meeting new people and winning them over and they derive satisfaction from breaking the ice and making a connection with another person." Strengths Test, "Clifton StrengthsFinder Themes," accessed 16 December 2014, http://www.strengthstest.com/theme _summary.php/.

after I stepped down from the chair position, from 2007 to 2010. While I was at UCLA, I also became chair of the Los Angeles meeting of the Southwest Oral History Association (SOHA) conference which was one of the most diverse meetings to date.

This overview delineates my academic library career, which took me to four Academic Level 1 institutions and six universities overall, including the State of New York at University at Buffalo in Amherst, New York; the University of Arizona Library in Tucson, Arizona; Texas A&M University in College Station, Texas; the Chicano Studies Research Center (CSRC) Library at UCLA; El Paso Community College; and the University of North Texas in Denton, Texas. In all of these places, I made friends and enjoyed working with diverse students, staff, and faculty.

As a result of all the micro-aggressions and things that happened to me while working at five predominantly white institutions, I could have easily become embittered, because I was often the only minority librarian, and more specifically I was often the only Latino male librarian on campus. After leaving my last position and instead of seeking another position, I decided to take time off to return to school and work towards a doctoral degree, something I had meant to do as early as my days at SUNY Buffalo when I was accepted into the doctoral program in American Studies. I decided to pass on the doctoral program at Buffalo and take the position as Fine Arts Librarian at the University of Arizona. In hindsight, my career could have been different if I had stayed and worked on my doctoral degree at Buffalo. Naively I thought that by working in a university, I would one day have the opportunity to take courses and obtain an advanced degree, but given the constraints of my positions, I never had the time to do so. The ability to take coursework and obtain additional graduate degrees is another opportunity that multicultural librarians often seek to supplement their MLS degrees, but because of workloads and other commitments, there is seldom time to pursue those additional credentials. Too often at many institutions librarians lack support in pursuing further graduate studies.

I believe that an enlightened academic library would be one that would allow actual time, as well provide support, both financial and release time, for academic librarians to seek and acquire those advanced degrees and not just pay lip service to the availability of the opportunity to take three hours of coursework per semester. The library profession is littered with people who didn't finish their academic coursework because they were given the perk of taking three hours per semester for the rest of their lives. Yet in contrast, due to white privilege, some individuals are able to engage in coursework full-time, while their supervisors look the other way.

Queering the Academic Library Profession

To diversify the academic library profession I feel we need to queer it. By queering the profession, I mean *othering* it. This means making it what it has not traditionally been, and this concept may upset our ideas regarding traditional academic librarians. *Othering* it means one must employ different techniques to attract, hire, and retain people who do not look or act like you. It means hiring people who are different from present-day librarians or from the present wave of baby boomer librarians who have not retired. Coincidentally, the exodus of baby boomer librarians has only now begun to occur. Queering the profession also means collecting in areas that are non-traditional. It means hiring people who think differently, people who may challenge established environments. It means hiring people who you would not necessarily hire. These changes are needed for the academic librarian profession or we will not represent the diversity of our great country and we will also miss out on building collections of underrepresented groups who one day will be the majority population. Queering collections and libraries means giving face to hidden areas of growth, to non-hetero-normative, to non-white, to class issues, to the unspoken realities in people's lives.

As recent events (such as Sandra Bland's mysterious death, systematic civil rights violations, the high number of incarcerated Latinos and Blacks, and the anti-immigration rhetoric) have revealed, there is already an engrained and deep-seated distrust of underrepresented groups; hence, the push towards Ethnic Studies in public school curriculums is an idea whose time has come. Yet changing the curriculum itself will not change the diversity of library staffs. In addition, much of the literature for diversifying academic libraries seems to focus on changing the environment for student success and not necessarily for staff and librarian success. But there have been some articles that showcase that diversity efforts have improved and that institutions are striving to "create inclusive communities." William C. Welburn in his article "Creating Inclusive Communities: Diversity and the Responses of Academic Libraries," sums up some of these advancements:

> Racial and ethnic diversity is far more common in the staffs of academic libraries in predominantly white colleges and universities now than 40 years. Associations such as ACRL and ARL have become more inclusive in both participation and programming, leading initiatives that have created opportunities for groups that have been historically underrepresented among professional and managerial ranks. The strategies employed in cultivating leadership are well known in the academic library community. They begin with scholarship support to recruit new librarians from underrepresented backgrounds and one- to two-year residency programs in academic libraries, and continue with leadership institutes, dissemination of ideas at national conferences on diversity in libraries, and development of inventive hiring strategies. These strategies have enjoyed some important successes, as the competition for scholarships has increased and involvement in institutes has received widespread support within the academic library community. While turning the tide on declining participation and gaining in frontline and middle management positions, higher education in its libraries will continue to struggle over diversifying senior leadership.[9]

Welburn's last phrase is key: "libraries will continue to struggle over diversifying senior leadership," meaning that there will continue to be a lack of diversity among those that lead academic libraries. It is one thing for organizations to "value diversity," and another to have diversity embedded in every level of the organization. What value is it to have entry-level non-tenured librarians from diverse backgrounds if the

---

9. William C. Welburn, "Creating Inclusive Communities: Diversity and the Responses of Academic Libraries," *portal: Libraries and the Academy* 10, no. 3 (2010): 360.

tenure-granting bodies and administrative levels are still pretty much represented by the dominant racial group?

There is also a significant amount of white privilege in academic libraries and unfortunately it is not going to go away any time soon. White colleagues often hire people who look and act like them. When libraries do hire someone who doesn't think or act like them, they use phrases to question their choices and state things like: "You may not be a good fit here." Academic libraries do not hire based on differences, but on similarities. But who determines "good fit" in an era of changing demographics and in an era of changing expectations, in a time of change and flux? Privilege in its many forms, racial, class, gender, etc., is a problem facing academic libraries and a topic that is not addressed because it is the elephant in the room. In order to diversify staffs, collections, and institutions, it must begin with the individuals who chart the course for the library—what are their biases, what do they value, what do they give importance to? Any time you address this issue in the academic library environment, it makes people uncomfortable because it challenges deeply held feelings and presents ideas that may not be in line with their personal beliefs.

For the most part, academic libraries and the librarians who work in them often see themselves as bastions of progressiveness, but too often they are not. This sense of false progressiveness often manifests itself in library activities such as who is hired to support librarians' and archivists' work. Of the libraries I worked in throughout my career I noticed that white librarians often hired students and temporary staff who looked like them—white students and white contract librarians, many with little or no experience in working with or assisting students and staff from diverse backgrounds. We must not forget issues such as class in hiring diversely. I remember hiring a white student who was majoring in history to process a collection. She had only worked at fast food places but her goal was to become an historian. Later, after she obtained some experience, I was able to intercede on her behalf and place her as an intern at the Alamo in San Antonio. Thus, what I also want to stress is that at every library I worked in, it was important that I not lose my ethnic identity but also my sense of fairness in providing opportunities for students, regardless of their ethnic backgrounds, class and/or situations. I purposefully made my ethnic identity, class, and interests part of my work in academic libraries, but it was also important that others be given the opportunity to learn about those who were different from themselves. As academic librarians of color, we cannot turn our backs against our cultures, or on students of color, just because we are trying to fit into a culture that oftentimes works against us.

Yet beyond who is hired and who is not, there are not enough minorities entering the profession to reflect growing multicultural populations.[10] So imagine, once a person of color enters the profession and they find out that they are maybe the only librarian of color or one of the few at their institutions, what impetus does that provide for them to remain in the profession? How do they develop a supportive environment and a network of allies?

Becoming an Information Activist and Building Diverse Online Communities

As I mentioned earlier in this essay, even before becoming a librarian I was a community activist at heart. Being an activist, I have also always been very social and everywhere I have worked and lived I have built networks. Thus when social media was introduced as one of our tools in librarianship, I took to it like a fish to water.

Librarianship and social networking are two aspects of my life that have become interrelated. As long as there is a need for mediated use of information and scholarly guidance for use of collections, there will be a need for librarians and curators. As long as the standard modalities of scholarly creation and dissemination of knowledge, and the publications, databases, e-scholarship, and other ways that information is organized and sold to consumers exist, there will be a need for librarians in the

---

10. Ricardo Andrade and Alexandra Rivera, "Developing a Diversity-Competent Workforce: The UA Libraries' Experience," *Journal of Library Administration* 51 (2011): 693..

knowledge economy. In the next phase of library services, we will have
to incorporate the data needs of faculty and researchers,[11] as well as
respond to emerging trends in how users access data and information.[12]

Social media expanded the notion of mediated use in other formats
and media. In many ways, librarianship has been a social media profession so the concept of social media is something we have worked with
for a number of years, only in different forms. Social media tools by
themselves will not replace librarianship but it will enrich it and make
us work in new mediated ways.

Librarians and curators will continue to play roles in selecting and
organizing information and collections for users, but now these roles
will be shared in new and more exciting forms. I have used social media
to engage with students, professors, and other users. I've used it to
communicate with possible donors of collections, to approach potential donors, and to post announcements of lectures and events that I
felt students and library users might be interested in. I also used this
medium to get a sense of what was happening in the community and
at venues around town (in the community).

I use social media to reach out to people in a non-obtrusive manner.
I have also used it to develop affinity groups and as a form of outreach,
as well as in the concept of "in-reach." In-reach is a form of communication with the people who already know, as opposed to the people
who don't know. I have also used social media's chat capacity to have
short and specific conversations with people in the same way that chat
in libraries is frequently used to answer specific reference questions. All
in all, social media is a good primer for librarians interested in learning
and researching user needs.

---

11. Deborah E. Keil, "Research Data Needs from Academic Libraries: The
Perspective of a Faculty Researcher," *Journal of Library Administration* 54, no.3
(2014): 233-240, DOI:10.1080/01930826.2014.915168.

12. Rajendra Madhavrao Kumbhar, "Academic Library's Responses to the
Emerging Trends in Higher Education," *DESIDOC Journal of Library & Information Technology* 34, no. 6 (2014): 477-485.

For me, as an information community builder and scholar, social media tools are about making connections and harnessing the power of these tools to create new forms of communication, associations, and learning. Sometimes people are fearful of things they don't understand. These new technologies challenge notions of the familiar. In a way, as one of my social media friends Chola Con Cello has theorized, these tools speed up the process of making connections in ways people are uncomfortable with or are not ready to accept. Anytime someone fuses polar opposites (the ways artists usually do), people are going to react to these things and not always in a positive way. Yet at the same time, this creates a space where new ways of doing things emerges. In addition, having a background in information studies, now also informed by U.S. History, Borderlands and Transnational Urban History, and Digital Humanities, has created a rich hybridity within my research interests.

At every institution I have worked in I have made it a point to be engaged in building community with faculty of color, and with the community at large that I believe is integral to being successful in such an environment. As librarians and curators of color we often find themselves in new cities and towns with no family, and often with no local support system and less cultural capital. Thus, it is important to build those social networks even if via social media, as many of us have done. My solution for maintaining engagement with librarians while pursuing a doctoral degree in a separate field has been creating affinity groups via social media. I have built two social media sites and am a member of many more groups where persons of color who are librarians, curators, and scholars, can come together to share ideas and projects, and where I remain tethered to colleagues in libraries and their institutions.

I'm the administrator of two social media groups where I engage with ethnic academic librarians: one is called "Latino/Chicano Academic Libraries" and includes 155 members and the other one is "Let's Build an Ethnic Studies Digital Archive," which has over 1,800 members who are librarians, archivists, faculty members, artists, writers, etc., all of whom are interested in ethnic studies, libraries, activism, arts, and more. I am also a member of other groups that include librarians: the

SUNY Buffalo Library Science Alumni; REFORMA Think Tank; Digital Frontiers; Ethnic and Multicultural Information Exchange Round Table (EMIERT); NACCS – National Association for Chicana and Chicano Studies; Archives Leadership Institute; Latina/o Studies Initiative; Teaching Face and Ethnic Studies; Latina/o Literature and Culture Society; ALA Think Tank; ALZAR; Social Responsibilities Round Table; *Archiveros, Documentalistas y C. Información;* Digital Humanities, Archives & Archivists; Critical Librarianship; *Bibliotecología Crítica para La Transformación Social;* SALALM; and *Archiveros en* Facebook, as well as others.

Climate & Karma: Why We Need a Diversity Report Card for Academic Libraries

I have suggested that departments initiate team building for new librarians in a department, without much success. It would be great if ALA or ARL or ACRL could create a diversity library report card for academic libraries that covers recruitment, retention, and attrition rates for librarians of color, so we could know where to apply and what libraries are challenged in these areas. The report card could mirror DiversityInc Magazine's "Top 50 Companies for Diversity," which features companies that "have publicly accessible materials on their diversity and inclusion initiatives" except in our case it would be for academic libraries.[13] The diversity library report card could be modeled in accord with the diversity standards that were developed by the ACRL Racial and Ethnic Diversity Committee and approved by the ACRL Board of Directors in April 2012.[14]

Thirteen members of the committee developed the following standards:

---

13. Alexia Hudson-Ward, "Diversity and Inclusion: Online Resources for Education," *C&RL News* 75, no. 6 (2014): 336.

14. ACRL Racial and Ethnic Diversity Committee, "Diversity Standards: Cultural Competency for Academic Librarians, Approved by the ACRL Board of Directors, April 2012," *C&RL News* 73, no. 9 (2012): 551-561.

Standard 1. Cultural awareness of self and others. Librarians and library staff shall develop an understanding of their own personal and cultural values and beliefs as a first step in appreciating the importance of multicultural identities in the lives of the people they work with and serve.

Standard 2. Cross-cultural knowledge and skills. Librarians and library staff shall have and continue to develop specialized knowledge and understanding about the history, traditions, values, and artistic expressions of colleagues, co-workers, and major constituencies served.

Standard 3. Organizational and professional values. Librarians and library staff shall develop and support organizational and professional values dedicated to culturally competent service.

Standard 4. Development of collections, programs, and services. Librarians and library staff shall develop collections and provide programs and services that are inclusive of the needs of all persons in the community the library serves.

Standard 5. Service delivery. Librarians and library staff shall be knowledgeable about and skillful in the use and provision of information services available in the community and broader society, and shall be able to make appropriate referrals for their diverse constituencies.

Standard 6. Language diversity. Librarians and library staff shall support the preservation and promotion of linguistic diversity, and work to foster a climate of inclusion aimed at eliminating discrimination and oppression based on linguistic or other diversities.

Standard 7. Workforce diversity. Librarians and library staff shall support and advocate for recruitment, admissions, hiring, and retention efforts in libraries, library associations, and LIS programs to increase diversity and ensure continued diversity in the profession.

Standard 8. Organizational dynamics. Librarians and library staff shall participate in and facilitate the development of organizational dynamics that enable individuals, groups, and organizations to continually develop and exercise cultural competence.

Standard 9. Cross-cultural leadership. Library leaders shall influence, support, and encourage the creation of proactive processes that increase diversity skills; empower colleagues, co-workers, and constituents from diverse backgrounds; share information about diverse populations; and advocate for their concerns.

Standard 10. Professional education and continuous learning. Librarians and library staff shall advocate for and participate in educational and training programs that help advance cultural competence within the profession.

Standard 11. Research shall be inclusive and respectful of non-Western thought and traditional knowledge reflecting the value of cultural ways of knowing.[15]

Quality controls that I would add would include the Diversity Competency Descriptions developed by the Millennium Report Oversight Committee (MROC) at the University of Arizona, both at the Entry and the Mastery levels.[16] These standards and competencies need to be part of the hiring stage and continue to the retention and promotion stages. They also need to be used in evaluating team leaders and library administrators. But by and large the aforementioned standards and competencies are not being practiced and are usually given lip service in academic libraries. Diversity efforts in academic libraries are highly fractured and inconsistent.

The creation of a tool for librarians to identify good places to work is essential in this day and age because that is how talented people decide where to work. As Alexia Hudson-Ward has stated in her article on recruitment and retention: "Potential employees desire meritocratic workplaces where the totality of an individual's diverse contributions and lifestyle choices matters as much as demographic differences."[17]

Numerous academic libraries embody cocoon-like environments not cognizant of the communities of color around them and this is reflected in lack of services for those communities or lack of collecting for and

---

15. Ibid., 552-553. Members of the 2012 Racial and Ethnic Diversity Committee included: Toni Anaya, University of Nebraska-Lincoln; Maria Carpenter, Northeastern University; Trevor Dawes, Princeton University; DeLoice Holliday, Indiana University; Emily Love, University of Illinois at Urbana-Champaign; Scott Mandernack, Marquette University; Charlene Maxey-Harris, University of Nebraska-Lincoln; Heleni Pedersoli, University of Maryland; Michelle Saunders, University of Arizona; Rayette Sterling, Eastern Washington University; Patrick Tomlin, University of Vermont; Melanee Vicedo, OCLC Fellow 2012; and Lesley Farmer, University of California-Long Beach, Editor.

16. Andrade and Rivera, "Developing a Diversity-Competent Workforce," 701-703.

17. Alexia Hudson-Ward, "Eyeing the New Diversity, An Emerging Paradigm for Recruitment and Retention," *American Libraries* July/August 2014, 32-35.

from them. My personal experiences suggest that institutions may talk the talk, but because of issues of white privilege and entrenched nepotism (and sometimes fear of the communities around them), although they mean well, they may not walk the talk. The situation is exacerbated by library organizations that supposedly exist to support academic libraries but have predominantly white boards.[18]

Sometimes there are signs that a certain position is not going to work out before one even starts. My advice is that if there are already signs that something does not sit right, it is best not to accept that position because usually those signs are spot on. When librarians take a new position, they are walking into a new culture; unless they have done their research or conferred with other librarians who have a history at that institution or if they are mentored by seasoned librarians who have the new librarian's best interest in mind, in the long run, the position might not work out.

Institutions should strive to hire diverse candidates but the reality is that in the present political climate, I feel diversity will continue to be a challenge to the profession. As this book of essays attests, a diverse environment is good for everyone: for students, for librarians, and for others. Even though demographics will continue to change and the country will strive to become more diverse, academic libraries need to reflect the communities they serve.

Efforts to diversify institutions begin with the people in those libraries; but most library directors and hiring committees are white, as well as predominantly straight. Just as these committees assess potential candidates in the hiring process, we too need to assess predominantly white academic libraries. In essence, we need to create a library report card

---

18. In 2014, the Association of Research Libraries (ARL), whose motto is "empowering the research library community," had a slate of fifteen white board members and no persons of color, as if diversity has taken a back seat: ARL, "Board of Directors," accessed December 11, 2014, http://www.arl.org/about/board-of-directors. On the other hand, the Association College and Research Libraries (ACRL) fared much better with three board members from underrepresented groups: ACRL, "Meet the ACRL Board of Directors," accessed December 11, 2014, http://www.ala.org/acrl/aboutacrl/directoryofleadership /board/meetboard.

on diversity, inclusiveness, and equity. Even when institutions become more diverse, the nature of white privilege is usually carried over in the library's culture from the period when the library was predominantly white, which in many institutions is still the status quo.

I wish this essay would become happier right about here and we could all hold hands across the library boardroom and sing *kumbaya*, but today's academic library environments seem to be breeding grounds for incessant micro-aggressions against librarians of color. Academic librarians go into the profession, not because they are going to get rich, but because they love what they do. But seemingly, the constant micro-aggressions day-in and day-out eventually cause many to leave the profession or seek other kinds of opportunities. I know several academic librarians who are practically at the end of their ropes, but because they are holding out until their retirements, they are enduring the barrage of actions against them. It is also an economic issue: jobs are scarce and tenure-track positions are slowly becoming a thing of the past. Yet even in an unstable economy we need to do more. As ALA President Barbara K. Stripling recently stated in her article on equity, diversity, and inclusion in *American Libraries*:

> What we know, however, is that we are not doing enough. Members of our communities and profession continue to face inequity and discrimination. We cannot pat ourselves on the back because we have groups to take action for us. Each one of us must accept personal responsibility to stand up for equity, diversity, and inclusion in our field and our communities.[19]

A solution would to devote our work to transforming specific areas in data and information science, and evolve the profession into what it needs to be. With this idea in mind, I am reminded of the work of fellow information studies scholar Dr. Zapopan Muela-Meza and his

---

19. Barbara K. Stripling, President's Message, "Equity, Diversity, and Inclusion: Standing Up for Our Values," *American Libraries*, May 5, 2014, http://americanlibrariesmagazine.org/2014/05/05/equity-diversity-and-inclusion/.

theories of social transformation via critical bibliography.[20] In other words, what good is information if it doesn't aid in changing the lives of our citizens and our civilization? I believe that this book is one step in that direction.

References

ACRL Racial and Ethnic Diversity Committee. "Diversity Standards: Cultural Competency for Academic Librarians, Approved by the ACRL Board of Directors, April 2012." *C&RL News* 73, no. 9 (2012): 551-561.

Andrade, Ricardo and Alexandra Rivera. (2011) "Developing a Diversity-Competent Workforce: The UA Libraries' Experience." *Journal of Library Administration* 51 (2011): 7-8, 692-727. DOI: 10.1080/01930826.2011.601271.

Association of College and Research Libraries (ACRL). "Meet the ACRL Board of Directors." Accessed December 11, 2014. http://www.ala.org/acrl/aboutacrl/ directoryofleadership/ board/meetboard.

Association of Research Libraries (ARL) "Board of Directors." Accessed December 11, 2014. http://www.arl.org/about/ board-of-directors.

Hudson-Ward, Alexia. "Diversity and Inclusion: Online Resources for Education." *C&RL News* 75, no. 6 (2014): 336-339, 345.

———. "Eyeing the New Diversity, An Emerging Paradigm for Recruitment and Retention." *American Libraries* (July/August 2014): 32-35.

---

20. Zapopan Martín Muela-Meza, in "Bibliotecología crítica para la transformación social," https://www.youtube.com/watch?v=uG2BPwIh_Pc, accessed 12 December 2014. Dr. Muela-Meza, Ph.D. in Information Studies, University of Sheffield, UK, presented his paper on 19 April 2008 at the 1st Conference of LIS Alumni of the undergraduate program at the School of Philosophy and Letters, in Nuevo Leon Autonomous University, San Nicolas de los Garza, Nuevo Leon, Mexico.

Juárez, Miguel. "De Frontera A Frontera/From Border to Border: The UB Library Internship/Residency Program." In *Diversity in Libraries: Academic Library Residency Programs*, edited by Raquel V. Cogell and Cindy A. Gruwell, 29-34. Westport, CT: Greenwood Press, 2001.

Keil, Deborah E. "Research Data Needs from Academic Libraries: The Perspective of a Faculty Researcher." *Journal of Library Administration* 54, no. 3 (2014): 233-240. DOI: 10.1080/01930826.2014.915168.

Kumbhar, Rajendra Madhavrao. "Academic Library's Responses to the Emerging Trends in Higher Education" *DESIDOC Journal of Library & Information Technology* 34, no. 6 (2014): 477-485.

Muela-Meza, Zapopan Martín. "Bibliotecología crítica para la transformación social." Accessed December 12, 2014. https://www.youtube.com/watch? v=uG2BPwIh_Pc.

Strengths Test. "Clifton StrengthsFinder Themes." Accessed 16 December 2014. http://www.strengthstest.com/theme_summary.php/.

Stripling, Barbara K. "Equity, Diversity, and Inclusion: Standing Up for Our Values." *American Libraries* (May 5, 2014). http://americanlibrariesmagazine. org/2014/05/05/equity-diversity-and-inclusion/.

University at Buffalo, The State University of New York. "Arthur A. Schomburg Fellowship Program." Accessed December 10, 2014. http://grad.buffalo.edu/ FinancialSupport/Scholarships_Fellowships/schomburg.html.

Welburn, William C. "Creating Inclusive Communities: Diversity and the Responses of Academic Libraries." *portal: Libraries and the Academy* 10, no. 3 (2010): 355-363.

Contributors Biographies

Jason Kelly Alston is a doctoral candidate at the School of Library and Information Science at the University of South Carolina. He attended the University of North Carolina at Wilmington for undergraduate school and earned his M.L.S. from North Carolina Central University. Alston was the first diversity resident librarian at the University of North Carolina at Greensboro and hopes to one day be a professor for a library school program with a personal research agenda focusing on diversity, cultural heritage, and how confirmation bias and other biases affect a user's acceptance and trust of information.

Tarida Anantachai is a Learning Commons Librarian at the Syracuse University Libraries, where she provides general and interdisciplinary reference, instruction, and outreach with an undergraduate focus. She also serves as the Libraries' liaison to her campus' international student services center, English language institute, and study abroad office. She received her MLIS from the University of Illinois at Urbana-Champaign and her BA in English and American Literature from Brandeis University. Tarida was an ALA Emerging Leader, a participant in the MN Institute for Early Career Librarians, and stays connected to the greater library profession as an active contributor to several national and regional library association committees, including those within ALA, ACRL, APALA, and the Eastern NY Chapter of ACRL. Prior to her stint in librarianship, Tarida also worked for several years in the academic publishing industry.

Roland Barksdale-Hall currently teaches in the Africana Studies Department at Youngstown State University and is director of the Quinby Street Resource Center Library. He has taught fulltime in the Clarion University Department of Library Science. Prior posts include Head Librarian at Penn State Shenango, Peabody Special Collections Librarian at Hampton University, Coordinator of Black Health History at the Howard University Health Sciences Library, Science/Engineering Librarian at Johns Hopkins University and Reference Librarian at NASA Headquarters Library. He has served on the executive committee of the Black Caucus of the American Library Association (BCALA) and former editor of the BCALA Newsletter. Publications include numerous scholarly essays in encyclopedias, journals and chapters in books. Published books include *African American Family's Guide to Tracing Our Roots: Healing, Understanding and Restoring Our Families, Under African Skies, Lion Pride, Farrell and African Americans in Mercer County.* He is the editor of the *Journal of the Afro-American Historical and Genealogical Society* and former editor of *QBR: The Black Book Review.* He is the recipient of numerous awards and holds master's degrees in history and leadership from Duquesne University and a masters in library science from the University of Pittsburgh.

Latrice Booker is the Coordinator of Library Instruction at Indiana University Northwest. She previously worked as the Interim Head of Cataloging/Serial Cataloger at Murray State University. Booker earned a Master of Library Science from Indiana University-Purdue University Indianapolis in 2006 and a Master of Business Administration from Indiana University Northwest in 2012. Very active in the profession, Booker is an ALA Councilor, Co-chair of the ACRL Scholarships Committee, Chair of the Indiana Library Federation District 1 Conference Planning Committee and President of the Indiana University Librarians' Association, in addition to serving on multiple professional committees.

Steven D. Booth is an Archivist at the U.S. National Archives in Washington, D.C. He previously served as project archivist for the Martin

Luther King, Jr. Papers at Boston University's Howard Gotlieb Archival Research Center while completing his graduate studies at Simmons College, where he earned a Master of Science in Library Science. An active member of the American Library Association and Society of American Archivists, Booth is involved with several outreach, diversity, and recruitment initiatives including the Spectrum Advisory Committee and Knowledge Alliance.

Agnes K. Bradshaw is the Human Resources Librarian for University Libraries at the University of North Carolina Greensboro in Greensboro, North Carolina. At UNCG, she has responsibility for library human resources concerns, including employee relations, recruitment, performance management, and staff development. She also serves as the Equal Opportunity Officer for the Libraries. She has more than 15 years of experience in several areas of Human Resources, including learning and development and employee benefits. Prior to becoming a librarian, she held a variety of Human Resources positions in the financial services industry as well as in higher education. Agnes earned a B.A. from Spelman College, a MS from the New School for Social Research in New York, and an M.L.I.S. from Rutgers University. She is also a certified Senior Professional in Human Resources (SPHR) through the Human Resources Certification Institute, a division of the Society of Human Resources Management and belongs to the College and University Professional Association for Human Resources. She is currently the Communications Director of the Triangle Chapter of the Human Resources Association, and has served on several committees with ALA's Library Leadership and Management Association (LLAMA.)

Stacy Brinkman is the Art & Architecture librarian and Asian Studies liaison librarian at Miami University in Ohio. Originally from Seattle, she earned a B.A. in comparative literature from Colorado College, an M.A. in East Asian Studies from Princeton University, and an M.L.I.S. from Rutgers University. Stacy's current research interests include diversity in libraries and higher education, learning and pedagogy, and the impact of

technology on information and librarianship. She has received a 2006
grant from the Japan Foundation Center for Global Partnership to fund
a cultural education program at Miami University Libraries promoting
Japanese children's literature, activities, and artifacts, as well as grants
from the Academic Library Association of Ohio to fund research on
information seeking behaviors of first-generation college students (2009)
and testing a prototype of an augmented reality shelf-reading application
(2012). Her conference presentations include the Association of College
and Research Libraries (ACRL), the Library Information Technology
Association (LITA), the Art Libraries Society of North America (ARLIS/
NA), the National Diversity in Libraries Conference, and the National
Conference on Race and Ethnicity (NCORE). She is an active member
of ARLIS/NA, where she has served as a member on the Education
Subcommittee, the Diversity Committee, and the Membership Com-
mittee, as well as the chair of the Professional Development Committee.
Currently, she is also a member of the ACRL Professional Development
Committee. Outside of libraries, Stacy enjoys being a mom, competing
in figure skating, taking on way too many DIY projects, and knitting.

Ava Iuliano Brillat graduated from the University of South Florida
with her MLS in 2010. She is currently the Instructional Design Librarian at Florida International University in Miami. Her research interests
center on instructional design and the professional experiences of new
librarians. Ava is involved in the American Library Association's Reference and User Services Association (RUSA). She is currently the chair
of the RUSA Reference Services Section Research & Statistics committee, which hosts an annual research forum at the ALA conference.

Emily K. Chan is Senior Assistant Librarian at San José State University. Previously, she was Sciences Librarian/Assistant Professor with
the University of the Pacific Library. Holding a BA in Biological Sciences
from Grinnell College and a MLIS from San José State University, Chan
is the liaison librarian to the departments of Kinesiology and Nutrition,
Food, and Packaging. Her research involves the use of technology to

streamline, improve, and document library services and processes. Chan is also interested in mentoring and diversity issues and is a recruiter for the Discovering Librarianship program.

Lori Driver is the Interim Department Head and Government Document Librarian at Florida International University in Miami. She received her MLIS degree from the University of South Florida and is an active member of the American Library Association, Association of College & Research Libraries, and Government Documents Round Table. Her research interests focus on the preservation and accessibility of historic document pertaining to under-served communities.

Rhonda E. Fowler, MILS, began her professional librarian career began in 1989 she I was hired to be a reference librarian in the university she currently works in. She soon moved into different roles throughout her career here including that of Education Librarian, and presently as the Government Documents/African American Studies Librarian. Her K-12 schooling was in a predominately African American environment where she played in the band, orchestra and jazz band. She always loved to read and throughout her high school and undergraduate years she searched for a career that would allow her to remain involved in reading. She enjoys helping children learn to love reading, and through her sorority's tutoring program she works with children on their reading and math skills. She is also active in her church's bookstore and also acts as the church librarian. She feels her mission is to help as many children of color learn how to appreciate reading and to realize that it an important skill to learn.

Rebecca Hankins, CA, MLIS, is an Associate Professor and a certified archivist/librarian. She received her graduate degree from Louisiana State University. She has been at Texas A&M University since 2003, receiving tenure in 2010. Her previous employment included 12 years as senior archivist at The Amistad Research Center at Tulane University in New Orleans, the premier research repository on Africana historical documentation. She teaches courses on the use of primary sources in research and research methodology. She has presented at numerous conferences and published in science fiction, library, archival, and other peer-reviewed journals. Her areas of expertise include building collections and scholarly resources for the study of the African Diaspora, Women & Gender Studies, and Arabic Language and Culture. Her latest publication is a book chapter titled "The Influence of Muslims and Islam in Science Fiction, Fantasy, and Comics" in the two-volume Praeger publication, *Muslims and American Popular Culture*.

Jacqueline Johnson is the Archivist of the Western College Memorial Archives. She earned her Bachelor's degree from Limestone College and master's from the University of South Carolina. Johnson has published *Finding Freedom: Memorializing the Voices of Freedom Summer* (Miami University Press 2013) and *The History of Western College* (Arcadia Press 2014). Her chapter on "Edgar Stillman Kelley, Dean of American Composers" was published in the book *Celebrating the Oxford, Ohio Bicentennial 1810-2010*. Her published works appear in the *Journal of Afro-American History and Genealogical Society*. Her research focuses on the history of Western College for Women and the Mississippi Summer Project. She is currently working on the manuscript *Ohio's First African American Graduates from Institutions of Higher Learning* (Mellen Press 2017). In January 2014 she traveled to Luxembourg and London, England and taught the class "A Comparative Look at Women's Historical Journals, Modern Day Blogging and Oral Histories." The course focused on journaling, oral history and blogging and the study of non-digital and digital communication. It utilized data from the Western College Female Seminary (1855-1974); National Archives of Luxembourg, University of London (Bedford College - Royal Holloway, 1849-1985); University of Oxford (St. Hughes College, 1832-1879); University of Cambridge (Girton College, 1827-1891). She has received grants from the Ohio Humanities Council to create the Mississippi Freedom Summer Project 1964 Digital Collection and to produce a documentary about the Mississippi Freedom Project and from the Academic Library Association of Ohio to research the life of noted Stone Mason Cephas Burn. She has collaborated with the Western College Alumnae Association on the Western Roundup Digital Newspaper Collection. Johnson has worked with the Society of Ohio Archivist in organizing state conferences and workshops. She enjoys reading, biking, ornithology, cross-stitch and loves cooking soul food and famous Johnson family recipes.

Miguel Juárez received a Bachelor of Arts degree in Liberal Arts from the University of Texas at El Paso in 1985 and took graduate studies in Arts Administration and Chicano Research Studies at California State University at Dominguez Hills and Museum Gallery coursework at California State University at Long Beach from 1989-1992. He is a 1998 graduate from the State University of New York (SUNY) School of Information and Library Science MLS program at the University at Buffalo. He also has an MA in Border Studies from the University of Texas at El Paso History Program (2012) and is currently working on his doctorate in U.S. History, Borderlands History, Transnational Urban History, and Digital Humanities at UT El Paso. In 1997, he published *Colors on Desert Walls: the Murals of El Paso* (Texas Western Press), a bilingual book, chronicling the region's rich mural movement and its artists. He has also published chapters in the following books: *Ordinary Women, Extraordinary Lives: American Women's History* (2000, Scholarly Press); *The Power of Language/el Poder de la Palabra: Selected Papers from the Second REFORMA National Conference* (2001, REFORMA and Libraries Unlimited); and *Diversity in Libraries: Academic Library Residency Programs* (2001, Greenwood Press). He has written about museums in Culturework, the University of Oregon, Arts Administration Program online newsletter and has published articles in the *REFORMA Newsletter;* the *Public Historian;* the *El Paso Herald Post;* the *El Paso Times;* Mujerestalk. org; and in *Dos Pueblos, Immigration Reform.*

Althea Lazzaro is a research and instruction librarian serving the University of Washington's Bothell campus and Cascadia Community College. She received an MLIS from the University of Washington's iSchool in 2011 and an MA from King's College, University of London in 2006. Since joining the University of Washington, she has actively worked to develop librarian cultural competency, and infuse the profession with a sense of how it can lead to more than just libraries. In service of this work, Lazzaro serves on a number of social justice and diversity committees at the libraries and institutional levels, is a member of the ACRL Diversity Committee, and is the co-author of publications about Whiteness, anti-racism, and diversity in academic libraries.

Vince Lee is the Archivist for the Carey C. Shuart Women's Archive and Research Collection at the University of Houston Libraries' Special Collections. In addition to the Shuart Women's Archive he also oversees and manages the collecting areas for Houston and Texas History as well as Architecture and Planning. He currently serves on the Library's Micro-grant Committee as its chair as well as on the University Commission on Women as one of its members. He was a former member of the Library's Strategic Directions Committee. In 2013, Vince curated the fall exhibit "Collective Herstory: A Mosaic Masterpiece, Exploring the Carey C. Shuart Women's Archive." He has also presented on Houston's Liberation and Feminist Movement at the Society of Southwest Archivists, as well published an article on the Houston Gorilla Girls in *Houston History Magazine*. Vince is the current Vice President/President Elect of the Archivists of the Houston Area, as well as a member of the Houston Area Rainbow Collective History (ARCH). Prior to joining the University of Houston he was the Lead Archivist and Assistant Manager at The African American Library at the Gregory School. Vince received his BA in Political Science from University of Michigan and his MLIS from Wayne State University. He currently resides with his wife and their five-year-old son in Sugar Land, Texas.

Jovanni Lota is currently the Information Literacy Coordinator as well as an adjunct professor at the University of Houston-Downtown. Previously, she served as the Curator/Librarian for the Melvin B. Tolson Black Heritage Library at Langston University. She received her B.A. in

Sociology from California State University Long Beach. Her graduate studies were completed at the University of California at Los Angeles, where she received her MLIS and a M.A. in Afro-American Studies. Lota is a 2008 Spectrum Scholar, and a 2012 Emerging Leader. She currently serves as a member of the of the Spectrum Scholar Advisory Committee and the Knowledge Alliance recruitment Initiative. Her research involves connecting new students to the library using augmented reality as a teaching tool in information literacy. Her interests include library instruction, diversity issues, and mentoring.

Akilah S. Nosakhere serves as Director of Library Services at New Mexico State University Carlsbad. She was a co-editor of the award winning book, *The 21st Century Black Librarian in America* published by Scarecrow Press in 2012. Ms. Nosakhere has held a variety of management positions in academic and special libraries during her 27-year career. She served as African American Studies subject editor for the seminal reference work, *Resources for College Libraries*, Managing Editor of *International Journal of Africana Studies* of the National Council of Black Studies (NCBS), and Past Chair of the African American Studies Librarian section of Association of College and Research Libraries (ACRL). A former board member of ALA Black Caucus, Ms. Nosakhere currently serves on the editorial board of the Association of College and Research Libraries' *Choice Reviews*. An advocate of the Open Access Movement, Ms. Nosakhere enjoys teaching information literacy and planning educational programs for NMSU and the Carlsbad community where she and husband, muralist Charles Freeman make their home.

Martha Parker is the current Librarian in Residence for the University of Arkansas at Fayetteville. Initially, she worked in cataloging and has worked in special collections for the past two years creating digital collections. Parker received an MLIS in 2011 from the University of North Carolina at Greensboro where she also received the prestigious UNCG's Academic and Cultural Enrichment (ACE) Scholarship, a Laura Bush 21st Century Librarian Program funded by a grant from the

Institute of Museum and Library Services (IMLS) and the UNCG-LIS Department. Parker also holds a B.A. in Business Administration from Queens University of Charlotte, and Elementary School Certification from Normal Miguel F. Martínez in México. A former educator and an experienced business executive, Parker has led several local and national committees since the beginning of her graduate school studies. Parker was the Charlotte representative for the UNCG's MLIS program from 2009-2011, an ALA-IRRT (International Relations Roundtable) member, and a REFORMA member. Since 2012, she has led the REFORMA Organizational Development and New Chapters committee, and is chair of the ACRL's Diversity Committee. She has been a driving force in promoting the 2012 ACRL's *Diversity Standards for Academic Libraries*, primarily to presentations at conferences, the creation of a diversity video, a diversity libguide at the University of Arkansas and finally, leading the creation of the ACRL's *Diversity Standards for Academic Libraries Toolkit*.

Karen Rogers-Collins, MSLS is an Electronic Resources and Serials Librarian who manages and maintains a wide range of licensed electronic resources. She is responsible for acquiring serials and electronic resources including databases and e-journals. Troubleshoots and resolves online applications and access problems. She compiles and analyzes statistics, develops unit goals and projects, establishes policies and procedures, and oversees training of staff. Her research interests include the changing role of the "traditional" technical services librarian in academic libraries, as well as the impact of changing job titles and descriptions and degree qualifications of librarians. Before accepting a tenure-track librarian position, she worked for 17 years as a librarian in special libraries (law, medical, pharmaceutical/corporate). She received her Master's degree in Library Science and a certificate in Archival Administration from Wayne State University in Detroit, MI.

Dr. Loriene Roy is Professor in the School of Information, the University of Texas at Austin. Her teaching areas are public librarianship, reference, library instruction/information literacy, and digital space design for popular music. She also teaches courses on indigenous librarianship for the Library and Information Science Program at the University of Hawai'i at Manoa. She has co-edited six monographs and written hundreds of articles, book chapters, newsletter articles, reviews, and reports. Her current advisory board service includes serving on the Library of Congress Literacy Awards and on the Rovelstad Scholarship Selection Committee for CLIR. She has given over 500 formal presentations in many venues across the world. She served as the 2007-2008 President of the American Library Association and the 1997-1998 President of the American Indian Library Association. She is Anishinabe, enrolled on the White Earth Reservation, a member of the Minnesota Chippewa Tribe.

Melody Royster received her MLIS from Florida State University in 2008. She is an Assistant University Librarian at the University of Florida, where she is the Instruction Coordinator and Agricultural Sciences subject specialist in the Marston Science Library. Melody is an active member of the United States Agricultural Information Network (USAIN) and serves as the Co-Chair of the Membership Committee. Her recent projects include the Association of Southeastern Research Libraries (ASERL) Cooperative Journal Retention Project and 3D printing technology grant.

David Schwieder is the Political Science Liaison and Humanities and Social Science Data Coordinator at Smathers Libraries, at the University of Florida. His interests include library instruction, information literacy, the psychology of the user experience, experimental and survey research design, and statistical methodology. His current projects include assessment at the University of Florida, library data, facilitating causal analysis in library scholarship, and re-conceptualizing information literacy.

Kwabena Sekyere is an Electronic Information Services Librarian. He develops electronic information systems and contribute to developing, designing and maintaining the Miami University Libraries' website.

He also manages the Black World Studies program's collection and serves as the Libraries' liaison to the program. He has master's degree in Information Science from State University of New York, Albany. Sekyere's research centers upon using emerging technologies to improve access to library resources and services. He has presented at many conferences and published in journals such as *Journal of Library & Information Services in Distance Learning* and *College & Undergraduate Libraries*. He has served on several national and international committees.

Holly A. Smith is currently the College Archivist at Spelman College. Previously she served as African American Materials Specialist in the Louis Round Wilson Special Collections Library at the University of North Carolina at Chapel Hill. She received her B.A. in History and Black Studies from The College of William and Mary, an M.A. in History from Yale University, and her M.S. in Library and Information Science, with concentration in Archival Management, from Simmons College. Ms. Smith is a member of the Archives and Archivists of Color Roundtable and the Society of American Archivists Diversity Committee.

Elías Tzoc, received his bachelor degree in Information Systems Management from Galileo University in Guatemala (2004) and a master degree in Information Studies from the School of Information at the University of Texas at Austin (2007). As Digital Initiatives Librarian, he assists the head of the Center for Digital Scholarship to provide Miami scholars with the facilities, services, and expertise to support the creation and use of digital scholarship. He serves as one of the main developers for the Miami Library's Digital Collections and Institutional Repository portals. In this role, he has implemented several web customization and plugins for DSpace and CONTENTdm -using PHP, CSS, XML, XSLT, HTML5, jQuery and JavaScript. Additionally, he has also served as co-Principal Investigator for several grant projects including: 2014 NEH Digital Humanities Start-Up, 2014 Miami Tech Fee, 2012 Miami Humanities Center, 2011 ALA/NEH Let's Talk About It, 2010 State Library of Ohio LSTA MiniGrant, and 2009 Ohio Humanities Council. His publications have appeared in journals such as *D-Lib Magazine*, *Code4Lib Journal*, and *College & Undergraduate Libraries*, among others. He is also serving as a reviewer for the *Revista Interamericana de Bibliotecología* based at the Universidad de Antioquia in Medellín, Colombia. His recent work with faculty includes prototyping and implementing web-based solutions for scholarly projects such as: a globally-accessible website for archiving bibliographic data on new media in the Middle East; an Omeka based website for managing three interdisciplinary databases of print and electronic materials for children, youth, and adults; a prototype and location-based game that interprets the Freedom Summer project on the site of the 1964 orientation at Western College; and the development of eBooks using open source standards. In the fall semesters, he is also an adjunct instructor in the Institute of Interactive Media Studies program where he teaches an IMS 201 class which focuses on Information Literacy and Information Technology.

Shaundra Walker is graduate of Spelman College where she received a Bachelor of Arts degree in history. She also earned the Masters in Library and Information Science from Clark-Atlanta University and is currently a doctoral student at Mercer University, in Educational Leadership with a concentration in Higher Education Administration. Her research focuses on leadership and organizational development in libraries at historically black colleges and universities. Shaundra serves as Associate Director of Instruction and Research Services at Georgia College in Milledgeville, Georgia.

INDEX

CPSIA information can be obtained at www.ICGtesting.com
Printed in the USA
BVOW02s0539220116

433721BV00002B/7/P

9 781936 117833